Contemporary Native American Literature

A Selected & Partially Annotated Bibliography

compiled by

ANGELINE JACOBSON

The Scarecrow Press, Inc.
Metuchen, N.J. 1977

Library of Congress Cataloging in Publication Data

Jacobson, Angeline, 1910-
Contemporary Native American literature.

Includes indexes.
1. Indian literature--North America--Bibliography. 2. American literature--Indian authors--Bibliography. 3. Eskimo literature--Bibliography.
I. Title.
Z7118.J32 [PM181] 016.8108'0054 77-5614
ISBN 0-8108-1031-X

Manufactured in the United States of America

CONTENTS

Part 1

INTRODUCTION

This bibliography has been compiled to bring together the literary works of Native American authors which have been written and published within the years from 1960 to mid-1976, and to give sources of such literature. An author's literary effort may be a single poem, a group of poems and/or short stories, or any other literary form. Such work or works may have been published in a periodical, in a collection of works by several authors, or as a title of an individual author's collected works, or as a single work. In the case of myths and legends they may be re-told or revised in some way by a native author, or edited by another authority in the subject. This is one area in which it seemed reasonable to relax the time limits stated above. It also seemed justifiable in some cases to include an author's works written earlier than 1960; e.g., N. Scott Momaday. The numbers of such entries in comparison with the total number is relatively small. Another relaxation of the time limit has been made by the inclusion of writers of the earlier years of the twentieth century. Many of these are autobiographies, "as told to" or through interpreters. As such they present first-hand accounts of Native American life and viewpoint. They are also useful in providing contrast or similarity of message with today's writers.

The term Native American has been chosen rather than American Indian in order to include Eskimo, Canadian and Mexican tribal writers. Eskimos are not Indians; but they are Native Americans. In addition to those Eskimo authors included, I have selected authors from the Kwakiutl tribe of the Northwest (Canada), from the Ojibway (Chippewa, or more accurately Anishinabe) in Canada as well as the Ojibway from Northern Minnesota and Northern Michigan, and the Yaqui from Northern Mexico. Also authors from Canadian-United States eastern border areas and other Eastern tribes--e.g. Iroquois, Mohawk, Seneca--are included. These may appear to be subjective decisions. However, the greatest concentration of authors seems to be from the area west of the Mississippi River. Each author seems to occupy a distinct niche in the panorama of Native American literature.

Because of the limits of time and human limitations this bibliography is a selected list.

* * *

During years of study and of being on the job, a Reference Librarian has little time to delve seriously into a particular subject of personal or contemporary interest. When, late in 1971, the opportunity arose for me to apply for a sabbatical leave, the time for such research became a possibility.

Sporadically the media had been calling our attention to the plight of the Native American. The Luther College community was experiencing twinges of concern, one result of which was an attempt to explore sources of contemporary Native American literature in support of and to enrich studies in Anthropology, Elementary Education and American Literature. In the latter field the American people have too long failed to recognize the indigenous literary roots embodied in the Native American's oral tradition. As a foundation for our literature, it is of equal importance, if not of greater import than our European literary heritage. Mary H. Austin was most likely the first, but not the last to write about our unwillingness to give the oral literature of Native Americans its rightful place in the study of what we define as American literature. The Cambridge History of American Literature, vol. 4, includes a chapter by her on the subject.

The areas of literature searched fall into the following categories: poetry; fiction; autobiography and personal reminiscences; biography; short stories; essays; and humor. Some liberties have been taken with the term contemporary, as noted above. Since 1960 more Native American writers have received recognition in the book world and in general periodicals. However, writers such as Charles Eastman, Francis La Flesche and others have been selected from earlier years of the twentieth century. They represent Native Americans who have been educated in the white system and who have achieved success according to white America's expectations of Indian assimilation. Their writings reflect in some measure that route of assimilation, with an obvious undercurrent of cynicism--an understandable response to white America's condescending acceptance of their capabilities. The Native Americans' inherent genius is apparent in all areas of their early oral literature as well as in their writings of today.

The route of preliminary planning began with a search of the Luther College Library holdings. Due to the efforts of Dr. Clark Mallam, Director of the Luther College Archaeological Research Center and an Assistant Professor in the Department of Anthropology, and with the cooperation of the Acquisitions Department, the Library was expanding and updating its holdings dealing with Native American culture. One of the first titles I discovered in my search which led to an emerging awareness of the impact and diversity of Native American literature was Arlene B. Hirschfelder's compilation, _American Indian Authors, a Representative Bibliography_, published in 1970 by the Association on American Indian Affairs, Inc. It provided a brief but valuable introduction to Native American authors of early and contemporary times in all subject areas. About the same time I learned of the newspaper-periodical, _Akwesasne Notes_, published by the Mohawk Nation. Each issue of this quarterly devotes one page (12" by 30") to the poetry of young Native Americans. I analyzed the poetry page of each issue back through 1970, and continued the process as each new issue arrived. The _Indian Historian_, a quarterly publication of the American Indian Historical Society which publishes current writings of Native Americans, was brought to my attention. I have had access to its back issues, and have analyzed them for literature. Other Native American periodicals have also been indexed for poetry. They are listed in Part 10.

The need for background became obvious. I continued a detailed search of the Luther College Library holdings and turned up numerous titles. Among them were re-published and recent compilations of excerpted traditional Native American songs and chants; e.g., Margot Astrov's _American Indian Prose and Poetry_, published by Capricorn Books in 1946 and re-published in 1962; Mary H. Austin's _The American Rhythm; Studies and Re-expressions of Amerindian Songs_ (Houghton, 1930), reprinted in a new and enlarged edition by Cooper Square in 1970; Natalie Curtis Burlin's _The Indian's Book_ (Harper, 1923), re-published by Dover in 1968; George W. Cronyn, _The Path on the Rainbow_ (Boni and Liveright, 1918), reprinted by Liveright in 1962 under the title, _American Indian Poetry; an Anthology of Songs and Chants_; and A. Grove Day's _The Sky Clears; Poetry of the American Indians_ (Macmillan, 1951).

The increased interest in the Native American encouraged the publication of new collections. William Brandon edited a collection entitled The Magic World (Morrow, 1971). John Bierhorst edited In the Trail of the Wind (Farrar, 1971). Virginia Armstrong compiled excerpts of famous Indian orations and gave it the apt title, I Have Spoken (Swallow, 1971). Jerome Rothenberg compiled Shaking the Pumpkin; Traditional Poetry of the Indian of the North Americas (Doubleday, 1972). And there are others. Shirley Witt, of Iroquois ancestry, together with Stan Steiner brought out a collection, The Way; an Anthology of American Indian Literature (Knopf, 1972). All except the last title are anthologies of traditional literature which fall outside my subject, but they gave me background on the significance of the oral tradition in the Native's life and culture and as fountain of the writer's inspiration.

Reference to the Annual Reports and Bulletins of the U. S. Bureau of American Ethnology yielded impressive results. They include translations and recordings of the oral traditional literature of the Native American: songs, chants, myths and legends, which together embody many of their religious beliefs and ceremonials.

My need to talk, discuss and ask questions about the subject became urgent. I went first to the University of South Dakota at Vermillion, primarily because it was not too far away--but I chose better than I had realized. Its Institute of Indian Studies was active in several areas. Dr. Joseph Cash, as Director of the American Indian Research Project, was collecting oral history of Native Americans with the assistance of the Institute's Native students: Oyate Iyechinka Woglakapi; an Oral History Collection (Vermillion: U. of S.D., 1970, 3 vols.). Dr. John R. Milton had published two collections of Native American authors: American Indian II (Dakota Pr., 1971); and American Indian Speaks (Dakota Pr., 1969). General Lloyd Moses, Native American Director of the Institute, advised me on locations of special interest, e.g., the Phillips Collection at the University of Oklahoma, Norman. Bob Carmack, University Librarian at South Dakota, offered the services of the library's collection in addition to his personal consideration.

Background reading and preliminary bibliographical study at the Luther College Library during the summer of 1972 enriched my semester study and gave me leads on the location of other sources. By correspondence, requests were made to use the research facilities of appropriate institutions. It became evident that universities and colleges with Native American Studies Institutes and/or special collections in the subject should be of first importance. Meeting librarians and directors of Institutes was a source of great inspiration and encouragement. Their personal contributions and suggested sources were extremely helpful. The following five universities and colleges were on my itinerary:

Institute of Indian Studies, University of South Dakota, Vermillion.

Department of American Indian Studies, University of Minnesota, Minneapolis.

Institute for Ethnic Studies, University of Nebraska, Lincoln.

Institute of Indian Studies, Bemidji State College, Bemidji, Minnesota.

Native American Studies, University of California, Berkeley.

The libraries of these Institutes provided valuable sources for my bibliography. Three university libraries house special collections in American Indian Bibliography:

Phillips Collection, University of Oklahoma, Norman.

University of Arizona, Tucson.

Arizona State University, Tempe.

The library at Stanford University yielded further material which had not surfaced before.

American Indian Junior Colleges contributed significantly to my research. Their library collections, although small in numbers of titles, in each case provided a rich concentration of sources. Those visited were:

Haskell Indian Junior College, Lawrence, Kansas.

Navajo Community Junior College, Many Farms, Arizona.

Institute of Indian Arts and Crafts, Santa Fe, New Mexico.

Cook Christian Training School for Indian Leadership, Tempe, Arizona.

A third group of institutions contacted were historical society and museum libraries.

Minnesota State Historical Society Library, St. Paul.

American Indian Historical Society Library, San Francisco, California.

Southwest Museum Library, Highland Park, Los Angeles, California.

Museum of Navajo Ceremonial Art Library, Sante Fe, New Mexico.

Usually historical society and museum libraries do not emphasize the contemporary, but those above were especially significant and were valuable sources of enrichment.

My professional and personal life has been enriched through this year of study. Meeting the directors of Native Studies programs was exciting and rewarding. Sincere thanks are due to the following Native American directors of university programs:

Roger Buffalohead, University of Minnesota, Minneapolis.

Richard Band, University of California, Berkeley.

Mrs. Alice Timmons, Phillips Collection, University of Oklahoma, Norman.

Lloyd Moses, University of South Dakota, Vermillion.

Don Bibeau, Bemidji State College, Bemidji, Minnesota.

Jeanette Henry, American Indian Historical Society, San Francisco, California.

In addition to the thanks due to the above named persons, the following persons deserve thanks for their courtesies:

Milton S. Overby, Librarian at Haskell Indian Junior College, Lawrence, Kansas.

Deborah Blouin, Reference Librarian at Arizona State, Tempe.

Gertrude Muir and Mrs. Ferral, Arizona State University, Tempe.

Del Delaware, Librarian, Cook Christian Training School for Indian Leadership, Tempe, Arizona.

Alix Lopez, Librarian at the American Indian Historical Society, San Francisco, California.

Ruth Christensen, Librarian at the Southwest Museum, Highland, Los Angeles, California.

Bernard Richardson, Librarian, Navajo Community College, Many Farms, Chinle, Arizona.

Janet Noll Naumer, Librarian, Institute of Arts & Crafts at Santa Fe, New Mexico.

Bertha Dutton, Director, Museum of Navajo Ceremonial Art, Santa Fe, New Mexico.

Frances Spadafore, Reference Librarian, Bemidji State College, Bemidji, Minnesota.

John R. Milton & Joseph Cash, Institute of Indian Studies, University of South Dakota, Vermillion.

Bob Carmack, Librarian, University of South Dakota, Vermillion.

Through them I was introduced to other Native Americans teaching in their departments. Their concern has been that the final bibliography be prepared for dissemination. Increased interest in anthropology, archaeology, environmental studies and back-to-nature styles of life which reflect the Native American's traditional way of life are all strong indications of the supportive role this bibliography occupies. For myself, a whole new world has been opened up during the last five years. Through reading Native American literature and related subject materials I have acquired a deep respect for the First Americans as a people and for their cultures.

Three years have passed all too quickly since the major portion of this work was done. The summer of 1976 was spent in updating the bibliography as far as time and circumstance would permit. Poetry from the 1973 to mid-1976 issues of Akwesasne Notes, Pembroke Magazine, Wassaja, and Blue Cloud Quarterly was indexed. Several poetry and story collections [see Part 8] published in 1974 and 1975 have been analyzed. Several fiction titles published since 1973 have been annotated. Also several titles in the area of biography and legend have been added. Revision was also necessary in some other areas.

Why have I not updated all of the periodicals listed? It would have been physically impossible and would have further lengthened the time before publication. The list of periodicals, as explained in Part 10, can suggest to the user of this bibliography sources of contemporary Native American prose and poetry. Several of the magazines indexed are produced by Native students of universities, e.g., Sun Tracks at the University of Arizona at Tucson.

Whenever possible I have indicated the writer's tribal affiliation. In some cases--e.g., Joseph Bruchac--the author does not wish to indicate his tribe. I have not included the writings of Frank Waters because he has not identified himself as a Native American. I respect his wishes as I do his scholarship and literary qualifications.

All omissions and errors are my responsibility.

Hearty thanks are due to many: to student assistants Deborah Carlson and Martha Grote; Reference assistant Deborah McCabe; Beverly Berg, who typed the first draft of the manuscript; Reference assistant Famie Berkeland, who worked on the indexes; and Linda Burri, Secretary to the Librarian, who typed the updated material and revisions.

Special thanks to Oivind Hovde, Head Librarian, for making possible the typing services, for other courtesies, and especially for pushing me when that was necessary. Thanks also to my library staff colleagues: Leona Alsaker, Elizabeth Kaschins, Martha Henzler, Duane Fenstermann and Harlan Sanderson, for their encouragement and understanding. Last but not least, a thank you to Clark Mallam for his continued enthusiasm.

Angeline Jacobson
Reference Librarian
Luther College Library
Decorah, Iowa
August 1976

Part 2

POETS AND THEIR POETRY

1. Ackley, Randall. (Pueblo) "Light Madness Is a Pleasant Way of Life." Pembroke Magazine no. 2 (1971) 23.

2. ______. "A Poem from Li Po to Tu Fu." Pembroke Magazine no. 2 (1971) 22.

3. ______. "A Troll Song." Pembroke Magazine no. 3 (1972) 65.

4. ______. "A Troll-Song for a Rainbowlove, for Brenda." Quetzal v. 2 (Summer, 1972) 5.

5. ______. Troll Songs. Bowling Green, Ohio: Tribal Pr., 1972.

6. ______. "Un Gritito." Quetzal v. 2 (Summer, 1972) 4.

7. Adams, Jane H. "you." [first line]. Akwesasne Notes v. 8 (Early Summer, 1976) 48.

8. Adams, Randy. "Touching Things." Angwamas Minosewag Anishinabeg. (Poets in the Schools Program) St. Paul Council of Arts and Sciences, Winter, 1973-74.

9. Aiello, Constance, ed. Oo-oonah Art, paintings with a few poems, by the Taos Pueblo Indian Schools 7th-8th grade pupils of 1967-68.

10. Alexander, Libby. (Spokane Tribal Group) "A Flight Called Love." Milton, John R., comp. The American Indian Speaks. Vermillion: U. of S.D., 1969, p. 138.

11. Alexander, Libby. (Spokane Tribal Group) "Humanity." Henry, Jeannette, ed., The American Indian Reader: Literature. Indian Historian Pr., 1973, p. 34.

12. ________. "This Man." In Henry, Jeannette, ed., The American Indian Reader: Literature. Indian Historian Pr., 1973, p. 34.

13. ________. "This Man." The Indian Historian v. 1 (Sept. 1968) 24.

14. Allen, Katharine H. (Choctaw) "Chahta Alla (Choctaw Child)." Blue Cloud Quarterly v. 20, no. 4.

15. Allen, Minerva. (Assiniboine) "Dawn was coming" [first line]. In Lourie, Dick, ed., Come to Power. The Crossing Press, 1974, p. 59.

16. ________. "Dog Soldier renounced life" [first line]. In Lourie, Dick, ed., Come to Power. The Crossing Press, 1974, p. 62.

17. ________. "For suns we traveled" [first line]. In Lourie, Dick, ed., Come to Power. The Crossing Press, 1974, p. 61.

18. ________. "Heavy clouds" [first line]. In Lourie, Dick, ed., Come to Power. The Crossing Press, 1974, p. 57.

19. ________. "The howling of the wind" [first line]. In Lourie, Dick, ed., Come to Power. The Crossing Press, 1974, p. 58.

20. ________. "In the dark of the night" [first line]. In Lourie, Dick, ed., Come to Power. The Crossing Press, 1974, p. 60.

21. ________. "Returning from" [first line]. In Lourie, Dick, ed., Come to Power. The Crossing Press, 1974, p. 63.

22. ________. "She is alone" [first line]. In Lourie, Dick, ed., Come to Power. The Crossing Press, 1974, p. 56.

23. ________. "A warm sunny day" [first line]. In Lourie,

Dick, ed., Come to Power. The Crossing Press, 1974, p. 55.

24. Allen, Paula Gunn. (Laguna-Sioux) "Crow Ambush (Song for '76)." In Milton, John R., ed., Four Indian Poets. Dakota Press, 1974, p. 44.

25. ______. "Deep Deep City Blues: Elegy for the Man Who Owned the Rain." In Milton, John R., ed., Four Indian Poets. Dakota Press, 1974, p. 33.

26. ______. "4 (The Dead Spider)." In Milton, John R., ed., Four Indian Poets. Dakota Press, 1974, p. 40.

27. ______. "Hoop Dancer." In Milton, John R., ed., Four Indian Poets. Dakota Press, 1974, p. 34.

28. ______. "Ikce Wichasha." In Milton, John R., ed., Four Indian Poets. Dakota Press, 1974, p. 35.

29. ______. "Jet Plane (Dhla-nuwa)." In Milton, John R., ed., Four Indian Poets. Dakota Press, 1974, pp. 47-8.

30. ______. "Lament of My Father, Lakota." In Dodge, Robert K. & Joseph B. McCullough, eds., Voices from Wah'kon-tah. International Publishers, 1974, p. 25.

31. ______. "Lament of My Father, Lakota." South Dakota Review v. 11 (Spring, 1973) 3.

32. ______. "Medicine Song." In Milton, John R., ed., Four Indian Poets. Dakota Press, 1974, p. 36.

33. ______. "Mountain Song." In Milton, John R., ed., Four Indian Poets. Dakota Press, 1974, p. 43.

34. ______. "1 (Shadow Way)." In Milton, John R., ed., Four Indian Poets. Dakota Press, 1974, p. 37.

35. ______. "Rain for Ke-waik Bu-ne-ya." In Milton, John R., ed., Four Indian Poets. Dakota Press, 1974, p. 41-2.

36. ______. "Sandia Crest, May, 1973." In Milton, John R., ed., Four Indian Poets. Dakota Press, 1974, p. 46.

37. Allen, Paula Gunn. (Laguna-Sioux) "Snowgoose." In Milton, John R., ed., Four Indian Poets. Dakota Press, 1974, p. 45.

38. ________. "3 (Lament)." In Milton, John R., ed. Four Indian Poets. Dakota Press, 1974, p. 39.

39. ________. "2 (The Duck-Billed God)." In Milton, John R., ed., Four Indian Poets. Dakota Press, 1974, p. 38.

40. Alta. (Mandan) "Thanksgiving." In Lowenfels, Walter, ed., From the Belly of the Shark. Vintage, 1973, p. 9.

41. Anderson, Andy. (Pomo) "Loneliness." Wassaja. v. 3 (March, 1975) 2.

42. Anderson, Vickie. "I am a Tree" [first line]. Angwamas Minosewag Anishinabeg. (Poets in the Schools Program) St. Paul Council of Arts and Sciences, Winter, 1973-74.

43. ________. "I am Blue" [first line]. Angwamas Minosewag Anishinabeg. (Poets in the Schools Program) St. Paul Council of Arts and Sciences, Winter, 1973-4.

44. Angaiak, John. (Eskimo) "My Native Land, the Beautiful." In Lowenfels, Walter, ed., From the Belly of the Shark. Vintage, 1973, p. 138.

45. Anon. "The End." Wassaja. v. 3 (September, 1975) 4.

46. Anon. (Nett Lake School) "My Feelings." Angwamas Minosewag Anishinabeg. (Poets in the Schools Program) St. Paul Council of Arts and Sciences, Winter, 1973-74.

47. Antelope, Verlys. "Frozen Promises" [first line]. The Blue Cloud Quarterly. v. 18, no. 3.

48. ________. "Illumination Meaning Nothing" [first line]. The Blue Cloud Quarterly. v. 18, no. 3.

49. ________. "The Shadowy Taste of Loneliness" [first

line]. The Blue Cloud Quarterly. v. 18, no. 3.

50. Antelope, Verlys. "Taos." The Blue Cloud Quarterly. v. 18, no. 3.

51. _______. "To Quote Rain." The Blue Cloud Quarterly. v. 18, no. 3.

52. _______. "You Think" [first line]. The Blue Cloud Quarterly. v. 18, no. 3.

53. Antene, David M. "Time." Akwesasne Notes. v. 3 (June, 1971) 46.

54. Arthur, Donald. (Alaska) "Dena Geleek: Song of the People." In Henry, Jeannette, ed., The American Indian Reader: Literature. Indian Historian Pr., 1973, p. 102-108.

55. Arviso, Cathy. (Navajo) "Magnificat." In Allen, T.D., ed., Arrow I. U.S. Bureau of Indian Affairs, Creative Writing Project, 1969, p. 11.

56. Atoni. (Choctaw) "Falling Tall." Sun Tracks. v. 1 (Fall, 1971) 24.

57. _______. "Fire Chant." Sun Tracks. v. 1 (Fall, 1971) 30.

58. _______. "The Promise Is Dead Grass." Sun Tracks. v. 1 (Fall, 1971) 24.

59. _______. "The Track of the Sun." Sun Tracks. v. 1 (June, 1971) 2.

60. awaninsgi ayu Udsdi hauhya. "look yonder and see" [first line]. Akwesasne Notes. v. 7 (Late Summer, 1975) 48.

61. Bacon, Bob. "The Child Awoke This Morning" [first line]. Akwesasne Notes. v. 5 (early Summer, 1973) 48.

62. _______. "Generation." Akwesasne Notes. v. 7 (Late Summer, 1975) 48.

63. _______. "The good die old" [first line]. Akwesasne

Notes. v. 7 (Late Summer, 1975) 48.

64. Bacon, Bob. "I Do Not Want to Die a White Man's Death." *Akwesasne Notes*. v. 6 (Early Spring, 1974) 48.

65. ________. "Indian Child." *Akwesasne Notes*. v. 4 (Early Spring, 1972) 48.

66. ________. "Poetic Advice." *Wassaja*. v. 3 (July, 1975) 13.

67. ________. "Priorities." *Akwesasne Notes*. v. 4 (Early Autumn, 1972) 48.

68. ________. "Tecumseh's Vision." *Akwesasne Notes*. v. 5 (Early Autumn, 1973) 3.

69. ________. "Turquoise Tears/Books & Jewelry." *Akwesasne Notes*. v. 5 (Early Autumn, 1973) 48.

70. Bacon, R. "Red Wine." *Akwesasne Notes*. v. 3 (April, 1971) 48.

71. Bacon, Robert. "Cree Cradle Song." *Akwesasne Notes*. v. 3 (Sept., 1971) 48.

72. ________. "Ghost Dance." *Akwesasne Notes*. v. 4 (Late Spring, 1972) 48.

73. ________. "He Also Had a Dream." *Akwesasne Notes*. v. 4 (Late Winter, 1972) 48.

74. ________. "Mister Scoutmaster." In Lowenfels, Walter, ed., *From the Belly of the Shark*. Vintage, 1973, p. 10.

75. ________. "Mister Scoutmaster." *Akwesasne Notes*. v. 3 (Oct./Nov., 1971) 48.

76. ________. "Plastic Paris Indians." *Akwesasne Notes*. v. 3 (July/Aug., 1971) 48.

77. ________. "Red/White ... and blue." *Akwesasne Notes*. v. 3 (May, 1971) 48.

78. ________. "Rushmore/Crazy Horse." *Akwesasne*

Notes. v. 3 (June, 1971) 48.

79. Bacon, Robert. "What Would You Give?" Akwesasne Notes. v. 3 (Dec., 1971) 48.

80. Badoni, Donald. "Dark Brown Navajo" [first line]. Akwesasne Notes. v. 2 (May, 1970) 48.

81. Bahe, Lee. "Home." Akwesasne Notes. v. 2 (May, 1970) 48.

82. ________. "Looking sad and lost" [first line]. Akwesasne Notes. v. 2 (May, 1970) 48.

83. Bahe, Liz Sohappy. (Yakima) "And What of Me?" In Niatum, Duane, ed., Carriers of the Dream Wheel. Harper, 1975, pp. 6-7.

84. ________. "Farewell." In Niatum, Duane, ed., Carriers of the Dream Wheel. Harper, 1975, p. 3.

85. ________. "Grandmother Sleeps." In Niatum, Duane, ed., Carriers of the Dream Wheel. Harper, 1975, p. 11.

86. ________. "Once Again." In Niatum, Duane, ed., Carriers of the Dream Wheel. Harper, 1975, pp. 12-13.

87. ________. "Printed Words." In Niatum, Duane, ed., Carriers of the Dream Wheel. Harper, 1975, pp. 4-5.

88. ________. "The Ration Card." In Niatum, Duane, ed., Carriers of the Dream Wheel. Harper, 1975, p. 8-9.

89. ________. "Talking Designs." In Niatum, Duane, ed., Carriers of the Dream Wheel. Harper, 1975, p. 10.

90. Bahe, Maggie. (Navajo) "On my Knees." In Allen, T.D., ed., Arrow III. U.S. Bureau of Indian Affairs, Creative Writing Project, 1971, pp. 5-6.

91. Baker, Jeanne. "My Life." In Witt, Shirley H., comp., The Way; an Anthology of American Indian Literature. Knopf, 1972, p. 146.

92. Ballard, Charles G. (Quapaw-Cherokee) "As Long as Rivers Flow." The Indian Historian. v. 5 (Fall, 1972) 24.

93. _______. "Changing of the Guard." In Dodge, Robert K. & Joseph B. McCullough, eds., Voices from Wah'kon-tah. International Publishers, 1974, p. 31.

94. _______. "During the Pageant at Medicine Lodge." In Dodge, Robert K. & Joseph B. McCullough, eds., Voices from Wah'kon-tah. International Publishers, 1974, p. 30.

95. _______. "Grandma Fire." The Indian Historian. v. 5 (Fall, 1972) 25.

96. _______. "The Man of Property." In Dodge, Robert K. & Joseph B. McCullough, eds., Voices from Wah'kon-tah. International Publishers, 1974, p. 29.

97. _______. "Navajo Girl of Many Farms." In Dodge, Robert K. & Joseph B. McCullough, eds., Voices from Wah'kon-tah. International Publishers, 1974, p. 27.

98. _______. "Now the People Have the Light." In Dodge, Robert K. & Joseph B. McCullough, eds., Voices from Wah'kon-tah. International Publishers, 1974, p. 33.

99. _______. "Old Fighter." The Indian Historian. v. 5 (Fall, 1972) 24.

100. _______. "Out on the Plains." The Indian Historian. v. 5 (Fall, 1972) 24.

101. _______. "Sand Creek." The Indian Historian. v. 5 (Fall, 1972) 25.

102. _______. "Time Was the Trail Went Deep." In Dodge, Robert K. & Joseph B. McCullough, eds., Voices from Wah'kon-tah. International Publishers, 1974, p. 32.

103. _______. "You Northern Girl." In Dodge, Robert K. & Joseph B. McCullough, eds., Voices from

Wah'kon-tah. International Publishers, 1974, p. 28.

104. Bantista, R. Michael. "West from the Railhead." In Levitas, Gloria, Frank Robert & Jacqueline J. Vivelo, eds., *American Indian Prose & Poetry.* Putnam, 1974, pp. 304-05.

105. Bantista, Rudy. (Kiowa) "Brothers." In Allen, T. D., ed., *Arrow III.* U.S. Bureau of Indian Affairs, Creative Writing Project, 1971, p. 22.

106. ________. "Indian Land." *Sun Tracks.* v. 1 (Winter, 1971/72) 15.

107. ________. "Looking North..." *Sun Tracks.* v. 1 (Winter 1971/72) 26.

108. ________. "My Father and My Son." In Allen, T. D., ed., *Arrow III.* U.S. Bureau of Indian Affairs, Creative Writing Project, 1971, p. 14.

109. ________. "Pony Song." In Allen, T.D., ed., *Arrow III.* U.S. Bureau of Indian Affairs, Creative Writing Project, 1971, p. 11.

110. ________. "Sweet Jesus." In Allen, T. D., ed., *Arrow III.* U.S. Bureau of Indian Affairs, Creative Writing Project, 1971. p. 1.

111. Baptiste, Jolyne. "I Am Free." *Wassaja.* v. 3 (April, 1975) 2.

112. Barefoot, Arthur T., Jr. (Federal Correctional Facility) "Does Anybody Know I'm Here?" *Akwesasne Notes.* v. 4 (Late Spring, 1972) 48.

113. Barnes, Jim. (Choctaw) "Autobiography: Last Chapter." In Niatum, Duane, ed., *Carriers of the Dream Wheel.* Harper, 1975, p. 27.

114. ________. "Bone Yard." In Niatum, Duane, ed., *Carriers of the Dream Wheel.* Harper, 1975, p. 21.

115. ________. "Camping Out on Rainy Mountain." In Niatum, Duane, ed., *Carriers of the Dream Wheel.* Harper, 1975, p. 19.

116. Barnes, Jim. (Choctaw) "The Captive Stone." In Niatum, Duane, ed., Carriers of the Dream Wheel. Harper, 1975, p. 23.

117. ________. "Halcyon Days." In Niatum, Duane, ed. Carriers of the Dream Wheel. Harper, 1975, p. 26.

118. ________. "Last Look at La Plata, Missouri." In Niatum, Duane, ed., Carriers of the Dream Wheel. Harper, 1975, p. 18.

119. ________. "Lying in a Yuma Saloon." In Niatum, Duane, ed., Carriers of the Dream Wheel. Harper, 1975, p. 24.

120. ________. "Paiute Ponies." In Niatum, Duane, ed., Carriers of the Dream Wheel. Harper, 1975, p. 25.

121. ________. "Sweating It Out on Winding Stair Mountain." In Niatum, Duane, ed., Carriers of the Dream Wheel. Harper, 1975, p. 22.

122. ________. "These Damned Trees Crouch." In Niatum, Duane, ed., Carriers of the Dream Wheel. Harper, 1975, p. 17.

123. ________. "Tracking Rabbits: Night." In Niatum, Duane, ed., Carriers of the Dream Wheel. Harper, 1975, p. 20.

124. Barsness, John. (Tuscarora) "Bearskin Wood." In Milton, John R., ed., Four Indian Poets. Dakota Press, 1974, p. 26.

125. ________. "Branding Spring." In Milton, John R., ed., Four Indian Poets. Dakota Press, 1974, p. 25.

126. ________. "Coor's Beer and the Rusty Canopener ..." In Milton, John R., ed., Four Indian Poets. Dakota Press, 1974, p. 27.

127. ________. "Crazy Woman." In Milton, John R., ed., Four Indian Poets. Dakota Press, 1974, p. 23.

128. Barsness, John. (Tuscarora) "Crazy Woman Rode a Dead Horse." In Milton, John R., ed., Four Indian Poets. Dakota Press, 1974, p. 22.

129. ________. "Deer Hunt 1971." In Milton, John R., ed., Four Indian Poets. Dakota Press, 1974, p. 21.

130. ________. "Hiline/U. S. Interstate Two." In Milton, John R., ed., Four Indian Poets. Dakota Press, 1974, p. 20.

131. ________. "Missouri River." Milton, John R., ed. Four Indian Poets. Dakota Press, 1974. p. 28-30.

132. ________. "There's a Man that Lives Alone in the Hills above the Yellowstone River." In Milton, John R., ed., Four Indian Poets. Dakota Press, 1974, pp. 17-9.

133. ________. "Walking in a Bear's Tracks." In Milton, John R., ed., Four Indian Poets. Dakota Press, 1974, p. 24.

134. Bass, Vincent. (Winnebago) "Waterfall." In Dance with Indian Children. Washington, D. C.: Center for the Arts of Indian Children, 1972, p. 27.

135. Batala, Art. "The Ceremony" (to dex westrum). Akwesasne Notes. v. 4 (Early Spring, 1972) 48.

136. Bautista, Robert. (Papago) "Fading Out." Sun Tracks. v. 1 (Spring, 1972) 30.

137. Bazhonoodah, Asa. "They Are Taking the Holy Elements from Mother Earth." In David, Jay, ed., The American Indian, the First Victim. Morrow, 1972, pp. 160-64.

138. Bazil, Frances. (Coeur d'Alène) "Loneliness." Sun Tracks. v. 1 (Winter, 1971/72) 25.

139. Beach, Marion "Tumbleweed." (Creek) "A Song to the Chicano Indian Village." In Lowenfels, Walter, ed., From the Belly of the Shark. Vintage, 1973, p. 11.

140. Beauchamp, Lewis. "Her Memories." Akwesasne Notes. v. 4 (Late Autumn, 1972) 48.

141. _______. "i walk tonight" [first line]. Akwesasne Notes. v. 6 (Early Summer, 1974) 48.

142. Bedoka, Sally. (Caddo) "Dew." In Allen, T. D., ed., Arrow III. U. S. Bureau of Indian Affairs, Creative Writing Project, 1971, p. 10.

143. Begay, Edward. "Happiness Is." Akwesasne Notes. v. 2 (May, 1970) 48.

144. Begay, Leland. (Navajo) "Decision." In Allen, T. D., ed., Arrow II. U. S. Bureau of Indian Affairs, Creative Writing Project, 1970, p. 20.

145. Begay, Terrence. "The Sheep Wandering" [first line]. Akwesasne Notes. v. 2 (May, 1970) 48.

146. Belgarde, Dallas. (Chippewa) "My Heavy Chevy." In Allen, T. D., ed., Arrow IV. U. S. Bureau of Indian Affairs, Creative Writing Project, 1972, p. 3.

147. Bell, Juanita. (Pima) "Indian Children Speak." In Lowenfels, Walter, ed., From the Belly of the Shark. Vintage, 1974, p. 12.

148. Bell, Richard. "The Indian." Akwesasne Notes. v. 3 (Oct./Nov., 1971) 48.

149. Beltrametti, Franco. "I Saw the Green Yuba River Flow." Akwesasne Notes. v. 5 (January, 1973) 48.

150. Benally, Ray. (Navajo) "Squaw." In Allen, T. D., ed., Arrow I. U. S. Bureau of Indian Affairs, Creative Writing Project, 1969, p. 4.

151. _______. "Ruins." In Allen, T. D., ed., Arrow I. U. S. Bureau of Indian Affairs, Creative Writing Project, 1969, p. 5.

152. Benally, Raymond. (Navajo) "Tourist." In Allen, T. D., ed., Arrow I. U. S. Bureau of Indian Affairs, Creative Writing Project, 1969, p. 6.

153. Benally, Raymond. (Navajo) "Indian." Sun Tracks. v. 1 (Spring, 1972) 3.

154. Bentley, Janis. (Absentee Shawnee) "Eagles, Hawks, Vultures" [first line]. In Allen, T. D., ed., Arrow IV. U.S. Bureau of Indian Affairs, Creative Writing Project, 1972, p. 3.

155. Benton, Sherrole. "Stirring the Evening Meal" [first line]. Angwamas Minosewag Anishinabeg. 1st issue. (Poets in the Schools Program) St. Paul Council of Arts and Sciences, [1973].

156. Berrigan, Ted. (Choctaw) "From Sonnets." In Rothenberg, J. & George Quasha, eds., America, a Prophecy ... Random, 1974, pp. 391-3.

157. _______. In the Early Morning Rain. Grossman, 1971.

158. _______. Many Happy Returns. Corinth Bks., 1968.

159. _______. "Peace." In Sanders, Thomas E. & Walter W. Peek, Literature of the American Indian. Glencoe Pr., 1973, p. 453.

160. _______. "Presence." In Sanders, Thomas E. & Walter W. Peek, Literature of the American Indian. Glencoe Pr., 1973, pp. 454-5.

161. _______. "Sonnet XXIII." In Haslam, Gerald W., Forgotten Pages of American Literature. Houghton, 1970, pp. 36-7.

162. _______. "Sonnet XXIII." In Dodge, Robert K. & Joseph B. McCullough, eds., Voices from Wah'kontah. International Publishers, 1974, p. 34.

163. _______. The Sonnets. Grove Press, 1967.

164. _______. "Tambourine Life." In Carroll, Paul. The Young American Poets. Big Table Pub., Co., 1968, pp. 93-119.

165. _______. "Words for Love; for Sandy." Poetry. v. 112 (June, 1968) 164-5.

166. Berrigan, Ted, Ron Padgett and Joe Brainard. (Choctaw) Spasms. N.Y.: Kulchur Pr., 1967.

167. Berry, Aaron. "Has Got to Fall." Akwesasne Notes. v. 3 (July/August, 1971) 48.

168. Bettles, Jody. "You've Given Too Much" [first line]. Akwesasne Notes. v. 3 (April, 1971) 48.

169. Big Eagle, Duane. (Osage) "Bidato [October Pomo Village]." In Lowenfels, Walter, ed., From the Belly of the Shark. Vintage, 1973, p. 13.

170. ________. Bidato: Ten Mile River Poems. The Workingman's Press, 1975.

171. ________. "My People." Akwesasne Notes. v. 5 (Early Autumn, 1973) 3.

172. ________. "Poems; IV, V, VI, VII." Quetzal. v. 2 (Winter/Spring, 1972) 28-9.

173. Bigbear, Joe. "Alcoholics." Angwamas Minosewag Anishinabeg. 1st issue. (Poets in the Schools Program) St. Paul Council of Arts and Sciences, [1973].

174. ________. "Loneliness." Angwamas Minosewag Anishinabeg. 1st issue. (Poets in the Schools Program) St. Paul Council of Arts and Sciences, [1972].

175. ________. "Old Man with Whiskers" [first line]. Angwamas Minosewag Anishinabeg. 1st issue. (Poets in the Schools Program) St. Paul Council of Arts and Sciences, [1972].

176. ________. "This Is Now" [first line]. Angwamas Minosewag Anishinabeg. 1st issue. (Poets in the Schools Program) St. Paul Council of Arts and Sciences, [1973].

177. ________. "Up in the North Woods" [first line]. Angwamas Minosewag Anishinabeg. 1st issue. (Poets in the Schools Program) St. Paul Council of Arts and Sciences, [1973].

178. Billy, Pfc. Jim N. [in Vietnam] "Happiness Was When." Akwesasne Notes. v. 2 (Nov./Dec., 1970) 48.

179. Bird, Dolly. "All the Old Hunters." Akwesasne Notes. v. 6 (Early Autumn, 1974) 48.

180. ______. "Can I Say." Akwesasne Notes. v. 4 (Late Spring, 1972) 48.

181. ______. "Can I Say." In Levitas, Gloria, Frank Robert & Jacqueline J. Vivelo, eds., American Indian Prose & Poetry. Putnam, 1974, pp. 288-90.

182. ______. "For the Animals as They Are Our Good Friends." Akwesasne Notes. v. 6 (Late Spring, 1974) 48.

183. ______. "Man of the Earth Red." Akwesasne Notes. v. 2 (October, 1970) 47.

184. ______. "Pa Sappa." Akwesasne Notes. v. 4 (Late Winter, 1972) 48.

185. ______. "Return to the Home We Made." Akwesasne Notes. v. 2 (Nov./Dec., 1970) 48.

186. ______. "Return to the Home We Made." In Lowenfels, Walter, ed., From the Belly of the Shark. Vintage, 1973, p. 14-17.

187. ______. "When the Leaves Circle." Akwesasne Notes. v. 5 (Early Winter, 1973) 48.

188. ______. "White Man's Got Guilt." Akwesasne Notes. v. 3 (March, 1971) 48.

189. ______. "The Worst Crime." Akwesasne Notes. v. 3 (April, 1971) 48.

190. Bird, Harold, or Littlebird. (Santo Domingo-Laguna) "Death in the Woods." In Dodge, Robert K. & Joseph B. McCullough, eds., Voices from Wah'kon-tah. International Publishers, 1974, p. 53.

191. Bird, Larry. (Santo Domingo-Laguna) "The Corn Awakens" [first line]. In Dance with Indian

Children. Washington, D. C.: Center for the Arts of Indian Children, 1972, p. 4.

192. Bird, Larry. (Santo Domingo Laguna) "I Sing a Song of Being" [first line]. Sun Tracks. v. 1 (Winter, 1971/72) 31.

193. Bissell, Brenda Jay. "Trees waved in freedom" [first line]. Akwesasne Notes. v. 3 (Oct./Nov., 1971) 48.

194. Bissonette, Pedro. "Give me the arrows" [first line]. Akwesasne Notes. v. 6 (Early Spring, 1974) 48.

195. Bitsui, Kee. "Proud Navajo." Akwesasne Notes. v. 1 (Nov., 1969) 33.

196. Black, Byron. "I the Fake Mad Bomber and Walking It Home Again." In Faderman, Lillian and Barbara Bradshaw, eds., Speaking for Ourselves: American Ethnic Writing. Scott, Foresman, 1969, pp. 505-6.

197. ________. "I, the Fake, Mad Bomber and Walking It Home Again." Prairie Schooner. v. 35 (Summer, 1961) 163-4.

198. ________. "I, the Fake Mad Bomber and Walking It Home Again." In Sanders, Thomas E. & Walter W. Peek, Literature of the American Indian. Glencoe Pr., 1973, pp. 456-7.

199. ________. "Ode to the Queen of Chrome, Fifty-Eight Buick." Prairie Schooner. v. 35 (Summer, 1961) 162.

200. ________. "Pressure Applied." Prairie Schooner. v. 35 (Summer, 1961) 162-3.

201. Blacketter, Brian. "I am dead" [first line]. Angwamas Minosewag Anishinabeg. (Poets in the Schools Program) St. Paul Council of Arts and Sciences, Winter, 1973-74.

202. ________. "The Moon Is Under Black Clouds" [first line]. Angwamas Minosewag Anishinabeg. (Poets in the Schools Program) St. Paul Council of Arts and Sciences, Winter, 1973-74.

203. Blackhat, Elva. "Cowboys and Indians" [first line]. Akwesasne Notes. v. 2 (May, 1970) 48.

204. Blackwater, Ray. "Loneliness." Akwesasne Notes. v. 2 (May, 1970) 48.

205. Blockcolski, Lew. (Cherokee-Choctaw) "The Five Year Indian." In Lourie, Dick, ed., Come to Power. The Crossing Press, 1974, p. 25.

206. ________. "Georgia's Champion." In Lourie, Dick, ed., Come to Power. The Crossing Press, 1974, p. 27.

207. ________. "The Life of Man." In Lourie, Dick, ed., Come to Power. The Crossing Press, 1974, p. 30.

208. ________. "Little Father Speaks." In Lourie, Dick, ed., Come to Power. The Crossing Press, 1974, p. 26.

209. ________. "Museum Exhibition." In Lowenfels, Walter, ed., From the Belly of the Shark. Vintage, 1973, p. 18.

210. ________. "Museum Exhibition." Akwesasne Notes. v. 3 (Oct./Nov., 1971) 48.

211. ________. "Poetry." In Lourie, Dick, ed., Come to Power. The Crossing Press, 1974, p. 29.

212. ________. "Pow-wow Remnants." Akwesasne Notes. v. 3 (July/Aug., 1971) 48.

213. ________. "Translation of a Prairie Band Pottawatomi Prayer." In Lourie, Dick, ed., Come to Power. The Crossing Press, 1974, p. 28.

214. Blue Cloud. "Crazy Horse Monument (to the sculptor)." Akwesasne Notes. v. 7 (Late Summer, 1975) 48.

215. ________. "Flying ... Turtles." Akwesasne Notes. v. 7 (Early Summer, 1975) 48.

216. ________. "For a Child." Akwesasne Notes. v. 7 (Early Summer, 1975) 48.

217. ________. "Sweat Lodge ... the Afterwards."

Akwesasne Notes. v. 7 (Early Autumn, 1975) 48.

218. Blue Cloud. "Turtle." Akwesasne Notes. v. 5 (Late Summer, 1973) 48.

219. ______. "Turtle." The Indian Historian. v. 7 (Summer, 1974) 61-2.

220. ______. "Yellowjacket (for Coyote)." Akwesasne Notes. v. 6 (Early Autumn, 1974) 48.

221. Blue Cloud, Peter, or Coyote 2. "Alcatraz Visions." In Tvedten, Benet, comp., An American Indian Anthology. Marvin, S. D.: Blue Cloud Abbey, 1971, pp. 49-50.

222. ______. "Turtle." Blue Cloud Quarterly. v. 19, no. 4.

223. ______. "When's the Last Boat to Alcatraz ... ?" Akwesasne Notes. v. 5 (January, 1973) 48.

224. Boney, Nancy. "Come to Darkest Eyes of the Horse" [first line]. Angwamas Minosewag Anishinabeg. (Poets in the Schools Program) St. Paul Council of Arts and Sciences, Winter, 1973-74.

225. Booth, Barbara. "In the Shallows." Akwesasne Notes. v. 6 (Early Summer, 1974) 48.

226. Brandi. "At the end of the day" [first line]. Akwesasne Notes. v. 5 (Late Summer, 1973) 48.

227. ______. "Chimborazo." Akwesasne Notes. v. 5 (Late Summer, 1973) 48.

228. ______. "Highland Song." Akwesasne Notes. v. 5 (January, 1973) 48.

229. ______. "We People Can't Think Straight." Akwesasne Notes. v. 6 (Late Spring, 1974) 48.

230. ______. "Where Is Ecuador?" Akwesasne Notes. v. 5 (Late Summer, 1973) 48.

231. Brigham, Besmilr. (Choctaw) "North from Tanyana." In Lowenfels, Walter, ed., From the Belly of the

Shark. Vintage, 1973, pp. 19-20.

232. Brown, Florence. "Waiting by Pyramid Lake." Akwesasne Notes. v. 3 (Dec., 1971) 48.

233. Brown, P. J. "On My Quest for Singing Stones" [first line]. Akwesasne Notes. v. 7 (Early Winter, 1975) 48.

234. Bruchac, Joseph. (Abnaki) "An African Town." In Lourie, Dick, ed., Come to Power. The Crossing Press, 1974, p. 47.

235. ______. "Bear Song No. 2." Pembroke Magazine. no. 7 (1976) 229.

236. ______. "Beaver Dam." Pembroke Magazine. no. 7 (1976) 227-8.

237. ______. "Canticle." Pembroke Magazine. no. 6 (1975) 76.

238. ______. "City." In Niatum, Duane, ed., Carriers of the Dream Wheel. Harper, 1975, p. 39.

239. ______. "Coming Back." In Niatum, Duane, ed., Carriers of the Dream Wheel. Harper, 1975, p. 41.

240. ______. "The Dolphin Burial." In Lourie, Dick, ed., Come to Power. The Crossing Press, 1974, p. 51.

241. ______. "Drum Songs." In Lourie, Dick, ed., Come to Power. The Crossing Press, 1974, pp. 48-9.

242. ______. "Elegy for Jack Bowman." In Niatum, Duane, ed., Carriers of the Dream Wheel. Harper, 1975, pp. 32-3.

243. ______. "Eyes in the Winter Cedar." Pembroke Magazine. no. 6 (1975) 74-6.

244. ______. "First Deer." In Lourie, Dick, ed., Come to Power. The Crossing Press, 1974, p. 50.

245. Bruchac, Joseph. (Abnaki) "Flower Children." Pembroke Magazine. no. 6 (1975) 76.

246. ______. "For a Winnebago Brave." In Niatum, Duane, ed., Carriers of the Dream Wheel. Harper, 1975, p. 43.

247. ______. "IV." In Niatum, Duane, ed., Carriers of the Dream Wheel. Harper, 1975, p. 40.

248. ______. "Frozen Hands." In Niatum, Duane, ed., Carriers of the Dream Wheel. Harper, 1975, p. 35.

249. ______. "Grain." Pembroke Magazine. no. 6 (1975) 76.

250. ______. "The Grandmother Came Down to Visit Us." In Niatum, Duane, ed., Carriers of the Dream Wheel. Harper, 1975, p. 31.

251. ______. "The Grandmother Came Down to Visit Us." Pembroke Magazine. no. 7 (1976) 227.

252. ______. "Grey Rock Poem." Pembroke Magazine. no. 7 (1976) 228-29.

253. ______. "Hiking." In Niatum, Duane, ed., Carriers of the Dream Wheel. Harper, 1975, p. 38.

254. ______. "The Immigrant." Pembroke Magazine. no. 7 (1976) 244.

255. ______. "Indian Mountain." In Lourie, Dick, ed., Come to Power. The Crossing Press, 1974, pp. 44-6.

256. ______. "Indian Mountain." In Lowenfels, Walter, ed., From the Belly of the Shark. Vintage, 1973, pp. 21-23.

257. ______. "Late February Snow." Pembroke Magazine. no. 7 (1976) 87.

258. ______. "The Manabozho Poems." Blue Cloud Quarterly. v. 20, no. 3.

259. Bruchac, Joseph. (Abnaki) "Maps." Pembroke Magazine. no. 7 (1976) 229.

260. ______. "Poem for Jan." In Niatum, Duane, ed., Carriers of the Dream Wheel. Harper, 1975, p. 44.

261. ______. "Red Jacket's Grave." Pembroke Magazine. no. 6 (1975) 74.

262. ______. "Second Skins--A Peyote Song." In Niatum, Duane, ed., Carriers of the Dream Wheel. Harper, 1975, p. 42.

263. ______. "The Seeds." Pembroke Magazine. no. 6 (1975) 74.

264. ______. "Stone Giant." In Niatum, Duane, ed., Carriers of the Dream Wheel. Harper, 1975, p. 34.

265. ______. "Three Poems for the Indian Steelworkers ...." In Niatum, Duane, ed., Carriers of the Dream Wheel. Harper, 1975, p. 36-7.

266. ______. "Walking." In Lourie, Dick, ed., Come to Power. The Crossing Press, 1974, p. 43.

267. ______. "Water." Pembroke Magazine. no. 6 (1975) 75.

268. ______. "Winter Poem." Pembroke Magazine. no. 7 (1976) 147.

269. Buckskin, Floyd. "I Am, I Am Not." Akwesasne Notes. v. 3 (Dec., 1971) 48.

270. ______. "I Am, I Am Not." In Henry, Jeannette, ed., The American Indian Reader: Literature. Indian Historian Pr., 1973, p. 32.

271. ______. "I Am, I Am Not." The Indian Historian. v. 2 (Fall, 1969) 34.

272. Budreau, Kim. "Crazy Dog Days." Angwamas Minosewag Anishinabeg. (Poets in the Schools

Program) St. Paul Council of Arts and Sciences, Winter, 1973-4.

273. Bullis, Janie. "Death." In Witt, Shirley H., comp., The Way: an Anthology of American Indian Literature, Knopf, 1972, p. 146.

274. Bunnell, David. "Alliance." Akwesasne Notes. v. 5 (January, 1973) 48.

275. Burnette, L. Sharon. (Sioux) "Entanglement." Sun Tracks. v. 1 (Winter, 1971/72) 25.

276. Burres, Lee Allan. "Homage to the Bear." Akwesasne Notes. v. 3 (March, 1971) 48.

277. Burson, Fred. (Ute) "Why Not? It's New Years!" [prose]. In Allen, T. D., ed., Arrow III. U.S. Bureau of Indian Affairs, Creative Writing Project, 1971, pp. 31-7.

278. Byerley, Fred. (Oglala Sioux) "I was born" [first line]. In Allen, T. D., ed. Arrow IV. U.S. Bureau of Indian Affairs, Creative Writing Project, 1972, p. 7.

279. ________. "We need" [first line]. In Allen, T. D., ed., Arrow IV. U.S. Bureau of Indian Affairs, Creative Writing Project, 1972, p. 14.

280. Cade, Scott R. "Warrior." Akwesasne Notes. v. 6 (Early Autumn, 1974) 48.

281. Calamity, Lawrence. (Navajo) "The Cliff Dwellers." In Allen, T. D., ed., Arrow IV. U.S. Bureau of Indian Affairs, Creative Writing Project, 1972, p. 22.

282. ________. "The Fates of War." In Allen, T. D., ed., Arrow IV. U.S. Bureau of Indian Affairs, Creative Writing Project, 1972, p. 12.

283. Calkins, Guy E. "A North American Indian Prayer." Akwesasne Notes. v. 1, Sec. 3 (Nov., 1969) 9.

284. Campbell, David. "Ancient mists shroud in silence" [first line]. Akwesasne Notes. v. 7 (Early Spring, 1975) 48.

285. Campbell, David. "At the Pyramids of Monte Alban." Akwesasne Notes. v. 7 (Early Spring, 1975) 48.

286. ________. "Momostenango shoe-shine boy" [first line]. Akwesasne Notes. v. 7 (Early Spring, 1975) 48.

287. Campbell, Janet. (Coeur d'Alène) "Nespelim Man." In Allen, Terry, ed., The Whispering Wind; Poetry by Young American Indians. Doubleday, 1972, p. 32.

288. ________. "Nespelim Man." In Dodge, Robert K. & Joseph B. McCullough, eds., Voices from Wah'kon-tah. International Publishers, 1974, p. 36.

289. ________. "Red Eagle." In Allen, Terry, ed., The Whispering Wind; Poetry by Young American Indians. Doubleday, 1972, p. 31.

290. ________. "Red Eagle." In Milton, John M., comp., The American Indian Speaks. Vermillion: U. of S. D., 1969, p. 137.

291. ________. "Red Eagle." In Dodge, Robert K. & Joseph B. McCullough, eds., Voices from Wah'kon-tah. International Publishers, 1974, p. 35.

292. Carden, Ramona. (Colville) "The Moccasins of an Old Man." In Dodge, Robert K. & Joseph B. McCullough, eds., Voices from Wah'kon-tah. International Publishers, 1974, p. 37.

293. ________. "The Moccasins of an Old Man." In Allen, Terry, ed., The Whispering Wind; Poetry by Young American Indians. Doubleday, 1972, p. 35.

294. ________. "Tumbleweed." In Dodge, Robert K. & Joseph B. McCullough, eds., Voices from Wah'kon-tah. International Publishers, 1974, p. 38.

295. ________. "Tumbleweed." In Allen, Terry, ed., The Whispering Wind; Poetry by Young American Indians. Doubleday, 1972, p. 36.

296. ________. "Tumble Weed." In Dance with Indian Children. Washington, D.C.: Center for the Arts of Indian Children, 1972, p. 19.

297. Carden, Ramona. (Colville) "Tumbleweed." In Milton, John R., comp., The American Indian Speaks. Vermillion: U. of S.D., 1969, p. 149.

298. Cardiff, Gladys. (Cherokee) "Carious Exposure." In Niatum, Duane, ed., Carriers of the Dream Wheel. Harper, 1975, p. 53.

299. ________. "Combing." In Niatum, Duane, ed., Carriers of the Dream Wheel. Harper, 1975, p. 50.

300. ________. "Dragon Skate." In Lowenfels, Walter, ed., From the Belly of the Shark. Vintage, 1973, pp. 23-4.

301. ________. "Dragon Skate." In Niatum, Duane, ed., Carriers of the Dream Wheel. Harper, 1975, p. 51-2.

302. ________. "Grey Woman." In Niatum, Duane, ed., Carriers of the Dream Wheel. Harper, 1975, p. 56.

303. ________. "Leaves Like Fish." In Niatum, Duane, ed., Carriers of the Dream Wheel. Harper, 1975, p. 47.

304. ________. "Long Person." In Niatum, Duane, ed., Carriers of the Dream Wheel. Harper, 1975, p. 49.

305. ________. "Swimmer." In Niatum, Duane, ed., Carriers of the Dream Wheel. Harper, 1975, p. 55.

306. ________. "Tlanusi'yi, the Leech Place." In Niatum, Duane, ed., Carriers of the Dream Wheel. Harper, 1975, p. 48.

307. ________. "To Frighten a Storm." In Niatum, Duane, ed., Carriers of the Dream Wheel. Harper, 1975, p. 54.

308. Carson, Mona. (Colville) "What Love Is." In Allen, T. D., ed., Arrow II. U.S. Bureau of Indian Affairs, Creative Writing Project, 1970, p. 30.

309. Carty, Susan. "Walk in the Old Ways." Akwesasne

Notes. v. 4 (Late Autumn, 1972) 48.

310. Castillo, Gloria. "The Life of a Leaf." In Henry, Jeannette, ed., The American Indian Reader: Literature. Indian Historian Pr., 1973, p. 26.

311. ________. "Life of a Leaf." The Indian Historian. v. 1 (Sept., 1968) 25.

312. Cesspooch (Dancing Eagle Plume). "Spirit Rock (Medicine)." Akwesasne Notes. v. 6 (Early Summer, 1974) 48.

313. Chaneg, Marion. (Seminole) "My Heart Was Black" [first line]. Akwesasne Notes. v. 3 (March, 1971) 48.

314. Charlie, Johnny. (Navajo) "Grandfather." Sun Tracks. v. 1 (Spring, 1972) 23.

315. Charlo, A. F. "Bars!!!!!!!!!" Native Nevadan. v. 9, no. 2, p. 6.

316. Chase, Betty. "Thin Poem." Akwesasne Notes. v. 2 (May, 1970) 48.

317. Chee, Laura. [Ft. Wingate H. S.] "Echoes of Tradition." Sun Tracks. v. 1 (June, 1971) 15.

318. ________. "Evening Was Coming Soon" [first line]. Sun Tracks. v. 1 (June, 1971) 15.

319. Cheman and Glen Fontaine. "The Red River, North Dakota." Akwesasne Notes. v. 5 (Late Summer, 1973) 48.

320. Chenay, John Vance. "Tears." Akwesasne Notes. v. 3 (Sept., 1971) 48.

321. Chippewa Jr. High Student. [Cloquet, Minn.] "Nobody Believes." Akwesasne Notes. v. 2 (Nov./Dec., 1970) 48.

322. Chosa, Martha. (Jemez Pueblo) "Drums." In Dodge, Robert K. & Joseph B. McCullough, eds., Voices from Wah'kon-tah. International Publishers, 1974, p. 39.

323. Chosa, Martha. (Jemez Pueblo) "Drums." In Milton, John R., comp., The American Indian Speaks. Vermillion: U. of S.D., 1969, p. 134.

324. Christian, Bob. "My eyes are blue, my skin is light" [first line]. Akwesasne Notes. v. 3 (June, 1971) 48.

325. Clancy. "Lesson to the Young." Akwesasne Notes. v. 4 (Late Spring, 1972) 48.

326. Clark, Paul. (Eskimo) "Prayer." In Allen, T. D., ed., Arrow IV. U.S. Bureau of Indian Affairs, Creative Writing Project, 1972, p. 5.

327. Clauschee, Lillian. "Lillian C." Akwesasne Notes. v. 2 (May, 1970) 48.

328. Cloutier, David. "The Moon of Blinding Snow." Akwesasne Notes. v. 5 (Early Spring, 1973) 48.

329. Cody, Lorraine. "Home." Akwesasne Notes. v. 2 (May, 1970) 48.

330. ________. "Homecoming." Akwesasne Notes. v. 2 (May, 1970) 48.

331. Coffee, Robin L. (Cherokee-Creek-Sioux) "i am the wind." In Allen, T. D., ed., Arrow IV. U.S. Bureau of Indian Affairs, Creative Writing Project, 1972, p. 4.

332. Cohoe, Grey. (Navajo) "Alone Together." In Allen, Terry, ed., The Whispering Wind; Poetry by Young American Indians. Doubleday, 1972, p. 26.

333. ________. "Ancestors." In Allen, Terry, ed., The Whispering Wind; Poetry by Young American Indians. Doubleday, 1972, p. 24.

334. ________. "Ancestors." Pembroke Magazine. no. 4 (1973) 11.

335. ________. "Ancestors." Sun Tracks. v. 1 (June, 1971) 9.

336. ________. "Dark Wind Over Me." Pembroke Magazine. no. 4 (1973) 12.

337. Cohoe, Grey. (Navajo) "The Folding Fan." In Dodge, Robert K. & Joseph B. McCullough, eds., Voices from Wah'kon-tah. International Publishers, 1974, p. 41.

338. ________. "The Folding Fan." In Allen, Terry, ed., The Whispering Wind; Poetry by Young American Indians. Doubleday, 1972, p. 25.

339. ________. "The Folding Fan." In Milton, John R., comp., The American Indian Speaks. Vermillion: U. of S.D., 1969, p. 133.

340. ________. "The Folding Fan." Pembroke Magazine. no. 4 (1973) 12.

341. ________. "The Folding Fan." Sun Tracks. v. 1 (June, 1971) 12.

342. ________. "The Male Voice of Thunder." Pembroke Magazine. no. 4 (1973) 11.

343. ________. "Mom." In Allen, Terry, ed., The Whispering Wind; Poetry by Young American Indians. Doubleday, 1972, p. 27.

344. ________. "Rainmakers." Pembroke Magazine. no. 4 (1973) 13.

345. ________. "Snowflakes." In Allen, Terry, ed., The Whispering Wind; Poetry by Young American Indians. Doubleday, 1972, p. 27.

346. ________. "Thirst." In Allen, Terry, ed., The Whispering Wind; Poetry by Young American Indians. Doubleday, 1972, p. 23.

347. Colfax, Greg. [from] "The River Never Named." In Lowenfels, Walter, ed., From the Belly of the Shark. Vintage, 1973, p. 25.

348. Concha, Carl. (Taos Pueblo) "Proud." The Blue Cloud Quarterly. v. 15, no. 3.

349. ________. "The Spirit Dreams." In Lowenfels, Walter, ed., From the Belly of the Shark. Vintage, 1973, p. 26.

350. Concha, Joseph. (Taos Pueblo) "Grandfather and I." In Witt, Shirley H., comp., The Way; an Anthology of American Indian Literature. Knopf, 1972, p. 136.

351. ______. "I Walked In." In Dance with Indian Children. Washington, D.C.: Center for the Arts of Indian Children, 1972, p. 7.

352. ______. Lonely Deer; Poems by a Pueblo Indian Boy. Illus. by author. Foreword by Constantine Aiello. Published by Taos Pueblo Council. [n.d.]

353. ______. Taos. "A Man after Lunch." Quetzal. v. 2 (Winter-Spring, 1972) 35-6.

354. ______. "A New Visitor (to the Pueblo)." In Witt, Shirley H., comp., The Way; an Anthology of American Indian Literature. Knopf, 1972, p. 137.

355. ______. "On Reading Books for Yourself" [first line]. In Future Directions in Native American Art. Sante Fe., N.M.: The Institute of American Indian Arts, [1973], p. 6.

356. ______. "The president of amerika" [first line]. In Allen, T. D., ed., Arrow III. U.S. Bureau of Indian Affairs, Creative Writing Project, 1971, p. 12.

357. ______. "Snow, the Last." In Witt, Shirley H., comp., The Way; an Anthology of American Indian Literature. Knopf, 1972, p. 136.

358. Conley, Robert J. (Cherokee) "Dancing Will No More." The Blue Cloud Quarterly. v. 18, no. 3.

359. ______. "I Hunt." Pembroke Magazine. no. 3 (1972) 52.

360. ______. "Song for the Shell Shaker." The Blue Cloud Quarterly. v. 18, no. 3.

361. ______. "Song of Ned Christie." Quetzal. v. 2 (Winter-Spring, 1972) 30-1.

362. ______. "War Dance." Pembroke Magazine. no. 3 (1972) 52.

363. Conley, Robert J. (Cherokee) "We Wait." In Lowenfels, Walter, ed., From the Belly of the Shark. Vintage, 1973, pp. 27-9.

364. ________. "Where Shall I Build My Fires?" The Blue Cloud Quarterly. v. 18, no. 3.

365. Connor, Allan. "Every Time I'm Lonely" [first line]. Angwamas Minosewag Anishinabeg. (Poets in the Schools Program) St. Paul Council of Arts and Sciences, Winter, 1973-74.

366. Coon, William. "I Want to Live." In Henry, Jeannette, ed., The American Indian Reader: Literature. Indian Historian Pr., 1973, p. 29.

367. ________. "I Want to Live." The Indian Historian. v. 2 (Fall, 1969) 34.

368. Coyote 2, or Blue Cloud. "Alcatraz." In Lowenfels, Walter, ed. From the Belly of the Shark. Vintage, 1973, p. 29-30.

369. ________. "Anthros." Akwesasne Notes. v. 4 (Late Spring, 1972) 48.

370. ________. "An Elegy to the American Way." In Levitas, Gloria, Frank Robert & Jacqueline J. Vivelo, eds., American Indian Prose & Poetry. Putman, 1974, pp. 291-92.

371. ________. "An Elegy to the American Way." Akwesasne Notes. v. 4 (Late Winter, 1972) 48.

372. Crawford, Shirley. (Kalispel Tribal Group) "Grandfather." Akwesasne Notes. v. 3 (April, 1971) 48.

373. ________. "Grandfather." In Henry, Jeannette, ed., The American Indian Reader: Literature. Indian Historian Pr., 1973, p. 53.

374. ________. "The River Took My Sister." In Milton, John R., comp., The American Indian Speaks. Vermillion: U. of S.D., 1969, p. 111.

375. Cuelho, Art, or Seven Buffaloes. "Gypsy Wine." Quetzal. v. 1 (Summer, 1971) 47.

376. Cuelho, Art, or Seven Buffaloes. "Nature Notes for a Song." Quetzal. v. 1 (Summer, 1971) 29.

377. Dacey, Philip. "Cottonwood Poem." South Dakota Review. v. 10 (Autumn, 1972) 72.

378. ______. "From the Book of Stones." South Dakota Review. v. 10 (Autumn, 1972) 73.

379. Daley, Paul. "The Vision of Two Eye." American Indian Crafts and Culture. v. 5 (March, 1972) 15.

380. David. [Nett Lake School] "My Stuff." Angwamas Minosewag Anishinabeg. (Poets in the Schools Program) St. Paul Council of Arts and Sciences, Winter, 1973-74.

381. David, Richard. (Navajo) "Hosteen Race Track was Shi Cheeh" [first line]. In Allen, T. D., ed., Arrow III. U.S. Bureau of Indian Affairs, Creative Writing Project, 1971, p. 9-10.

382. ______. "Somewhere off to the Rising Sun" [first line]. In Allen, T. D., ed., Arrow III. U.S. Bureau of Indian Affairs, Creative Writing Project, 1971, p. 8.

383. DeFoe, Roy. "The Circle of Life." Angwamas Minosewag Anishinabeg. 1st issue. (Poets in the Schools Program) St. Paul Council of Arts and Sciences, [1973].

384. Defoe, Steve. "I was riding my Bike" [first line]. Angwamas Minosewag Anishinabeg. (Poets in the Schools Program) St. Paul Council of Arts and Sciences. Winter, 1973-74.

385. De Witt, Leddy. "Now I'm dead" [first line]. Angwamas Minosewag Anishinabeg. (Poets in the Schools Program) St. Paul Council of Arts and Sciences, Winter, 1973-74.

386. ______. "Our People are Learning" [first line]. Angwamas Minosewag Anishinabeg. (Poets in the Schools Program) St. Paul Council of Arts and Sciences, Winter 1973-74.

387. Dixon, Edith. (Navajo) "Home." Akwesasne Notes. v. 2 (May, 1970) 48.

388. ________. "Untitled." In Allen, T. D., ed., Arrow I. U.S. Bureau of Indian Affairs, Creative Writing Project, 1969, p. 13.

389. Dixon, R. S. "Pine Ridge, South Dakota." Akwesasne Notes. v. 4 (Early Autumn, 1972) 48.

390. Dnynia. "Charlie Wenjack Projected." Akwesasne Notes. v. 5 (Early Winter, 1973) 48.

391. Donald, Carolyn. "The Sky." Angwamas Minosewag Anishinabeg. (Poets in the Schools Program) St. Paul Council of the Arts and Sciences, Winter, 1973-74.

392. Doolittle, Anna. "Sand Creek." The Warpath. v. 4, no. 9, p. 5.

393. Dorris, Michael. "Bicentennial." Wassaja. v. 3 (September 20, 1975) 10.

394. Downing, Linda. (Cherokee) "The Dark." In Allen, T. D., ed., Arrow II. U.S. Bureau of Indian Affairs, Creative Writing Project, 1970, p. 15.

395. Doyle, Bruce. (Cherokee-Creek) "Thus Spoke the Establishment." In Allen, T. D., ed., Arrow II. U.S. Bureau of Indian Affairs, Creative Writing Project, 1970, pp. 31-35.

396. Duggleby, John. "American Eagle." Akwesasne Notes. v. 4 (Late Autumn, 1972) 48.

397. Edmo, Ed. "I'm not going to get burnt out" [first line]. Akwesasne Notes. v. 3 (Sept., 1971) 48.

398. ________. "I'm not Going to Get Burn't Out." In Lowenfels, Walter, ed., From the Belly of the Shark. Vintage, 1973, pp. 31-2.

399. Edwards, Susan. (Colville) "Her Food Was Her Song" [first line]. In Future Directions in Native American Art. Sante Fe, N.M.: The Institute of American Indian Arts, [1973], p. 25.

400. Edwards, Susan. (Colville) "his emotions" [first line]. In Allen, T. D., ed., Arrow IV. U.S. Bureau of Indian Affairs, Creative Writing Project, 1972, p. 2.

401. ________. "In the Short Time" [first line]. In Future Directions in Native American Art. Sante Fe, N.M.: The Institute of American Indian Arts, [1973], [1].

402. ________. "Paint Is Like the Smile" [first line]. In Future Directions in Native American Art. Sante Fe, N.M.: The Institute of American Indian Arts, [1973], p. 25.

403. ________. "Where Hidden Fires Burn." In Levitas, Gloria, Frank Robert & Jacqueline J. Vivelo, eds., American Indian Prose & Poetry. Putman, 1974, pp. 302-03.

404. El Teatro. "The Tlamatinime Questions." Akwesasne Notes. v. 5 (Early Winter, 1973) 48.

405. Ellis, Gail. (Oneida) "For My Uncle Jimmy." Quetzal. v. 2 (Winter-Spring, 1972) 36.

406. Emerson, Gloria. "Lady, with Shawl." In Henry, Jeannette, ed., The American Indian Reader: Literature. Indian Historian Pr., 1973, pp. 43-46.

407. ________. "Lady, with Shawl" [first line]. The Indian Historian. v. 4 (Summer, 1971) 8-9.

408. ________. "A Navajo Prayer." United Scholarship Service News. v. 1 (July, 1969) 3.

409. Emerson, Larry. "A Tale of Two Worlds." Sun Tracks. v. 1 (Spring, 1972) 11-21.

410. Endrezze, Anita. (Yaqui) "Eclipse." Blue Cloud Quarterly. v. 19, no. 4.

411. ________. "Manifest Destiny." Blue Cloud Quarterly. v. 19, no. 4.

412. ________. "The Plague." Blue Cloud Quarterly. v. 19, no. 4.

413. Endrezze, Anita. (Yaqui) "Yaqui Cry." Blue Cloud Quarterly. v. 19, no. 4.

414. Esparza, Phil. "Cantina y Restaurant." Akwesasne Notes. v. 7 (Early Spring, 1975) 48.

415. Eteeyan, Warren H. "Now I lay me down to die" [first line]. Akwesasne Notes. v. 3 (Sept., 1971) 48.

416. Eureka Indian Pre-School Children. "I am a deer" [first line]. Akwesasne Notes. v. 8 (Early Summer, 1976) 48.

417. Evaloardjuak, Lucy. "In the Spring When the Sun Never Sets." In Lewis, Richard, comp. I Breathe a New Song. Simon, 1971, p. 108.

418. Evans, Alice. "My Horse Galloping" [first line]. Akwesasne Notes. v. 2 (May, 1970) 48.

419. Fallis, Laurence S. (Cree) "The Apache Hide-out at Whitewater Canyon, New Mexico." Akwesasne Notes. v. 6 (Early Spring, 1974) 48.

420. ______. "Geronimo: If I Must Die in Bondage." Blue Cloud Quarterly. v. 19, no. 3.

421. Farabaugh, Ruth. "Countdown." Akwesasne Notes. v. 6 (Early Autumn, 1974) 48.

422. Finley, Deborah. (Colville) "Grandfather." Blue Cloud Quarterly. v. 15, no. 3.

423. Fisher, Mary Lu. "Say he was sad" [first line]. Akwesasne Notes. v. 3 (Jan./Feb., 1971) 48.

424. Fisher, Thomas Michael. (Sioux) "Dancing Music." Blue Cloud Quarterly. v. 19, no. 4.

425. ______. "Power Came to Them." Blue Cloud Quarterly. v. 19, no. 4.

426. ______. "Shall My Prayer Rise?" Blue Cloud Quarterly. v. 19, no. 4.

427. ______. "That My Heart Be Touched." Blue Cloud Quarterly. v. 19, no. 4.

428. Flores, Diane. (Papago) "Cooking." In Allen, T. D., ed., Arrow III. U.S. Bureau of Indian Affairs, Creative Writing Project, 1971, p. 20.

429. Flores, Manuel Chavarria. "Indian, you travel all the roads of America" [first line]. Akwesasne Notes. v. 3 (Sept., 1971) 48.

430. Flynn, Darline. (Sioux) "A Tribute to our Great Chief Crazy Horse." Quetzal. v. 2 (Winter-Spring, 1972) 39.

431. Fools Crow, Frank. (Oglala Sioux) "A Prayer for Peace." Wassaja. v. 3 (October, 1975) 1.
This prayer was given by Chief Frank Fools Crow, holy man of the Oglala Sioux, as the opening prayer in the U.S. Senate, September 5, 1975.

432. Francisco, Bertha. (Navajo) "Poem." In Levitas, Gloria, Frank Robert & Jacqueline J. Vivelo, eds., American Indian Prose & Poetry. Putman, 1974, p. 304.

433. ________. "Relations." In Levitas, Gloria, Frank Robert & Jacqueline J. Vivelo, eds., American Indian Prose & Poetry. Putnam, 1974, p. 304.

434. ________. "The Sun Eloped with You" [first line]. In Allen, T. D., ed., Arrow III. U.S. Bureau of Indian Affairs, Creative Writing Project, 1971, p. 7.

435. Frazier, Carol. (Paiute) "Dancing Tree." In Dance with Indian Children. Washington, D.C.: Center for the Arts of Indian Children, 1972, p. 21.

436. Frazier, Danny. (Navajo) "I Say It." In Allen, T. D., ed., Arrow IV. U.S. Bureau of Indian Affairs, Creative Writing Project, 1972, p. 10.

437. Fyten, Leah. "Dreaming." Angwamas Minosewag Anishinabeg. (Poets in the Schools Program) St. Paul Council of Arts and Sciences, Winter, 1973-74.

438. Gali, Isidro, Jr. "The People." Akwesasne Notes. v. 7 (Late Summer, 1975) 48.

439. Garcia, Rosey E. (Pueblo at Santo Domingo) "Then and Now." In Milton, John R., comp., *The American Indian Speaks*. Vermillion: U. of S. D., 1969, p. 148.

440. Garrett, Lance. "Graduation Song." *Akwesasne Notes*. v. 4 (Late Winter, 1972) 48.

441. ________. "Reunion." *Akwesasne Notes*. v. 4 (Early Spring, 1972), 48.

442. Garter, Tony. (Sioux) "Bison." In Allen, T. D., ed., *Arrow III*. U.S. Bureau of Indian Affairs, Creative Writing Project, 1971, p. 13.

443. Gaseoma, Lee Roy. (Hopi) "A Dream, Yet So Real." In Allen, T. D., ed., *Arrow IV*. U.S. Bureau of Indian Affairs, Creative Writing Project, 1972, p. 7.

444. Geeshuzhan. "Progress Is This Now." *Akwesasne Notes*. v. 4 (Early Autumn, 1972) 48.

445. Gemmill, Renee. "This Time." *Akwesasne Notes*. v. 6 (Early Autumn, 1974) 48.

446. George, Phil. (Nez Perce) "Ambition." In Milton, John R., comp., *The American Indian Speaks*. Vermillion: U. of S. D., 1969, p. 113.

447. ________. "Ask the Mountains." In Allen, Terry, ed., *The Whispering Wind; Poetry by Young American Indians*. Doubleday, 1972, pp. 124-5.

448. ________. "Ask the Mountains." In Dodge, Robert K. & Joseph B. McCullough, eds., *Voices from Wah'kon-tah*. International Publishers, 1974, p. 46.

449. ________. "Battle Won Is Lost." In Dodge, Robert K. & Joseph B. McCullough, eds., *Voices from Wah'kon-tah*. International Publishers, 1974, p. 48.

450. ________. "Battle Won Is Lost." In Allen, Terry, ed., *The Whispering Wind; Poetry by Young American Indians*. Doubleday, 1972, p. 114.

451. ________. "Child Rest." In Allen, Terry, ed., *The Whispering Wind; Poetry by Young American*

Indians. Doubleday, 1972, p. 117.

452. George, Phil. (Nez Perce) "Coyote's Night." In Allen, Terry, ed., The Whispering Wind; Poetry by Young American Indians. Doubleday, 1972, p. 128.

453. ________. "Monument in Bone." In Allen, Terry, ed., The Whispering Wind; Poetry by Young American Indians. Doubleday, 1972, p. 122.

454. ________. "Morning Beads." In Allen, Terry, ed., The Whispering Wind; Poetry by Young American Indians. Doubleday, 1972, p. 127.

455. ________. "My Indian Name." Sun Tracks. v. 1 (Winter, 1971/72) 21-24.

456. ________. "Night Blessing." In Allen, Terry, ed., The Whispering Wind; Poetry by Young American Indians. Doubleday, 1972, pp. 118-9.

457. ________. "Night Blessing." Blue Cloud Quarterly. v. 15, no. 3.

458. ________. "Night Blessing." In Dodge, Robert K. & Joseph B. McCullough, eds., Voices from Wah'kon-tah. International Publishers, 1974, p. 44.

459. ________. "Old Man, the Sweat Lodge." In Dodge, Robert K. & Joseph B. McCullough, eds., Voices from Wah'kon-tah. International Publishers, 1974, p. 42.

460. ________. "Old Man, the Sweat Lodge." In Allen, Terry, ed., The Whispering Wind; Poetry by Young American Indians. Doubleday, 1972, p. 115.

461. ________. "Old Man, the Sweat Lodge." In Gooderham, Kent, ed., I Am an Indian. Toronto: Dent, 1969, pp. 68-9.

462. ________. "Old Man's Plea." In Allen, Terry, ed., The Whispering Wind; Poetry by Young American Indians. Doubleday, 1972, p. 126.

463. ________. "Poetess." In Milton, John R., comp.,

The American Indian Speaks. Vermillion: U. of S. D., 1969, p. 112.

464. George, Phil. (Nez Perce) "Proviso." In Allen, Terry, ed., The Whispering Wind; Poetry by Young American Indians. Doubleday, 1972, p. 113.

465. ________. "Proviso." In Future Directions in Native American Art. Sante Fe, N. M.: The Institute of American Indian Arts, [1973], p. 21.

466. ________. "Self." In Allen, Terry, ed., The Whispering Wind; Poetry by Young American Indians. Doubleday, 1972, p. 122.

467. ________. "Shadows and Song." In Allen, Terry, ed., The Whispering Wind; Poetry by Young American Indians. Doubleday, 1972, p. 123.

468. ________. "Song of a New Cradleboard." In Allen, Terry, ed., The Whispering Wind; Poetry by Young American Indians. Doubleday, 1972, p. 116.

469. ________. "Song of a New Cradleboard." Sun Tracks. v. 1 (Winter, 1971/72) 8.

470. ________. "Through Dawn's Pink Aurora." In Allen, Terry, ed., The Whispering Wind; Poetry by Young American Indians. Doubleday, 1972, p. 127.

471. ________. "Until Then." In Allen, Terry, ed., The Whispering Wind; Poetry by Young American Indians. Doubleday, 1972, p. 126.

472. George, Willie. (Yuchi) "In the Hot Sun We Dance." In Dance with Indian Children. Washington, D. C.: Center for the Arts of Indian Children, 1972, p. 24.

473. ________. "Pop, Crackle, Hiss!" [first line]. In Dance with Indian Children. Washington, D. C.: Center for the Arts of Indian Children, 1972, p. 17.

474. ________. "War Signs." In Dance with Indian Children. Washington, D. C.: Center for the Arts of Indian Children, 1972, p. 25.

475. George, Willie. (Yuchi) "War Signs." In Witt, Shirley H., comp., The Way; an Anthology of American Indian Literature. Knopf, 1972, p. 147.

476. Gilbert, El. "With My Crayons." Akwesasne Notes. v. 6 (Early Autumn, 1974) 48.

477. ______. "With My Kachina." Akwesasne Notes. v. 7 (Early Autumn, 1975) 48.

478. Gonier, Bonita. "Bring to me the Moose out of the Water" [first line]. Angwamas Minosewag Anishinabeg. (Poets in the Schools Program) St. Paul Council of Arts and Sciences, Winter, 1973-74.

479. Gonzales, Paul Allen. "Navajo." New Mexico Quarterly. v. 34 (Autumn, 1964) 283-4.

480. Good Iron, Vance. (Mandan) "Clouds." Sun Tracks. v. 1 (Spring, 1972) 26.

481. ______. "Complaining to the Gods in the Springtime." In Tvedten, Benet, comp., An American Indian Anthology. Marvin, S. D.: Blue Cloud Abbey, 1971, pp. 40-1.

482. ______. "Complaints to the Gods." The Indian Historian. v. 3 (Spring, 1970) 48.

483. ______. "Dreams." Akwesasne Notes. v. 1, no. 7 (July, 1969) p. 32. [reprinted from United Scholarship Service News. v. 1, no. 5]

484. ______. "The History of Good Fur Robe." The Indian Historian. v. 3 (Spring, 1970) 48.

485. ______. "The History of Good Fur Robe." In Tvedten, Benet, comp., An American Indian Anthology. Marvin, S. D.: Blue Cloud Abbey, 1971, p. 41.

486. ______. "Song of Dust and Clouds." The Indian Historian. v. 3 (Spring, 1970) 48.

487. ______. "The Spring Rain." Sun Tracks. v. 1 (Spring, 1972) 22.

488. Good Iron, Vance. (Mandan) "Untitled." Akwesasne Notes. v. 1, no. 7 (July, 1969) p. 32.

489. ________. "Untitled." The Indian Historian. v. 3 (Spring, 1970) 48.

490. ________. "Untitled." In Witt, Shirley H., The Way: an Anthology of American Indian Literature. Knopf, 1972, p. 138.

491. Gordon, Donna. "Sailing" [first line]. Angwamas Minosewag Anishinabeg. (Poets in the Schools Program) St. Paul Council of Arts and Sciences, Winter, 1973-74.

492. Govan, Donald. "Courage." In Lowenfels, Walter, ed., From the Belly of the Shark. Vintage, 1973, p. 32.

493. Guardipee, Francix X. (Blackfoot) "A Prayer." In Henry, Jeannette, ed., The American Indian Reader: Literature. Indian Historian Pr., 1973, p. 13.

494. Gwin, Lillian. (Gros Ventre-Arikara) "I Wish." In Allen, T. D., ed., Arrow III. U.S. Bureau of Indian Affairs, Creative Writing Project, 1971, p. 19.

495. Gyalog, Ron. "Red Bark Willow Shaven" [first line]. Akwesasne Notes. v. 5 (Early Autumn, 1973) 48.

496. Haley, Ayron. (Cherokee) "Red Man, Old Man." In Rickards, Montana H., Literature for the Native American. Atlanta: Nat'l. Counc. of Teachers of English, Nov. 1970, p. 11.

497. Haley, Jon. (Navajo) "Trail of Beauty." In Allen, T. D., ed., Arrow II. U.S. Bureau of Indian Affairs, Creative Writing Project, 1970, pp. 27-8.

498. Hampton, Sherry. (Choctaw) "Beau Geste." In Allen, T. D., ed., Arrow II. U.S. Bureau of Indian Affairs, Creative Writing Project, 1970, pp. 11-12.

499. ________. "A Gift." In Allen, T. D., ed., Arrow I.

U. S. Bureau of Indian Affairs, Creative Writing Project, 1969, p. 1.

500. Hampton, Sherry. (Choctaw) "A Gift." Sun Tracks. v. 1 (Winter, 1971/72) 27.

501. Harjo, Patty Leah. (Seneca-Seminole) "In Restless Dreams..." [first line]. Sun Tracks. v. 1 (Spring, 1972) 22.

502. ________. "The Journey." Sun Tracks. v. 1 (June, 1971) 5-7.

503. ________. "The Mask." In Dance with Indian Children. Washington, D. C.: Center for the Arts of Indian Children, 1972, p. 7.

504. ________. "The Mask." Sun Tracks. v. 1 (Fall, 1971) 21.

505. ________. "Musings." In Dodge, Robert K. & Joseph B. McCullough, eds., Voices from Wah'kon-tah. International Publishers, 1974, p. 49.

506. ________. "Musings." In Milton, John R., comp., The American Indian Speaks. Vermillion, South Dakota, 1969, p. 151.

507. ________. "Musings." In Sanders, Thomas E. & Walter W. Peek, Literature of the American Indian. Glencoe Pr., 1973, p. 458.

508. ________. "My Heart Is Full of Words" [first line]. Sun Tracks. v. 1 (Winter, 1971/72) 25.

509. ________. "My Heart Is Sad With Remembering." Sun Tracks. v. 1 (Spring, 1972) 9.

510. ________. "Walk Proud, Walk Straight, Let Your Thoughts Race." In Witt, Shirley H., The Way: An Anthology of American Indian Literature. Knopf, 1972, p. 141-2.

511. ________. "Wisps of Cedar Smoke Stripe the Air" [first line]. Blue Cloud Quarterly. v. 15, no. 3.

512. ________. "Wisps of Cedar Smoke" [first line].

Sun Tracks. v. 1 (Winter, 1971/72) 19.

513. Harner, Michael. "Wounded Knee." Akwesasne Notes. v. 5 (Early Spring, 1973) 41.

514. Harvey, Johnny. "To Hold on to Something." Sun Tracks. v. 1 (Winter, 1971/72) 19.

515. Harvey, Roberta. "Poem." Akwesasne Notes. v. 1, no. 7 (July, 1969) 32.

516. Haven, Ernest. "Gray." Akwesasne Notes. v. 2, (May, 1970) 48.

517. Haycock, Todd. (Navajo) "Above Alkali Spring." In Milton, John R., ed., Four Indian Poets. Dakota Press, 1974, p. 52.

518. ______. "Days Come Through as White Dust Arrives." In Milton, John R., ed., Four Indian Poets. Dakota Press, 1974, p. 56.

519. ______. "Lited a Smoke to Grind Some Sorrow." In Milton, John R., ed., Four Indian Poets. Dakota Press, 1974, p. 51.

520. ______. "Navajoland." In Milton, John R., ed., Four Indian Poets. Dakota Press, 1974, p. 57.

521. ______. "Rain." In Milton, John R., ed., Four Indian Poets. Dakota Press, 1974, p. 54.

522. ______. "Time Flew in a Manner of Birds." In Milton, John R., ed., Four Indian Poets. Dakota Press, 1974, p. 53.

523. ______. "Wild Flowers." In Milton, John R., ed., Four Indian Poets. Dakota Press, 1974, p. 55.

524. Hellmuth, Thane. "There Was a World of Earth and Sky..." [first line]. Akwesasne Notes. v. 3 (May, 1971) 48.

525. ______. "The Visit." Akwesasne Notes. v. 3 (March, 1971) 48.

526. Hendricks, Edmond. "It Was Beautiful." In Henry,

Jeannette, ed., The American Indian Reader: Literature. Indian Historian Pr., 1973, p. 27.

527. Hendricks, Edmond. "It was Beautiful." The Indian Historian. v. 1 (Sept., 1968) 26.

528. Henry, Dennis. "Long Walk." Akwesasne Notes. v. 2 (May, 1970) 48.

529. Henson, Lance. (Cheyenne) "The Cold." In Niatum, Duane, ed., Carriers of the Dream Wheel. Harper, 1975, p. 63.

530. _______. "Dawn in January." In Niatum, Duane, ed., Carriers of the Dream Wheel. Harper, 1975, p. 60.

531. _______. "Grandfather." In Niatum, Duane, ed., Carriers of the Dream Wheel. Harper, 1975, p. 62.

532. _______. "Last Words, 1968." In Niatum, Duane, ed., Carriers of the Dream Wheel. Harper, 1975, p. 61.

533. _______. "Moon at Three A.M." In Niatum, Duane, ed., Carriers of the Dream Wheel. Harper, 1975, p. 64.

534. _______. "Our Smoke Has Gone Four Ways." In Niatum, Duane, ed., Carriers of the Dream Wheel. Harper, 1975, p. 59.

535. _______. "Wish." In Niatum, Duane, ed., Carriers of the Dream Wheel. Harper, 1975, p. 65.

536. Herman, Jake. (Sioux) "Cowboy Joe." In Henry, Jeannette, ed., The American Indian Reader: Literature. The Indian Historian Pr., 1973, pp. 140-2.

537. High Pines, Gayle. "Gifts." Akwesasne Notes. v. 5 (Early Autumn, 1973) 3.

538. Hight, Louise. (Ute) "Rain." In Allen, T. D., ed., Arrow I. U.S. Bureau of Indian Affairs, Creative Writing Project, 1969, p. 14.

539. Hill, Howard. "Some Do." Akwesasne Notes. v. 3 (March, 1971) 48.

540. Hill, Roberta. (Oneida) "Beginning the Year at Rosebud, S. D." In Niatum, Duane, ed., Carriers of the Dream Wheel. Harper, 1975, p. 76.

541. ________. "Direction." In Niatum, Duane, ed., Carriers of the Dream Wheel. Harper, 1975, pp. 70-71.

542. ________. "Dream of Rebirth." In Niatum, Duane, ed., Carriers of the Dream Wheel. Harper, 1975, p. 77.

543. ________. "Falling Moon." In Niatum, Duane, ed., Carriers of the Dream Wheel. Harper, 1975, pp. 72-73.

544. ________. "In the Madison Zoo." In Niatum, Duane, ed., Carriers of the Dream Wheel. Harper, 1975, p. 84.

545. ________. "Lines for Marking Time." In Niatum, Duane, ed., Carriers of the Dream Wheel. Harper, 1975, p. 78.

546. ________. "Midnight on Front Street." In Niatum, Duane, ed., Carriers of the Dream Wheel. Harper, 1975, pp. 82-3.

547. ________. "A Nation Wrapped in Stone." In Niatum, Duane, ed., Carriers of the Dream Wheel. Harper, 1975, p. 74.

548. ________. "Night along the Mackinac Bridge." In Niatum, Duane, ed., Carriers of the Dream Wheel. Harper, 1975, p. 69.

549. ________. "Sleeping with Foxes." In Niatum, Duane, ed., Carriers of the Dream Wheel. Harper, 1975, p. 75.

550. ________. "Song for Healing." In Niatum, Duane, ed., Carriers of the Dream Wheel. Harper, 1975, p. 80.

551. Hill, Roberta. (Oneida) "Star Quilt." In Niatum, Duane, ed., Carriers of the Dream Wheel. Harper, 1975, p. 79.

552. ______. "Whispers." In Niatum, Duane, ed., Carriers of the Dream Wheel. Harper, 1975, p. 81.

553. Hin-sha-agli-win, or Beatrice Medicine. "The Big Foot Trail to Wounded Knee." The Indian Historian. v. 6 (Fall, 1973) 23-5.

554. Holt, Rochelle. (Kiowa) A Ballet of Oscillations. Sioux City, Iowa: Ragnarok Pr., 1972.

555. ______. The Bare Tissue of Her Soul. N.Y.: Folder Editions, 1972.

556. ______. "The Dancer." Quetzal. v. 1 (Summer, 1971) 17.

557. ______. "Night Rendevous." Quetzal. v. 1 (Summer, 1971) 17.

558. ______. A Seismograph of Feeling. Sioux City, Iowa: Ragnarok Pr., 1972.

559. ______. "What He Told Me." Quetzal. v. 1 (Summer, 1971) 32.

560. Horn, Gabriel. (Onondaga) "A Chant to Lure Honor." In Sanders, Thomas E. & Walter W. Peek, Literature of the American Indian. Glencoe Pr., 1973, pp. 524-5.

561. Hosay, Stacey. "I Have Wasted Many" [first line]. Akwesasne Notes. v. 4 (Late Autumn, 1972) 48.

562. Hosh, Koi. "The Whippoorwill Calls." Wassaja. v. 4, no. 1 (January, 1976) 20.

563. ______. "The Wonderer." Wassaja. v. 3 (September 20, 1973) 10.

564. Huckaby, Gerald. "There are Some Indians They say..." [first line]. Akwesasne Notes. v. 2 (October, 1970) 47.

565. Hummingbird, Don. (Cherokee) "Words." In Allen,

T. D., ed., Arrow IV. U.S. Bureau of Indian Affairs, Creative Writing Project, 1972, p. 1.

566. Humphrey, P. [in Vietnam] "If I Die in Vietnam." Akwesasne Notes. v. 3 (Jan./Feb., 1971) 48.

567. Ignacio, Bruce. (Ute) "Dancing." Sun Tracks. v. 1 (Winter, 1971/72) 18.

568. ______. "Lost." in Dodge, Robert K. & Joseph B. McCullough, eds., Voices from Wah'kon-tah. International Publishers, 1974, p. 50.

569. ______. "Lost. In Milton, John R., comp., The American Indian Speaks. Vermillion, South Dakota, 1969, p. 150.

570. ______. "Lost." In Sanders, Thomas E. & Walter W. Peek, Literature of the American Indian. Glencoe Pr., 1973, p. 457.

571. ______. "When I Was Young My Father Said." In Witt, Shirley H., The Way; an Anthology of American Indian Literature. Knopf, 1972, pp. 142-3.

572. Ignacio, Leonard. (Navajo) "Life." In Allen, T. D., ed., Arrow IV. U.S. Bureau of Indian Affairs, Creative Writing Project, 1972, p. 6.

573. Inman, William. "Arrows of Resonance." Akwesasne Notes. v. 7 (Early Autumn, 1975) 48.

574. Inman, Will. "SIWLOKI." Akwesasne Notes. v. 7 (Early Winter, 1975) 48.

575. iron priest, tsi ka-gi. "If You Meet My Father." Akwesasne Notes. v. 7 (Early Winter, 1975) 48.

576. Irving, Patricia. "Going Where." In Allen, Terry, ed., The Whispering Wind; Poetry by Young American Indians. Doubleday, 1972, p. 78.

577. ______. "Goodbye and Run." In Allen, Terry, ed., The Whispering Wind; Poetry by Young American Indians. Doubleday, 1972, p. 81.

578. Irving, Patricia. "Legend." In Allen, Terry, ed., The Whispering Wind; Poetry by Young American Indians. Doubleday, 1972, p. 79.

579. ________. "A Silver Mist Creeps Along the Shore." In Allen, Terry, ed., The Whispering Wind; Poetry by Young American Indians. Doubleday, 1972, p. 80.

580. ________. "Sun Dancers." In Allen, Terry, ed., The Whispering Wind; Poetry by Young American Indians. Doubleday, 1972, p. 80.

581. ________. "Sweet Winds of Love." In Allen, Terry, ed., The Whispering Wind; Poetry by Young American Indians. Doubleday, 1972, p. 77.

582. ________. "Why." In Allen, Terry, ed., The Whispering Wind; Poetry by Young American Indians. Doubleday, 1972, p. 81.

583. ________. "Why?; Legend." Sun Tracks. v. 1 (Fall, 1971) 5.

584. ________. "You Too." In Allen, Terry, ed., The Whispering Wind; Poetry by Young American Indians. Doubleday, 1972, p. 79.

585. Isaac, Marzine. (Choctaw) "Life." In Allen, T. D., ed., Arrow IV. U.S. Bureau of Indian Affairs, Creative Writing Project, 1972, p. 9.

586. Issaluk, Luke. (Eskimo) "I See Your Face" [first line]. In Lewis, Richard, I Breathe A New Song. Simon, 1971, p. 85.

587. Janis, Vincent. "Sacred Earth." Wassaja. v. 3 (May, 1975) 2.

588. Jendrzejczyk, L. M. "Exhibit." Akwesasne Notes. v. 6 (Early Autumn, 1974) 48.

589. Johnson, Cecil E., Jr. (Pima) "Gah-Chacalis." In Allen, T. D., ed., Arrow IV. U.S. Bureau of Indian Affairs, Creative Writing Project, 1972, p. 5.

590. Johnson, E. Pauline. (Mohawk) "The Corn Husker."

In Gooderham, Kent, ed., I Am an Indian. Toronto: Dent, 1969, p. 151.

591. Johnson, E. Pauline. (Mohawk) "Ojistosh." In Gooderham, Kent., ed., I Am an Indian. Toronto: Dent, 1969, pp. 161-3.

592. Johnson, Jay Ralph. (Navajo) "Cherished." In Milton, John R., comp. American Indian II. Vermillion: U. of S. Dak., 1971, p. 145.

593. ________. "A Dying Boy." In Milton, John R., comp., American Indian II. Vermillion: U. of S. Dak., 1971, p. 146.

594. ________. "Fort Wingate." In Milton, John R., comp., American Indian II. Vermillion: U. of S. Dak., 1971, p. 145.

595. ________. "A Hidden Bird Sings Softly." In Milton, John R., comp., American Indian II. Vermillion: U. of S. Dak., 1971, p. 142.

596. ________. "I Was Born as a Yucca." In Milton, John R., comp., American Indian II. Vermillion: U. of S. Dak., 1971, p. 138.

597. ________. "An Indian." Sun Tracks. v. 1 (Spring, 1972) 3.

598. ________. "An Indian." In Milton, John R., comp., American Indian II. Vermillion: U. of South Dakota, 1971, p. 137.

599. ________. "Me." In Milton, John R., comp., American Indian II. Vermillion: U. of South Dakota, 1971, p. 144.

600. ________. "Medicine Song." Sun Tracks. v. 1 (Winter, 1971/72) 15.

601. ________. "My Lovely Stars." In Milton, John R., comp., American Indian II. Vermillion: U. of S. Dak., 1971, p. 143.

602. ________. "Rose Full of Lorretta and Bruce." In Milton, John R., comp., American Indian II.

Vermillion: U. of S. Dak., 1971, p. 140.

603. Johnson, Jay Ralph. (Navajo) "The Unfortunate Flower." In Milton, John R., comp., American Indian II. Vermillion: U. of S. Dak., 1971, p. 139.

604. Johnson, Leigh. "You." Akwesasne Notes. v. 4 (Summer, 1972) 48.

605. ________. "You Who Grows Tall Like the Corn." In Levitas, Gloria, Frank Robert & Jacqueline J. Vivelo, eds., American Indian Prose & Poetry. Putman, 1974, pp. 297-98.

606. Johnson, Ralph Ray. (Navajo) "Battle Song." In Allen, T. D., ed., Arrow I. U.S. Bureau of Indian Affairs, Creative Writing Project, 1969, p. 3.

607. ________. "Medicine Song." In Allen, T. D., ed., Arrow I. U.S. Bureau of Indian Affairs, Creative Writing Project, 1969, p. 2.

608. Johnson, Sandra. (Makah) "We Sprang from Salt Water." In Lowenfels, Walter, ed., From the Belly of the Shark. Vintage, 1973, pp. 34-5.

609. Johnson, Yvonne. "Yvonne ii shi ii nish ye." Akwesasne Notes. v. 7 (Late Summer, 1975) 48.

610. Johnston, Basil H. "Dreamers' Rock." Akwesasne Notes. v. 8 (Early Summer, 1976) 48.

611. Jones, Tiger. "When I Die." Angwamus Minosewag Anishinabeg. 1st issue. (Poets in the Schools Program) St. Paul Council of Arts and Sciences, [1973].

612. Jordan, Don. (Chippewa-Cherokee-Choctaw-Iroquois) Curios of K'oS Naahaabii. Roseville, Calif: Blue Oak Pr., 1970.

613. Julian, Bob. "Indian Power." Wassaja. v. 4, no. 5 (May, 1976) 8.

614. Junge, M. "Upon Submitting Proposals for Federally

Funded Summer Programs." Akwesasne Notes. v. 3 (April, 1971) 48.

615. Kakakaway, Bill. [from New Breed] "Loneliness." Akwesasne Notes. v. 4 (Summer, 1972) 48.

616. Kale, Kenneth. "Sorry about That." In Witt, Shirley H., The Way; an Anthology of American Indian Literature. Knopf, 1972, pp. 144-6.

617. Kamp, Wayne Ian. "Arrested at the Southwest Museum." Akwesasne Notes. v. 3 (June, 1971) 48.

618. Karoniaktatie. (Mohawk) "between the two of us" [first line]. In Lourie, Dick, ed., Come to Power. The Crossing Press, 1974, pp. 69-70.

619. ________. "Bridge Poem." In Lourie, Dick, ed., Come to Power. The Crossing Press, 1974, pp. 76-7.

620. ________. "child of mine" [first line]. Akwesasne Notes. v. 6 (Late Spring, 1974) 48.

621. ________. "Forgive Me" [first line]. Akwesasne Notes. v. 5 (Early Summer, 1973) 48.

622. ________. "From the Sequence 'Confessions of the Grand Manipulator.' " In Lourie, Dick, ed., Come to Power. The Crossing Press, 1974, pp. 73-4.

623. ________. "From the Sequence 'Megalomaniac.' " In Lourie, Dick, ed., Come to Power. The Crossing Press, 1974, p. 71.

624. ________. "Hostages." Akwesasne Notes. v. 5 (Early Spring, 1973) 13.

625. ________. "I am" [first line]. Akwesasne Notes. v. 4 (Summer, 1972) 48.

626. ________. "I am the Dance" [first line]. Akwesasne Notes. v. 5 (Early Autumn, 1973) 3.

627. ________. "I can not be still" [first line]. Akwesasne Notes. v. 5 (Early Spring, 1973) 13.

628. Karoniaktatie. (Mohawk) "i have seen." In Lourie, Dick, ed., Come to Power. The Crossing Press, 1974, p. 75.

629. ________. "i lost the song" [first line]. In Lourie, Dick, ed., Come to Power. The Crossing Press, 1974, p. 67.

630. ________. "I Was Young" [first line]. Akwesasne Notes. v. 4 (Late Spring, 1972) 48.

631. ________. "Lookin' up" [first line]. Akwesasne Notes. v. 4 (Early Autumn, 1972) 48.

632. ________. "Lost and Lonely Child." Akwesasne Notes. v. 5 (January, 1973) 48.

633. ________. "The Maniac." Akwesasne Notes. v. 5 (Late Summer, 1973) 48.

634. ________. "The Moon Will Rise." Akwesasne Notes. v. 5 (Early Autumn, 1973) 48.

635. ________. "the moon will rise" [first line]. In Levitas, Gloria, Frank Robert & Jacqueline J. Vivelo, eds., American Indian Prose & Poetry. Putnam, 1974, p. v.

636. ________. Native Colours. Rooseveltown, N.Y.: Akwesasne Notes, 1974.

637. ________. "Night-walker." Akwesasne Notes. v. 4 (Late Autumn, 1972) 48.

638. ________. "Sneakin' into Wounded Knee" [first line]. Akwesasne Notes. v. 5 (Early Spring, 1973) 35.

639. ________. "There Are Bridges." Akwesasne Notes. v. 5 (Early Winter, 1973) 48.

640. ________. "To Mary." In Lourie, Dick, ed., Come to Power. The Crossing Press, 1974, p. 68.

641. ________. "Troll Song." In Lourie, Dick, ed., Come to Power. The Crossing Press, 1974. p. 72.

642. Karoniaktatie. (Mohawk) "War." Akwesasne Notes. v. 5 (Early Summer, 1973) 11.

643. Keams, Gerri. (Navajo) "Cry of Nature." Sun Tracks. v. 1 (Spring, 1972) 8.

644. Kee, James. (Navajo) "Cold." In Allen, T. D., ed., Arrow IV. U.S. Bureau of Indian Affairs, Creative Writing Project, 1972, p. 24.

645. Keene, Veronica. "See the Eagle Die." Akwesasne Notes. v. 3 (Dec., 1971) 48.

646. _______. "Sioux Chief." Akwesasne Notes. v. 3 (Jan./Feb., 1971) 48.

647. Keeshig, John. "Life Is a Circle." Akwesasne Notes. v. 6 (Early Summer, 1974) 48.

648. _______. "An Old Lie." Akwesasne Notes. v. 6 (Early Summer, 1974) 48.

649. Kegg, Roxanne. "Home." Wassaja. v. 3 (May, 1975) 10.

650. _______. "One Poem on War." Wassaja. v. 3 (May, 1975) 10.

651. _______. "Reflections." Wassaja. v. 3 (May, 1975) 10.

652. Kelsey, A. "Great White Indian." Akwesasne Notes. v. 2 (Nov./Dec., 1970) 48.

653. _______. "My Indian Son." Akwesasne Notes. v. 3 (March, 1971) 48.

654. Kempton, Karl. "&th beat of that heart" [first line]. Akwesasne Notes. v. 5 (Early Autumn, 1973) 3.

655. Kenny, Maurice. (Mohawk) "Corn-Planter." Blue Cloud Quarterly. v. 21, no. 4.

656. _______. "Father I Come" [first line]. Akwesasne Notes. v. 5 (Early Spring, 1973) 48.

657. _______. "I became a man" [first line]. Akwesasne

Notes. v. 6 (Early Spring, 1974) 48.

658. Kenny, Maurice. (Mohawk) "Indian Burial Grounds." Blue Cloud Quarterly. v. 21, no. 4.

659. ________. "Monahsetah ... A Cheyenne Girl." Akwesasne Notes. v. 4 (Late Autumn, 1972) 48.

660. ________. "Monahsetah ... A Cheyenne Girl." In Lowenfels, Walter, ed., From the Belly of the Shark. Vintage, 1973, pp. 35-6.

661. Keon, Orville Wayne & Ronald Keon. Sweetgrass; a Modern Anthology of Indian Poetry. Selected by Wayne Keon. Elliot Lake, Ontario: W. O. K. Books, 1971.

662. Khanshendel, Chiron [pseud.] [Bronwen Elizabeth Edwards, or Schiacalega]. (Hopi-Comanche) "Grandfather Pipestone Soul." In Lowenfels, Walter, ed., From the Belly of the Shark. Vintage, 1973, pp. 36-7.

663. ________. "Grebes at Sunset." In Faderman, Lillian & Barbara Bradshaw, eds., Speaking for Ourselves: American Ethnic Writing. Foresman, 1969, p. 511.

664. ________. "Grebes at Sunset." In Sanders, Thomas E. & Walter W. Peek, Literature of the American Indian. Glencoe Pr., 1973, pp. 458-9.

665. ________. "Hopi Roadrunner, Dancing, Dancing." In Faderman, Lillian & Barbara Bradshaw, eds., Speaking for Ourselves: American Ethnic Writing. Foresman, 1969, p. 511.

666. ________. "I Mourned for My Land" [first line]. The Warpath. v. 4, no. 7, p. 11.

667. ________. "West Side of the Valley." In Faderman, Lillian & Barbara Bradshaw, eds., Speaking for Ourselves: American Ethnic Writing. Foresman, 1969, pp. 501-2.

668. King, Bruce. [SP4] "They Came" [first line]. Akwesasne Notes. v. 4 (Late Winter, 1972) 48.

669. King, Ronald. (Navajo) "No Days." In Allen, T. D., ed., Arrow I. U.S. Bureau of Indian Affairs, Creative Writing Project, 1969, pp. 15-16.

670. Kingbird, Bonnie. "Clouds past slowly" [first line]. Angwamus Minosewag Anishinabeg. (Poets in the Schools Program) St. Paul Council of Arts and Sciences, Winter, 1973-74.

671. ________. "Worms and Storms" [first line]. Angwamas Minosewag Anishinabeg. (Poets in the Schools Program) St. Paul Council of Arts and Sciences, Winter, 1973-74.

672. Kisto, Frances. (Papago) "I Am a Papago Girl." In Witt, Shirley H., The Way; an Anthology of American Indian Literature. Knopf, 1972, p. 141.

673. Knoxsah, Jimmy. "For Angel." Akwesasne Notes. v. 6 (Early Autumn, 1974) 48.

674. Koeppel, Heather. "Wounded Knee 1890-?" Akwesasne Notes. v. 5 (Early Winter, 1973) 48.

675. Koskiway, Diane. (Otoe) "I Believe in" [first linc]. In Allen, T. D., ed., Arrow IV. U.S. Bureau of Indian Affairs, Creative Writing Project, 1972, p. 8.

676. Kuka, King D. (Blackfoot) "Ego Swamp." In Allen, Terry, ed., The Whispering Wind; Poetry by Young American Indians. Doubleday, 1972, p. 74.

677. ________. "The Strong Hearts." Sun Tracks. v. 1 (Winter, 1971/72) 9-12.

678. ________. "A Taste of Honey." In Allen, Terry, ed., The Whispering Wind; Poetry by Young American Indians. Doubleday, 1972, p. 73.

679. ________. "A Taste of Honey." In Dodge, Robert K. & Joseph B. McCullough, eds., Voices from Wah'kon-tah. International Publishers, 1974, p. 51.

680. L., O. H. "The Indian's Soliloquy." In Levitas, Gloria, Frank Robert & Jacqueline J. Vivelo, eds.,

American Indian Prose & Poetry. Putman, 1974, p. 287.

681. LaBlanc, Tom. "Where You Going Little Indian Boy?" [first line]. Akwesasne Notes. v. 4 (Early Spring, 1972) 48.

682. La Farge, Peter. "Autumn 1964." In Lowenfels, Walter, ed., From the Belly of the Shark. Vintage, 1973, pp. 38-9.

683. ________. "Vision of a Past Warrior." In Faderman, Lillian & Barbara Bradshaw, eds., Speaking for Ourselves: American Ethnic Writing. Foresman, 1969, p. 500.

684. ________. "Vision of a Past Warrior." In Sanders, Thomas E. & Walter W. Peek, Literature of the American Indian. Glencoe Pr., 1973, p. 459.

685. Laitinen, Kim. "A Man Once Tall and Proud" [first line]. Angwamas Minosewag Anishinabeg. (Poets in the Schools Program) St. Paul Council of Arts and Sciences, Winter, 1973-74.

686. ________. "My Spirit Has Been Lifted to the Pound of a Drum" [first line]. Angwamas Minosewag Anishinabeg. (Poets in the Schools Program) St. Paul Council of Arts and Sciences, Winter, 1973-74.

687. LaMere, Frank. "Come Home, Mister Chairman." Akwesasne Notes. v. 3 (Sept., 1971) 48.

688. Lane, Donald Rex. "Fragment." Akwesasne Notes. v. 3 (Oct./Nov., 1971) 48.

689. ________. "Fragment." In Levitas, Gloria, Frank Robert & Jacqueline J. Vivelo, eds., American Indian Prose & Poetry. Putnam, 1974, p. 288.

690. ________. "Talking from a Cage." Akwesasne Notes. v. 3 (April, 1971) 48.

691. Laroque, Florence. "The Beading of Chippewa" [first line]. Angwamas Minosewag Anishinabeg. (Poets in the Schools Program) St. Paul Council of Arts and Sciences, Winter, 1973-74.

692. Larson, Chris. "Dead Men Do Not Sing." In Henry, Jeannette, ed., The American Indian Reader: Literature. Indian Historian Pr., 1973, p. 28.

693. Lassaw, Denise. "Alaska '70." Akwesasne Notes. v. 3 (June, 1971) 48.

694. ______. "Alaska '70." Akwesasne Notes. v. 4 (Early Spring, 1972) 48.

695. ______. "N.Y.C. '69." Akwesasne Notes. v. 3 (May, 1971) 48.

696. Laughing Wolf, John. "Prayer." Akwesasne Notes. v. 7 (Early Winter, 1975) 48.

697. Laursen, Ross. "Beyond the Sun." Akwesasne Notes. v. 7 (Early Autumn, 1975) 48.

698. ______. "My Kind of Guy." Akwesasne Notes. v. 6 (Late Spring, 1974) 48.

699. ______. "An Old Chief's Vision of the Spirit World." Akwesasne Notes. v. 6 (Early Spring, 1974) 48.

700. Lawless, Gary. "We Came and Chanted" [first line]. Akwesasne Notes. v. 4 (Summer, 1972) 48.

701. Lee, Latie, and Frank Wright. "Echo Cliffs." [poem and photo]. Arizona Highways. v. 34 (1958) 25.

702. Lee, Roger. (Navajo) "Long ago there were Giants ..." [first line]. Sun Tracks. v. 1 (Spring, 1972) 27.

703. Leivas, June. (Chemehuevi) "America." American Indian Culture Center Journal. v. 2 (Winter, 1971) 14.

704. ______. "The Battle's Not Over Yet." Akwesasne Notes. v. 3 (June, 1971) 48.

705. ______. "Don't Let Time's Conquest Be Final." American Indian Culture Center Journal. v. 2 (Winter, 1971) 15.

706. ______. "No Indians Here." Akwesasne Notes. v. 3 (Oct./Nov., 1971) 48.

707. Leivas, June. (Chemehuevi) "No Indians Here." In Lowenfels, Walter, ed., From the Belly of the Shark. Vintage, 1973, pp. 39-42.

708. ________. "Rest in Peace." Akwesasne Notes. v. 5 (Early Autumn, 1973) 48.

709. ________. "Shadow People." Akwesasne Notes. v. 3 (May, 1971) 48.

710. ________. "Thoughts from Navajo Country." American Indian Culture Center Journal. v. 3 (Fall/Winter, 1971/72) 31.

711. ________. "Two-Line Autobiography." American Indian Culture Center Journal. v. 3 (Fall/Winter, 1971/72) 30.

712. ________. "Yesterday." Akwesasne Notes. v. 3 (Jan./Feb., 1971) 48.

713. Leonard, Augustine. "The Spinning Wind." Akwesasne Notes. v. 2 (May, 1970) 48.

714. Levantonio, Harry. "The Last Battle." Sun Tracks. v. 1 (Winter, 1971/72) 14.

715. Levine, Anna Marie. "Riddle: Who Am I." Akwesasne Notes. v. 2 (Nov./Dec., 1970) 48.

716. Levitas, Gloria, Frank Robert & Jacqueline J. Vivelo. "Out of the Darkness." In Levitas, Gloria, Frank Robert & Jacqueline J. Vivelo, eds., American Indian Prose & Poetry. Putnam, 1974, p. 306.

717. Lincoln. "I Am an Indian Soul." Akwesasne Notes. v. 5 (Early Summer, 1973) 48.

718. Link, Virgil Curtis. "Remember Yesterday." Sun Tracks. v. 1 (Fall, 1971) 7-15.

719. Linklater, Harold. "On Watching a Hockey Game in a Pub." Akwesasne Notes. v. 3 (April, 1971) 48.

720. Litson, George. "I'm Called Navajo." Akwesasne Notes. v. 3 (Sept., 1971) 48.

721. Little One, Bob Maldonado. "An Indian Thought." Pembroke Magazine. no. 2 (1971) 16.

722. Littlebird. (Santo Domingo & Laguna) "Death in the Woods." In Milton, John R., comp., The American Indian Speaks. Vermillion: U. of South Dakota, 1969, p. 135.

723. ________. "Death in the Woods." In Momaday, Natachee Scott. American Indian Authors. Houghton, 1972, pp. 117-118.

724. Littlebird, Harold. (Santo Domingo Pueblo) "Everywhere You Looked Was Singing." Pembroke Magazine. no. 6 (1973) 32.

725. ________. "For Tom Tumkena, Hopi-Spokane." Pembroke Magazine. no. 6 (1975) 32-3.

726. Littlebud, Larry. "Hands That Kissed the Earth." In Levitas, Gloria, Frank Robert & Jacqueline J. Vivelo, eds., American Indian Prose & Poetry. Putnam, 1974, p. 303.

727. Livingston, John. "Dccr Hidc Flap Open" [first line]. Angwamas Minosewag Anishinabeg. (Poets in the Schools Program) St. Paul Council of Arts and Sciences, Winter, 1973-74.

728. ________. "Fly Slow for Your Heart Guides You" [first line]. Angwamas Minosewag Anishinabeg. (Poets in the Schools Program) St. Paul Council of Arts and Sciences, Winter, 1973-74.

729. ________. "To Think of Being a Bird Is Hard" [first line]. Angwamas Minosewag Anishinabeg. (Poets in the Schools Program) St. Paul Council of Arts and Sciences, Winter, 1973-74.

730. Lone Pine, Sonny. "The End." Akwesasne Notes. v. 5 (Early Autumn, 1973) 48.

731. Long, Charles C. (Navaho) "Yei-ie's Child." Blue Cloud Quarterly. v. 15, no. 3.

732. ________. "Yei-ie's Child." In Dodge, Robert K. & Joseph B. McCullough, eds., Voices from Wah'kontah. International Publishers, 1974, p. 55.

733. Long, Charles C. (Navajo) "Yei-ie's Child." In Future Directions in Native American Art. Santa Fe, N.M.: The Institute of American Indian Arts, [1973], p. 39.

734. ________. "Yei-Ie's Child." Wassaja. v. 3 (August, 1975) 13.

735. Lopez, Alonzo. (Papago) "Celebration." In Allen, Terry, ed., The Whispering Wind; Poetry by Young American Indians. Doubleday, 1972, p. 3.

736. ________. "Celebration." In Dance with Indian Children. Washington, D.C.: Center for the Arts of Indian Children, 1972, p. 23.

737. ________. "Direction." Akwesasne Notes. v. 1, sec. 3 (Nov., 1969) 9.

738. ________. "Direction." In Allen, Terry, ed., The Whispering Wind; Poetry for Young American Indians. Doubleday, 1972, p. 10.

739. ________. "Direction." In Dodge, Robert K. & Joseph B. McCullough, eds., Voices from Wah'kon-tah. International Publishers, 1974, p. 56.

740. ________. "Direction." In Lowenfels, Walter, ed., From the Belly of the Shark. Vintage, 1973, p. 43.

741. ________. "Direction." In Milton, John R., comp., The American Indian Speaks. Vermillion: U. of South Dakota, 1969, p. 107.

742. ________. "Direction." In Momaday, Natachee Scott, American Indian Authors. Houghton, 1972, p. 69.

743. ________. "Direction." In Sanders, Thomas E. & Walter W. Peek, Literature of the American Indian. Glencoe Pr., 1973, p. 460.

744. ________. "Dry and Parched." In Allen, Terry, ed., The Whispering Wind; Poetry for Young American Indians. Doubleday, 1972, p. 9.

745. ________. "Dry and Parched" [first line]. In Dance

with Indian Children. Washington, D.C.: Center for the Arts of Indian Children, 1972, p. 4.

746. Lopez, Alonzo. (Papago) "Eagle Flight." In Allen, Terry, ed., The Whispering Wind; Poetry for Young American Indians. Doubleday, 1972, p. 7.

747. ________. "Eagle Flight." In Dance with Indian Children. Washington, D.C.: Center for the Arts of Indian Children, 1972, p. 4.

748. ________. "An Eagle Wings Gracefully Through the Sky" [first line]. Akwesasne Notes. v. 4 (Late Spring, 1972) 48.

749. ________. "Endless Search." In Allen, Terry, ed., The Whispering Wind; Poetry for Young American Indians. Doubleday, 1972, p. 7.

750. ________. "Hypochondriac." In Milton, John R., comp., The American Indian Speaks. Vermillion: U. of S. Dak., 1969, p. 108.

751. ________. "I Am Crying from Thirst." In Allen, Terry, ed., The Whispering Wind; Poetry for Young American Indians. Doubleday, 1972, p. 8.

752. ________. "I Am Crying from Thirst" [first line]. In Dance with Indian Children. Washington, D.C.: Center for the Arts of Indian Children, 1972, p. 7.

753. ________. "I Am Crying from Thirst." In Dodge, Robert K. & Joseph B. McCullough, eds., Voices from Wah'kon-tah. International Publishers, 1974, p. 59.

754. ________. "I Am Crying from Thirst." In Milton, John R., comp., The American Indian Speaks. Vermillion: U. of S. Dak., 1969, p. 107.

755. ________. "I Am Crying from Thirst." In Sanders, Thomas E. & Walter W. Peek, Literature of the American Indian. Glencoe Pr., 1973, p. 459.

756. ________. "I Called Out." In Henry, Jeannette, ed., The American Indian Reader: Literature. Indian Historian Pr., 1973, pp. 52-3.

757. Lopez, Alonzo. (Papago) "I Go Forth to Move About the Earth." In Allen, Terry, ed., The Whispering Wind; Poetry for Young American Indians. Doubleday, 1972, p. 8.

758. ______. "I Go Forth to Move About the Earth" [first line]. In Dance with Indian Children. Washington, D.C.: Center for the Arts of Indian Children, 1972, p. 15.

759. ______. "I Journey Westward." Sun Tracks. v. 1 (Winter, 1971/72) 32.

760. ______. "I See a Star." In Allen, Terry, ed., The Whispering Wind; Poetry for Young American Indians. Doubleday, 1972, p. 4.

761. ______. "I See a Star" [first line]. In Dance with Indian Children. Washington, D.C.: Center for the Arts of Indian Children, 1972, p. 13.

762. ______. "The Lavender Kitten." In Allen, Terry, ed., The Whispering Wind; Poetry for Young American Indians. Doubleday, 1972, p. 11-12.

763. ______. "The Lavendar Kitten." In Dodge, Robert K. & Joseph B. McCullough, eds., Voices from Wah'kon-tah. International Publishers, 1974, p. 57.

764. ______. "A Question." In Allen, Terry, ed., The Whispering Wind; Poetry for Young American Indians. Doubleday, 1972, p. 6.

765. ______. "The Rainbow Faded into the Sky" [first line]. In Dance with Indian Children. Washington, D.C.: Center for the Arts of Indian Children, 1972, p. 7.

766. ______. "Raise Your Hands to the Sky." In Allen, Terry, ed., The Whispering Wind; Poetry for Young American Indians. Doubleday, 1972, p. 9.

767. ______. "Raise Your Hands to the Sky" [first line]. In Dance with Indian Children. Washington, D.C. Center for the Arts of Indian Children, 1972, p. 24

768. ______ "Separation." In Allen, Terry, ed., The

Whispering Wind; Poetry for Young American Indians. Doubleday, 1972, p. 4.

769. Lopez, Alonzo. (Papago) "Tears." In Allen, Terry, ed., The Whispering Wind; Poetry for Young American Indians. Doubleday, 1972, p. 3.

770. _______. "Untitled." In Allen, Terry, ed., The Whispering Wind; Poetry for Young American Indians. Doubleday, 1972, p. 5.

771. _______. "Whirlwind." In Henry, Jeannette, ed., The American Indian Reader: Literature. Indian Historian Pr., 1973, p. 56.

772. Loretto, Phillip. "A Place in the Sun." In Henry, Jeannette, ed., The American Indian Reader: Literature. The Indian Historian Pr., 1973, p. 30.

773. _______. "A Place in the Sun." The Indian Historian. v. 2 (Fall, 1969) 34.

774. Louis, Adrian C. (Paiute) "Equine Stars." Blue Cloud Quarterly. v. 21, no. 4.

775. _______. "Old Chief Treebark and His Honda." Blue Cloud Quarterly. v. 21, no. 4.

776. _______. "Sodom, Gomorrah and Kansas?" Blue Cloud Quarterly. v. 21, no. 4.

777. Lourie, Dick, ed. Come to Power; Eleven Contemporary American Indian Poets. Intro. by Joseph Bruchac. The Crossing Press, 1974.

778. Luckenbach. "I Don't mean to imply dead seagull squacks." Akwesasne Notes. v. 4 (Early Autumn, 1972) 48.

779. McGinnis, Duane, or Duane Niatum. (Klallam) After the Death of an Elder Klallam; Contemporary Poems. Phoenix: Baleen Pr., 1970.

780. _______. "Indian Prayer." In Dodge, Robert K. & Joseph B. McCullough, eds., Voices from Wah'kontah. International Publishers, 1974, p. 63.

781. McGinnis, Duane, or Duane Niatum. (Klallam) "The Novelty Shop." Akwesasne Notes. v. 3 (Jan./ Feb., 1971) 48.

782. ________. "Song for Yellow Leaf Moon." In Dodge, Robert K. & Joseph B. McCullough, eds., Voices from Wah'kon-tah. International Publishers, 1974, p. 66.

783. ________. "Street Kid." In Levitas, Gloria, Frank Robert & Jacqueline J. Vivelo, eds., American Indian Prose & Poetry. Putnam, 1974, p. 290.

784. ________. "Train Rhythms and the Color Wheel." In Dodge, Robert K. & Joseph B. McCullough, eds., Voices from Wah'kon-tah. International Publishers, 1974, p. 65.

785. MacGuire, Deirdre. "Museum." Akwesasne Notes. v. 4 (Late Autumn, 1972) 48.

786. ________. "Poem." Akwesasne Notes. v. 5 (Early Summer, 1973) 48.

787. Machukay, Tony. "The First Apache Christmas." The Indian Historian. v. 7 (Fall, 1974) 3-4.

788. McIntosh, Vicki. (Creek) "Autumn." In Allen, T. D., ed., Arrow II. U.S. Bureau of Indian Affairs, Creative Writing Project, 1970, p. 29.

789. Madgequommoqua. "Wounded Knee 1890--Wounded Knee 1973." Akwesasne Notes. v. 5 (Early Summer, 1973) 20.

790. Magnuson, Lynn. "Remember." Akwesasne Notes. v. 4 (Late Spring, 1972) 48.

791. Maho, Lucille. (Hopi) "The Park." In Allen, T. D., ed., Arrow II. U.S. Bureau of Indian Affairs, Creative Writing Project, 1970, p. 6.

792. Mahto, Ted. (Chippewa) "Jim Runs-Along-the-Bank" [first line]. In Abuse. Minneapolis: Training Resource and Developmental Assistance Center, [n.d.] p. 97-8.

793. Mahto, Ted. (Chippewa) "Uncle Tomahawk." In Vizenor, Gerald. The Everlasting Sky. Crowell, 1972, pp. 66-69.

794. Many Feathers. "Distant Drums." Akwesasne Notes. v. 3 (Sept., 1971) 48.

795. ________. "Lost Cause... ?" Akwesasne Notes. v. 3 (March, 1971) 48.

796. Martin Nez, Dave, or Martinez, David W. (Navajo) "New Way, Old Way." Blue Cloud Quarterly. v. 15, no. 3.

797. ________. "New Way, Old Way." In Dodge, Robert K. & Joseph B. McCullough, eds., Voices from Wah'kon-tah. International Publishers, 1974, p. 60.

798. ________. "New Way, Old Way." In Future Directions in Native American Art. Santa Fe, N.M.: The Institute of American Indian Arts, [1973], p. 11.

799. ________. "New Way, Old Way." In Witt, Shirley H., The Way; an Anthology of American Indian Literature. Knopf, 1972, pp. 143-4.

800. ________. "This Is Today." Blue Cloud Quarterly. v. 15, no. 3.

801. ________. "This Is Today." In Dodge, Robert K. & Joseph B. McCullough, eds., Voices from Wah'kon-tah. International Publishers, 1974, p. 62.

802. Maryanne. "If I Seen a Mouse" [first line]. Angwamas Minosewag Anishinabeg. (Poets in the Schools Program) St. Paul Council of Arts and Sciences, Winter, 1973-74.

803. Mason, Winston. "Just a Minute." In Lourie, Dick, ed., Come to Power. The Crossing Press, 1974, p. 106.

804. ________. "The Raven." In Lourie, Dick, ed., Come to Power. The Crossing Press, 1974, p. 105.

805. ________. "Suicide." In Lourie, Dick, ed., Come to Power. The Crossing Press, 1974, p. 107.

806. Mattson, Joyce. (Blackfoot) "Morning Air Stillness" [first line]. In Allen, T. D., ed., Arrow I. U.S. Bureau of Indian Affairs, Creative Writing Project, 1972, p. 10.

807. MawHeeShen. "Indian Summer." Akwesasne Notes. v. 4 (Late Spring, 1972) 48.

808. Mayne, Brian. "Nisgas." Akwesasne Notes. v. 7 (Late Summer, 1975) 48.

809. Means, Vivian. (Sioux) "And Dance." In Dance with Indian Children. Washington, D.C.: Center for the Arts of Indian Children, 1972, p. 41.

810. Meryl. "The Wolf." Akwesasne Notes. v. 4 (Early Spring, 1972) 48.

811. Milk, Albert R., Jr. (Sioux) "Self-Image." Blue Cloud Quarterly. v. 15, no. 3.

812. Mitchell, Emerson Blackhorse. (Navajo) "The Drifting Lonely Seed." In Faderman, Lillian & Barbara Bradshaw, eds., Speaking for Ourselves: American Ethnic Writing. Foresman, 1969, p. 513.

813. ________. "The Four Directions." In Allen, Terry, ed. The Whispering Wind; Poetry by Young American Indians. Doubleday, 1972, p. 95.

814. ________. "The Four Directions." In Dodge, Robert K. & Joseph B. McCullough, eds., Voices from Wah'kon-tah. International Publishers, 1974, p. 71.

815. ________. "Miracle Hill." In Allen, Terry, ed., The Whispering Wind; Poetry by Young American Indians. Doubleday, 1972, p. 93.

816. ________. "Miracle Hill." In Dodge, Robert K. & Joseph B. McCullough, eds., Voices from Wah'kon-tah. International Publishers, 1974, p. 68.

817. ________. "Miracle Hill." In Future Directions in Native American Art. Santa Fe, N.M.: The Institute of American Indian Arts, [1973], [i].

818. ________. "Miracle Hill." In Milton, John R., comp.,

The American Indian Speaks. Vermillion: U. of S. Dak. Pr., 1969, p. 110.

819. Mitchell, Emerson Blackhorse. (Navajo) "The New Direction." In Milton, John R., comp., *The American Indian Speaks*. Vermillion: U. of S. Dak. Pr., 1969, p. 109.

820. ______. "The New Direction." *The Native Nevadan*. v. 9 (Nov.-Dec., 1973) 4.

821. ______. "The New Direction." In Sanders, Thomas E. & Walter W. Peek, *Literature of the American Indian*. Glencoe Pr., 1973, pp. 460-1.

822. ______. "The Path I Must Travel." In Allen, Terry, ed., *The Whispering Wind; Poetry by Young American Indians*. Doubleday, 1972, p. 94.

823. ______. "The Path I Must Travel." In Dodge, Robert K. & Joseph B. McCullough, eds., *Voices from Wah'kon-tah*. International Publishers, 1974, p. 70.

824. ______. "Talking to His Drum." In Allen, Terry, ed., *The Whispering Wind; Poetry by Young American Indians*. Doubleday, 1972, p. 96.

825. Modesto, Jamay Lube. "I Can Feel the Movement." *Akwesasne Notes*. v. 7 (Early Autumn, 1975) 48.

826. Mokiyuk, Ernestine. (Eskimo) "Eskimo." In Allen, T. D., ed., *Arrow IV*. U.S. Bureau of Indian Affairs, Creative Writing Project, 1972, p. 8.

827. Momaday, N. Scott. (Kiowa-Cherokee) "Angle of Geese." In Dodge, Robert K. & Joseph B. McCullough, eds., *Voices from Wah'kon-tah*. International Publishers, 1974, p. 73.

828. ______. "Angle of Geese." In Haslam, Gerald W. *Forgotten Pages of American Literature*. Houghton, 1970, pp. 59-60.

829. ______. "Angle of Geese." *New Mexico Quarterly*. v. 38 (Spring, 1968) 105.

830. Momaday, N. Scott. (Kiowa-Cherokee) "Angle of Geese." In Niatum, Duane, ed., Carriers of the Dream Wheel. Harper, 1975, p. 106.

831. ______. "Angle of Geese." In Sanders, Thomas E. & Walter W. Peek, Literature of the American Indian. Glencoe Pr., 1973, p. 461.

832. ______. Angle of Geese and Other Poems. David R. Godine, 1974.

833. ______. "The Bear." In Dodge, Robert K. & Joseph B. McCullough, eds., Voices from Wah'kon-tah. International Publishers, 1974, p. 72.

834. ______. "The Bear." In Faderman, Lillian & Barbara Bradshaw, eds., Speaking for Ourselves; American Ethnic Writing. Foresman, 1969, p. 515.

835. ______. "The Bear." New Mexico Quarterly. v. 31 (Spring, 1961) 46.

836. ______. "The Bear." New Mexico Quarterly. v. 38 (Spring, 1968) 104.

837. ______. "The Bear." In Niatum, Duane, ed., Carriers of the Dream Wheel. Harper, 1975, p. 91.

838. ______. "The Bear & The Colt." In Faderman, Lillian & Barbara Bradshaw, eds., Speaking for Ourselves: American Ethnic Writing. Foresman, 1969, pp. 472-76.

839. ______. "Before an Old Painting of the Crucifixion." In Haslam, Gerald W. Forgotten Pages of American Literature. Houghton, 1970, pp. 58-9.

840. ______. "Before an Old Paitning of the Crucifixion." New Mexico Quarterly. v. 38 (Spring, 1968) 106-7.

841. ______. "Before an Old Painting of the Crucifixion." In Sanders, Thomas E. & Walter W. Peek, Literature of the American Indian. Glencoe Pr., 1973, p. 462.

842. ______. "Before an Old Painting of the Crucifixion." Southern Review. v. 1 (Spring, 1965) 421-423.

843. Momaday, N. Scott. (Kiowa-Cherokee) "The Burning." Pembroke Magazine. no. 6 (1975) 31.

844. ________. "But Then and There the Sun Bore Down." In Niatum, Duane, ed., Carriers of the Dream Wheel. Harper, 1975, p. 105.

845. ________. "Buteo Regalis." In Dodge, Robert K. & Joseph B. McCullough, eds., Voices from Wah'kon-tah. International Publishers, 1974, p. 77.

846. ________. "Buteo Regalis." In Faderman, Lillian & Barbara Bradshaw, eds., Speaking for Ourselves: American Ethnic Writing. Foresman, 1969, p. 515.

847. ________. "Buteo Regalis." New Mexico Quarterly. v. 31 (Spring, 1961) 47.

848. ________. "Buteo Regalis." New Mexico Quarterly. v. 38 (Spring, 1968) 104.

849. ________. "Carriers of the Dream Wheel." In Niatum, Duane, ed., Carriers of the Dream Wheel. Harper, 1975, p. 87.

850. ________. "The Delight Song of Tsoai-Talee." In Niatum, Duane, ed., Carriers of the Dream Wheel. Harper, 1975, p. 89.

851. ________. "The Eagle-Feather Fan." In Niatum, Duane, ed., Carriers of the Dream Wheel. Harper, 1975, p. 98.

852. ________. "The Eagles of the Valle Grande." In Faderman, Lillian & Barbara Bradshaw, eds., Speaking for Ourselves: American Ethnic Writing. Foresman, 1969, pp. 476-81.

853. ________. "Earth and I Gave You Turquoise." In Dodge, Robert K. & Joseph B. McCullough, eds., Voices from Wah'kon-tah. International Publishers, 1974, p. 74.

854. ________. "Earth and I Gave You Turquoise." In Lowenfels, Walter, ed., From the Belly of the Shark. Vintage, 1973, p. 44.

855. Momaday, N. Scott. (Kiowa-Cherokee) "Earth and I Gave You Turquoise." New Mexico Quarterly. v. 29 (Summer, 1959) 156.

856. ________. "Earth & I Gave You Turquoise." New Mexico Quarterly. v. 38 (Spring, 1968) 103.

857. ________. "Earth and I Gave You Turquoise." In Niatum, Duane, ed., Carriers of the Dream Wheel. Harper, 1975, pp. 96-7.

858. ________. "For the Old Man Mad for Drawing, Dead at Eighty-Nine." Pembroke Magazine no. 6 (1975) 31.

859. ________. "Forms of the Earth at Abiquiu." In Niatum, Duane, ed., Carriers of the Dream Wheel. Harper, 1975, p. 88.

860. ________. "The Gourd Dancer." In Niatum, Duane, ed., Carriers of the Dream Wheel. Harper, 1975, pp. 94-5.

861. ________. "Los Alamos." New Mexico Quarterly. v. 29 (Autumn, 1959) 306.

862. ________. "Pit Viper." In Dodge, Robert K. & Joseph B. McCullough, eds., Voices from Wah'kon-tah. International Publishers, 1974, p. 76.

863. ________. "Pit Viper." New Mexico Quarterly. v. 31 (Spring, 1961) 47.

864. ________. "Pit Viper." New Mexico Quarterly. v. 38 (Spring, 1968) 102.

865. ________. "Pit Viper." In Niatum, Duane, ed., Carriers of the Dream Wheel. Harper, 1975, p. 100.

866. ________. "Plainview: 3." In Niatum, Duane, ed., Carriers of the Dream Wheel. Harper, 1975, p. 103.

867. ________. "Rainy Mountain Cemetery." New Mexico Quarterly. v. 38 (Spring, 1968) 107.

868. ________. "Rainy Mountain Cemetery." In Niatum,

Duane, ed., Carriers of the Dream Wheel. Harper, 1975, p. 99.

869. Momaday, N. Scott. (Kiowa-Cherokee) "Simile." New Mexico Quarterly. v. 38 (Spring, 1968) 108.

870. ________. "Simile." In Niatum, Duane, ed., Carriers of the Dream Wheel. Harper, 1975, p. 101.

871. ________. "The Story of a Well-Made Shield." In Niatum, Duane, ed., Carriers of the Dream Wheel. Harper, 1975, p. 104.

872. ________. "To a Child Running..." In Niatum, Duane, ed., Carriers of the Dream Wheel. Harper, 1975, p. 92.

873. ________. "Trees and Evening Sky." In Niatum, Duane, ed., Carriers of the Dream Wheel. Harper, 1975, p. 102.

874. ________. "Wide Empty Landscape..." In Niatum, Duane, ed., Carriers of the Dream Wheel. Harper, 1975, p. 90.

875. ________. "Winter Holding Off the Coast..." In Niatum, Duane, ed., Carriers of the Dream Wheel. Harper, 1975, p. 93.

876. Mooney, Elsie. "Eagle Pride." Wassaja. v. 3 (September 20, 1975) 9.

877. Moore, Gordon. (Cree) "The Spell of the Windego." In Gooderham, Kent, ed., I Am an Indian. Toronto, Dent, 1969, pp. 107-8.

878. Moore, Janice Lee. (Cherokee-Powhatan) "Spirit Free..." [first line]. Akwesasne Notes. v. 7 (Early Winter, 1975) 48.

879. Mora, Ricardo. "Eighteen." Akwesasne Notes. v. 3 (December, 1971) 48.

880. Moyah, Courtney. (Pima-Apache) "In One Day My Mother Grew Old." In Witt, Shirley H., The Way; an Anthology of American Indian Literature. Knopf, 1972, p. 137.

881. Moyah, Courtney. (Pima-Apache) "Twisting." In Dance with Indian Children. Washington, D.C.: Center for the Arts of Indian Children, 1972, p. 4.

882. Nahsonhoya, Julie. (Hopi) "Butterflies." In Allen, T. D., ed., Arrow III. U.S. Bureau of Indian Affairs, Creative Writing Project, 1971, p. 6.

883. Namingha, Kathleen. (Hopi) "The Last Supper." In Allen, T. D., ed., Arrow II. U.S. Bureau of Indian Affairs, Creative Writing Project, 1970, p. 5.

884. Nasewytewa, Agustin. (Yaqui-Pima-Hopi) "Alone and Weary" [first line]. Sun Tracks. v. 1 (Spring, 1972) 23.

885. The Native Brotherhood of Indians and Metis. "Prayer of the Brotherhood." Sun Tracks. v. 1 (Winter, 1971/72) 32.

886. Nelson, Mary, or Snena of the Skoylep. "The History of Good Fur Robe." In Henry, Jeannette, ed., The American Indian Reader: Literature. Indian Historian Pr., 1973, p. 50.

887. ________. "Ode to the Future." The Indian Historian. v. 3 (Fall, 1970) 31.

888. ________. "Ode to the Future: Boarding Schools for Whites on Indian Reservations." In Henry, Jeannette, ed., The American Indian Reader: Literature. Indian Historian Pr., 1973, pp. 49-50.

889. Niatum, Duane, or Duane McGinnis. (Klallam) "After the Death of an Elder Klallam." In Lourie, Dick, ed., Come to Power. The Crossing Press, 1974, pp. 112-3.

890. ________. "After the Death of an Elder Klallam." In Niatum, Duane, ed., Carriers of the Dream Wheel. Harper, 1975, pp. 137-39.

891. ________. Ascending Red Cedar Moon. Harper, 1973.

892. ________. "Ascending Red Cedar Moon." In Lowenfels, Walter, ed., From the Belly of the Shark. Vintage, 1973, pp. 45-6.

893. Niatum, Duane, or Duane McGinnis. (Klallam) "Ascending Red Cedar Moon." In Niatum, Duane, ed., Carriers of the Dream Wheel. Harper, 1975, pp. 118-19.

894. ________. "Chief Leschi of the Nisquallies." In Lourie, Dick, ed., Come to Power. The Crossing Press, 1974, p. 114.

895. ________. "Chief Leschi of the Nisqually." In Niatum, Duane, ed., Carriers of the Dream Wheel. Harper, 1975, p. 117.

896. ________. "Crow's Way." In Niatum, Duane, ed., Carriers of the Dream Wheel. Harper, 1975, p. 133.

897. ________. "Elegy for Chief Sealth (1786-1866)." In Niatum, Duane, ed., Carriers of the Dream Wheel. Harper, 1975, p. 121.

898. ________. "Elegy for Chief Sealth (1786-1866)." In Tvedten, Benet, comp., An American Indian Anthology. Marvin, S. D.: Blue Cloud Abbey, 1971, p. 44.

899. ________. "Homage to Chagall." In Lourie, Dick, ed., Come to Power. The Crossing Press, 1974, p. 111.

900. ________. "Homage to Chagall." In Niatum, Duane, ed., Carriers of the Dream Wheel. Harper, 1975, p. 135.

901. ________. "I, Joseph of the Nez Perce." In Tvedten, Benet, comp., An American Indian Anthology. Marvin, S. D.: Blue Cloud Abbey, 1971, p. 43.

902. ________. "Indian Prayer." Prairie Schooner. v. 44 (Spring, 1970) 19.

903. ________. "Indian Rock, Bainbridge Island, Washington." In Niatum, Duane, ed., Carriers of the Dream Wheel. Harper, 1975, p. 120.

904. ________. "No One Remembers Abandoning the Village ..." In Niatum, Duane, ed., Carriers of the Dream Wheel. Harper, 1975, pp. 124-26.

905. Niatum, Duane, or Duane McGinnis. (Klallam) "The Novelty Shop." In Niatum, Duane, ed., Carriers of the Dream Wheel. Harper, 1975, p. 132.

906. ______. "Old Tillicum." In Lourie, Dick, ed., Come to Power. The Crossing Press, 1974, p. 115-6.

907. ______. "Old Woman Awaiting..." In Niatum, Duane, ed., Carriers of the Dream Wheel. Harper, 1975, p. 127.

908. ______. "Old Woman Awaiting the Greyhound Bus." Prairie Schooner. v. 44 (Spring, 1970) 20.

909. ______. "On Hearing the Marsh Bird's Water Cry." In Niatum, Duane, ed., Carriers of the Dream Wheel. Harper, 1975, pp. 122-23.

910. ______. "On Leaving Baltimore." In Niatum, Duane, ed., Carriers of the Dream Wheel. Harper, 1975, pp. 128-29.

911. ______. "On Visiting My Son..." In Niatum, Duane, ed., Carriers of the Dream Wheel. Harper, 1975, pp. 130-31.

912. ______. "Poem for the People Who Came from the Moon." In Tvedten, Benet, comp., An American Indian Anthology. Marvin, S. D.: Blue Cloud Abbey, 1971, p. 42.

913. ______. "The Rhythm." Pembroke Magazine. no. 4 (1973) 14.

914. ______. "Slow Dancer That No One Hears..." In Niatum, Duane, ed., Carriers of the Dream Wheel. Harper, 1975, p. 136.

915. ______. "To Your Question." In Niatum, Duane, ed., Carriers of the Dream Wheel. Harper, 1975, p. 134.

916. ______. "Train Rhythms & the Color Wheel." Prairie Schooner. v. 44 (Spring, 1970) 20.

917. Noder, Leonard. "Long time ago my grandfather

travel by canoe and snowshoes" [first line]. Akwesasne Notes. v. 3 (Jan. / Feb., 1971) 48.

918. Nofchissey, Alberta. (Navajo) "Five Haiku." Sun Tracks. v. 1 (Winter, 1971/72) 7.

919. No-Nee. (Pima) "In Coming Rain Comes You" [first line]. Sun Tracks. v. 1 (Spring, 1972) 22.

920. Northsun, Nila. (Shoshoni-Chippewa) "Indian Dancer." Pembroke Magazine. no. 7 (1976) 223.

921. O.Y.S. "A Silent Messenger." Akwesasne Notes. v. 4, no. 3 (Late Spring, 1972) 48.

922. O'John, Calvin. (Ute-Navajo) "Afternoon and His Unfinished Poem." In Allen, Terry, ed., The Whispering Wind; Poetry by Young American Indians. Doubleday, 1972, p. 66.

923. ________. "Dancing Teepees." In Allen, Terry, ed., The Whispering Wind; Poetry by Young American Indians. Doubleday, 1972, p. 61.

924. ________. "Dancing Teepees." In Dodge, Robert K. & Joseph B. McCullough, eds., Voices from Wah'kon-tah. International Publishers, 1974, p. 78.

925. ________. "Dirt Road." In Allen, Terry, ed., The Whispering Wind; Poetry by Young American Indians. Doubleday, 1972, p. 61.

926. ________. "Doldrums." In Allen, Terry, ed., The Whispering Wind; Poetry by Young American Indians. Doubleday, 1972, p. 65.

927. ________. "Good or Bad." In Allen, Terry, ed., The Whispering Wind; Poetry by Young American Indians. Doubleday, 1972, p. 68.

928. ________. "Half of My Life." In Allen, Terry, ed., The Whispering Wind; Poetry by Young American Indians. Doubleday, 1972, p. 64.

929. ________. "Problems." In Allen, Terry, ed., The Whispering Wind; Poetry by Young American Indians. Doubleday, 1972, p. 65.

930. O'John, Calvin. (Ute-Navajo) "Song and Flight." In Milton, John R., ed., The American Indian Speaks. Vermillion: U. of South Dakota, 1969, p. 113.

931. ________. "Speak to Me." In Allen, Terry, ed., The Whispering Wind; Poetry by Young American Indians. Doubleday, 1972, p. 64.

932. ________. "A Tear Rolled Down My Cheek." In Allen, Terry, ed., The Whispering Wind; Poetry by Young American Indians. Doubleday, 1972, p. 63.

933. ________. "A Tear Rolled Down My Cheek" [first line]. In Future Directions in Native American Art. Santa Fe, N.M.: The Institute of American Indian Arts, [1973], p. 1.

934. ________. "That Lonesome Place." In Allen, Terry, ed., The Whispering Wind; Poetry by Young American Indians. Doubleday, 1972, p. 68.

935. ________. "That Mountain Clear" [first line]. In Dance with Indian Children. Washington, D.C.: Center for the Arts of Indian Children, 1972, p. 4.

936. ________. "This Day Is Over." In Allen, Terry, ed., The Whispering Wind; Poetry by Young American Indians. Doubleday, 1972, p. 67.

937. ________. "Three Poems." In Witt, Shirley H., The Way; an Anthology of American Indian Literature. Knopf, 1972, p. 140.

938. ________. "Trees." In Allen, Terry, ed., The Whispering Wind; Poetry by Young American Indians. Doubleday, 1972, p. 69.

939. ________. "Water Baby." In Allen, Terry, ed., The Whispering Wind; Poetry by Young American Indians. Doubleday, 1972, p. 62.

940. ________. "You Smiled." In Allen, Terry, ed., The Whispering Wind; Poetry by Young American Indians. Doubleday, 1972, p. 63.

941. Okimow, Robert. "Blaze Me a Trail." Akwesasne Notes. v. 4 (Summer, 1972) 48.

942. Oliva, Leo E. "White Buffalo Cow Woman." Akwesasne Notes. v. 7 (Early Summer, 1975) 48.

943. Oliver, Betty. "The People call for justice" [first line]. Akwesasne Notes. v. 3 (Oct./Nov., 1971) 48.

944. ______. "The People Call for Justice." In Lowenfels, Walter, ed., From the Belly of the Shark. Vintage, 1973, p. 47.

945. Oliver, Floyd K. (Rosebud Sioux) "The Answer." Akwesasne Notes. v. 3 (Jan./Feb., 1971) 48.

946. ______. "The Journey." Akwesasne Notes. v. 3 (Oct./Nov., 1971) 48.

947. Oppenheim, Clarence. (Coldwater Band) "Loss for Progress." In Gooderham, Kent, ed., I Am an Indian. Toronto, Dent, 1969, pp. 38-9.

948. Orlando. "Peyote." Akwesasne Notes. v. 8 (Early Summer, 1976) 48.

949. Ortiz, Simon J. (Acoma Pueblo) "And the Land Is Just as Dry" [line from song by Peter LaFarge]. In Sanders, Thomas E. & Walter W. Peek, Literature of the American Indian. Glencoe Pr., 1973, pp. 464-5.

950. ______. "Apache Love." Quetzal. v. 2 (Winter-Spring, 1972) 5-6.

951. ______. "Back into the Womb, the Center." Pembroke Magazine. no. 7 (1976) 214-6.

952. ______. "Believing It Will Rain Soon." Pembroke Magazine. no. 3 (1972) 11.

953. ______. "Between Albuquerque and Sante Fe." Pembroke Magazine. no. 7 (1976) 211.

954. ______. "Blessing." The Indian Historian. v. 3 (Winter, 1970) 58.

955. ______. "Bony." In Niatum, Duane, ed., Carriers of the Dream Wheel. Harper, 1975, p. 158.

956. Ortiz, Simon J. (Acoma Pueblo) "Buck Nez." Quetzal. v. 2 (Summer, 1972) 34.

957. ________. "The Creation: According to Coyote." In Niatum, Duane, ed., Carriers of the Dream Wheel. Harper, 1975, p. 144-45.

958. ________. "The Creek Nation East of the Mississippi." The Indian Historian. v. 3 (Fall, 1970) 27-8.

959. ________. "Crossing the Border: Georgia into Florida." The Indian Historian. v. 3 (Fall, 1970) 29-30.

960. ________. "A Designated National Park: Arizona." Pembroke Magazine. no. 3 (1972) 3-4.

961. ________. "Earth's and Gods, the Planet's and Sun." Quetzal. v. 2 (Winter-Spring, 1972) 3.

962. ________. "Fingers Talking in the Wind." Pembroke Magazine. no. 7 (1976) 211.

963. ________. "For Gary: How to Make a Good Chili Stew on July 16, Saturday, Indian 1971." Quetzal. v. 2 (Winter-Spring, 1972) 7-8.

964. ________. "Forming Child Poems." In Niatum, Duane, ed., Carriers of the Dream Wheel. Harper, 1975, pp. 153-55.

965. ________. "Gifts." Pembroke Magazine. v. 7 (1976) 217.

966. ________. "Gifts." Pembroke Magazine. no. 3 (1972) 5.

967. ________. "Grand Canyon Christmas Eve 1969." Pembroke Magazine. no. 4 (1973) 3-4.

968. ________. "Having Left Round Rock." Pembroke Magazine. no. 3 (1972) 6.

969. ________. "Hunger." Pembroke Magazine. no. 3 (1972) 8.

970. ________. "I Like Indians." In Henry, Jeannette,

ed., The American Indian Reader: Literature. Indian Historian Pr., 1973, p. 40.

971. Ortiz, Simon J. (Acoma Pueblo) "I Shall Go and Touch My Fingers to Stones and a Tree." Pembroke Magazine. no. 3 (1972) 10.

972. ______. "I Tell You Now." Pembroke Magazine. no. 7 (1976) 218-9.

973. ______. "I Told You." In Henry, Jeannette, ed., The American Indian Reader: Literature. Indian Historian Pr., 1973, p. 39.

974. ______. "I Told You, Flagler Beach, Florida." The Indian Historian. v. 3 (Fall, 1970) 30.

975. ______. "In Your House: Made for Mary." Pembroke Magazine. no. 3 (1972) 9.

976. ______. "Irish Poems on Saturday and an Indian." In Milton, John R., comp., The American Indian Speaks. Vermillion: U. of S.D., 1969, p. 6.

977. ______. "Like Mississippi." Pembroke Magazine. no. 7 (1976) 212.

978. ______. "Listen to Them." The Indian Historian. v. 3 (Winter, 1970) 59.

979. ______. "The Long House Valley Poem." Pembroke Magazine. no. 3 (1972) 7-8.

980. ______. "Lumbee Country, June 1971." Quetzal. v. 2 (Winter-Spring, 1972) 4.

981. ______. "Missing that Indian Name of Roy or Ray." In Witt, Shirley H., The Way; an Anthology of American Indian Literature. Knopf, 1972, pp. 85-7.

982. ______. "A Morning Prayer and Advice for a Rainbowdaughter." Quetzal. v. 2 (Winter-Spring, 1972) 13.

983. ______. "My Home." Quetzal. v. 2 (Summer, 1972) 35.

984. Ortiz, Simon J. (Acoma Pueblo) "Naming Things." The Indian Historian. v. 3 (Winter, 1970) 58.

985. _______. "A New Mexico Place Name." Pembroke Magazine. no. 7 (1976) 213-4.

986. _______. "Out of the Canyon Near Two Turkey Ruin." Alcheringa. v. 2 (Summer, 1971) 18.

987. _______. Poems from Naked in the Wind. Quetzal-Vihio Pr., 1971.

988. _______. "A Pretty Woman." In Niatum, Duane, ed., Carriers of the Dream Wheel. Harper, 1975, p. 150.

989. _______. "Relocation." In Dodge, Robert K. & Joseph B. McCullough, eds., Voices from Wah'kon-tah. International Publishers, 1974, p. 82.

990. _______. "Relocation." In Witt, Shirley H., The Way; an Anthology of American Indian Literature. Knopf, 1972, pp. 84-5.

991. _______. "A San Diego Poem: January-February 1973." In Niatum, Duane, ed., Carriers of the Dream Wheel. Harper, 1975, p. 146-49.

992. _______. "The Serenity in Stones." In Niatum, Duane, ed., Carriers of the Dream Wheel. Harper, 1975, p. 156.

993. _______. "The Serenity Possible in Stones." Pembroke Magazine. no. 3 (1972) 10.

994. _______. "Sighting in on Montana, for James Welch." Quetzal. v. 2 (Winter-Spring, 1972) 12.

995. _______. "Smoking My Prayers." In Dodge, Robert K. & Joseph B. McCullough, eds., Voices from Wah'kon-tah. International Publishers, 1974, p. 81.

996. _______. "Smoking My Prayers." In Milton, John R., comp., The American Indian Speaks. Vermillion: U. of S.D., 1969, p. 8.

997. _______. "Smoking My Prayers." In Sanders,

Thomas E. & Walter W. Peek, Literature of the American Indian. Glencoe Pr., 1973, p. 466.

998. Ortiz, Simon J. (Acoma Pueblo) "Survival This Way." In Niatum, Duane, ed., Carriers of the Dream Wheel. Harper, 1975, p. 159.

999. ______. "Teach Me Your Song." The Indian Historian. v. 3 (Winter, 1970) 58.

1000. ______. "Telling about Coyote." Alcheringa. v. 4 (Autumn, 1972) 15-19.

1001. ______. "Telling about Coyote." In Quasha, George & Jerome Rothenberg, eds., America, a Prophecy. Vintage Books, 1974, pp. 235-8.

1002. ______. "Ten O'Clock News." In Dodge, Robert K. & Joseph B. McCullough, eds., Voices from Wah'kon-tah. International Publishers, 1974, p. 79.

1003. ______. "Ten O'Clock News." In Milton, John R., comp., The American Indian Speaks. Vermillion: U. of South Dakota, 1969, p. 5.

1004. ______. "Ten O'Clock News." In Sanders, Thomas E. & Walter W. Peek, Literature of the American Indian. Glencoe Pr., 1973, p. 465.

1005. ______. "That Time." New Mexico. v. 51 (March/April, 1973) 30.

1006. ______. "This American." The Indian Historian. v. 3 (Winter, 1970) 59.

1007. ______. "This Is for My Brothers, Blue Jay, Gold Finch, Flicker and Squirrel, Who Perished, Lately, Victims in this Unnecessary of All Wars." Quetzal. v. 2 (Winter-Spring, 1972) 11.

1008. ______. "This Preparation." In Dodge, Robert K. & Joseph B. McCullough, eds., Voices from Wah'kon-tah. International Publishers, 1974, p. 80.

1009. ______. "This Preparation." In Milton, John R.,

comp., The American Indian Speaks. Vermillion: U. of S.D., 1969, p. 7.

1010. Ortiz, Simon J. (Acoma Pueblo) "This Preparation." In Sanders, Thomas E. & Walter W. Peek, Literature of the American Indian. Glencoe Pr., 1973, p. 467.

1011. ______. "To Insure Survival." In Niatum, Duane, ed., Carriers of the Dream Wheel. Harper, 1975, p. 143.

1012. ______. "Traveling in the Wind." Pembroke Magazine. no. 7 (1976) 211-23.

1013. ______. "Two Old Man at Ft. Lyons Vah." Pembroke Magazine. no. 7 (1976) 220-3.

1014. ______. "Various Texas Places." In Henry, Jeannette, ed., The American Indian Reader: Literature. Indian Historian Pr., 1973, p. 35-39.

1015. ______. "Various Texas Places." The Indian Historian. v. 3 (Fall 1970) 26.

1016. ______. "Vision Shadows." Pembroke Magazine. no. 3 (1972) 4-5.

1017. ______. "Waiting for You to Come By." In Niatum, Duane, ed., Carriers of the Dream Wheel. Harper, 1975, p. 152.

1018. ______. "Waking." Pembroke Magazine. no. 7 (1976) 217-8.

1019. ______. "War Poem [Oct. 15, Moratorium Day]." In Lowenfels, Walter, ed., From the Belly of the Shark." Vintage, 1973, pp. 49-50.

1020. ______. "Watching Salmon Jump." In Niatum, Duane, ed., Carriers of the Dream Wheel. Harper, 1975, p. 157.

1021. ______. "West: Grants to Gallup, New Mexico." In Witt, Shirley H., The Way; an Anthology of American Indian Literature. Knopf, 1972, pp. 88-9.

1022. Ortiz, Simon J. (Acoma Pueblo) "What I Tell Him." In Niatum, Duane, ed., Carriers of the Dream Wheel. Harper, 1975, p. 151.

1023. ________. "Wind on Snow." Pembroke Magazine. no. 7 (1976) 217.

1024. Palmanteer, Ted. (Colville) "Chinook Dance." Sun Tracks. v. 1 (Winter, 1971/72) 28-30.

1025. ________. "Hit!" In Allen, Terry, ed., The Whispering Wind; Poetry by Young American Indians. Doubleday, 1972, pp. 39-40.

1026. ________. "Judgment." In Allen, Terry, ed., The Whispering Wind; Poetry by Young American Indians. Doubleday, 1972, p. 46.

1027. ________. "Spring Dew." In Allen, Terry, ed., The Whispering Wind; Poetry by Young American Indians. Doubleday, 1972, p. 43.

1028. ________. "The Strings of Time." In Allen, Terry, ed., The Whispering Wind; Poetry by Young American Indians. Doubleday, 1972, p. 47.

1029. ________. "This Is Real." In Allen, Terry, ed., The Whispering Wind; Poetry by Young American Indians. Doubleday, 1972, pp. 44-5.

1030. ________. "We Saw Days." In Allen, Terry, ed., The Whispering Wind; Poetry by Young American Indians. Doubleday, 1972, pp. 41-42.

1031. Panegoosho, M. (Eskimo) "Morning Mood." In Lewis, Richard, comp., I Breathe a New Song. Simon, 1971, p. 22.

1032. Paredes, Jose Maria. "Eternal Dust." Akwesasne Notes. v. 4 (Early Spring, 1972) 48.

1033. Parisien, Darlene. (Chippewa) "Rain." In Allen, T. D., ed., Arrow III. U.S. Bureau of Indian Affairs, Creative Writing, 1971, p. 18.

1034. ________. "Stream." In Allen, T. D., ed., Arrow III. U.S. Bureau of Indian Affairs, Creative Writing Project, 1971, p. 18.

1035. Patkotak, Ethel. (Eskimo) "The Help Rain Gives Me." In Allen, T. D., ed., *Arrow II*. U.S. Bureau of Indian Affairs, Creative Writing Project, 1970, p. 19.

1036. Pauly, William. "For David White Bear, son of Time." *Akwesasne Notes*. v. 3 (Jan./Feb., 1971) 48.

1037. ________. "Notice in Grand Canyon National Park." *Akwesasne Notes*. v. 3 (Oct./Nov., 1971) 48.

1038. Paulzine, Niki. "I Am the Fire of Time" [first line]. *Akwesasne Notes*. v. 5 (January, 1973) 48.

1039. ________. "Untitled." In Lowenfels, Walter, ed., *From the Belly of the Shark*. Vintage, 1973, p. 57.

1040. Pawo Pawo, Haihai. (Ojibwa) "Alcatraz...Lives!!" *Akwesasne Notes*. v. 3 (June, 1971) 48.

1041. ________. "Alcatraz...Lives!!" In Lowenfels, Walter, ed., *From the Belly of the Shark*. Vintage, 1973, p. 33.

1042. Peacock, Dozer. "The Very Old Woman Sitting on a Rug" [first line]. *Angwamas Minosewag Anishinabeg*. 1st issue. (Poets in the Schools Program) St. Paul Council of Arts and Sciences, [1973].

1043. Pepion, Betty. "Humanity." *The Indian Historian*. v. 1 (Sept., 1968) 27.

1044. ________. "Yesterday." In Henry, Jeannette, ed., *The American Indian Reader: Literature*. Indian History Pr., 1973, p. 58.

1045. Peynetsa, Andrew. (Zuni) "When the Old Timers Went Deer Hunting." ed. by Dennis Tedlock. *Alcheringa*. v. 3 (Winter, 1971) 76-81.

1046. Pickernall, Clarence. (Eskimo) "This Is My Land." In Lowenfels, Walter, ed., *From the Belly of the Shark*. Vintage, 1973, pp. 140-1.

1047. Pineapple. "Coyote." *Akwesasne Notes*. v. 7 (Early Summer, 1975) 48.

1048. Pineapple. "Massacre." Akwesasne Notes. v. 4 (Late Autumn, 1972) 48.

1049. ________. "Native Child/Moment in a Life." Akwesasne Notes. v. 5 (Early Autumn, 1973) 3.

1050. ________. "Sacrificial Thought." Akwesasne Notes. v. 5 (January, 1973) 48.

1051. ________. "1778--Capt. James Cook Discovers the Hawaiian Islands." Akwesasne Notes. v. 6 (Late Spring, 1974) 48.

1052. ________. "tree--my brother" [first line]. Akwesasne Notes. v. 6 (Early Spring, 1974) 48.

1053. ________. "Who has given us back our spirit" [first line]. Akwesasne Notes. v. 5 (Early Summer, 1973) 48.

1054. Pinto, Yvonne. (Navajo) "Feeling Your Presence" [first line]. In Allen, T. D., ed., Arrow III. U.S. Bureau of Indian Affairs, Creative Writing Project, 1971, p. 8.

1055. Pipe On Head, Diana. (Oglala Sioux) "Meadows." In Allen, T. D., ed., Arrow IV. U.S. Bureau of Indian Affairs, Creative Writing Project, 1972, p. 9.

1056. Platta, Charles. (Mescalero Apache) "Mescalero." In Allen, T. D., ed., Arrow IV. U.S. Bureau of Indian Affairs, Creative Writing Project, 1972, p. 6.

1057. Platte, Lori. "He Who Casts a Shadow." [first line]. Akwesasne Notes. v. 5 (Early Autumn, 1973) 3.

1058. Posey, Alex. (Creek) "Ode to the Sequoyah." In Foreman, Grant, ed., Sequoyah. U. of Okla. Pr., 1959 [1938], p. 82.

1059. Pratt, Agnes T. (Suquamish) "Bremerton, January 18, 1969." In Allen, Terry, ed., The Whispering Wind; Poetry by Young American Indians. Doubleday, 1972, pp. 99-100.

1060. ________. "Death Takes Only a Minute." In Allen,

Terry, ed., The Whispering Wind; Poetry by Young American Indians. Doubleday, 1972, p. 106.

1061. Pratt, Agnes. (Suquamish) "Death Takes Only a Minute." In Dodge, Robert K. & Joseph B. McCullough, eds., Voices from Wah'kon-tah. International Publishers, 1974, p. 84.

1062. ________. "Empathy." In Dodge, Robert K. & Joseph B. McCullough, eds., Voices from Wah'kon-tah. International Publishers, 1974, p. 85.

1063. ________. "Empathy." In Allen, Terry, ed., The Whispering Wind; Poetry by Young American Indians. Doubleday, 1972, p. 107.

1064. ________. "Fishing." In Allen, Terry, ed., The Whispering Wind; Poetry by Young American Indians. Doubleday, 1972, p. 101.

1065. ________. "Fragments of Spring." In Allen, Terry, ed., The Whispering Wind; Poetry by Young American Indians. Doubleday, 1972, p. 108.

1066. ________. "Hope to Keep." In Allen, Terry, ed., The Whispering Wind; Poetry by Young American Indians. Doubleday, 1972, p. 109.

1067. ________. "I'm Going to Wash My Face" [first line]. In Future Directions in Native American Art. Santa Fe, N.M.: The Institute of American Indian Arts, [1973], [i].

1068. ________. "I'm Only Going to Tell You Once." In Allen, Terry, ed., The Whispering Wind; Poetry by Young American Indians. Doubleday, 1972, p. 106.

1069. ________. "Inspiration." In Milton, John R., comp., The American Indian Speaks. Vermillion: U. of S.D., 1969, p. 130.

1070. ________. "Lamentation." In Allen, Terry, ed., The Whispering Wind; Poetry by Young American Indians. Doubleday, 1972, p. 108.

1071. Pratt, Agnes T. (Suquamish) "Lamentation." In Milton, John R., comp., The American Indian Speaks. Vermillion: U. of S. Dak., 1969, p. 131.

1072. ________. "Question." In Allen, Terry, ed., The Whispering Wind; Poetry by Young American Indians. Doubleday, 1972, p. 103.

1073. ________. "Quietly I Shout." In Allen, Terry, ed., The Whispering Wind; Poetry by Young American Indians. Doubleday, 1972, p. 110.

1074. ________. "The Sea Is Melancholy." In Allen, Terry, ed., The Whispering Wind; Poetry by Young American Indians. Doubleday, 1972, p. 103.

1075. ________. "So Quickly Came the Summer." In Allen, Terry, ed., The Whispering Wind; Poetry by Young American Indians. Doubleday, 1972, p. 109.

1076. ________. "Sympathy." In Allen, Terry, ed., The Whispering Wind; Poetry by Young American Indians. Doubleday, 1972, p. 105.

1077. ________. "Twilight's Feet." In Allen, Terry, ed., The Whispering Wind; Poetry by Young American Indians. Doubleday, 1972, p. 102.

1078. ________. "Untitled." In Allen, Terry, ed., The Whispering Wind; Poetry by Young American Indians. Doubleday, 1972, p. 104.

1079. Presley, John Woodrow. (Choctaw) "In My Father's House." Blue Cloud Quarterly. v. 21, no. 4.

1080. ________. "Landscape: White on White." Blue Cloud Quarterly. v. 21, no. 4.

1081. ________. "A Lover's Lesson." Blue Cloud Quarterly. v. 21, no. 4.

1082. Pretty Voice Hawk, Chaske. "I Talk with the Wind." Akwesasne Notes. v. 3 (Dec., 1971) 48.

1083. ________. "Whispering Thunder." Akwesasne Notes. v. 5 (Early Summer, 1973) 48.

1084. Pretty Voice Hawk, Chaske. "Whiteman Killer." Akwesasne Notes. v. 6 (Early Autumn, 1974) 48.

1085. Probst, Anita Endrezze. (Yaqui) "Canto Llano." In Niatum, Duane, ed., Carriers of the Dream Wheel. Harper, 1975, pp. 176-77.

1086. ________. "Eclipse." In Niatum, Duane, ed., Carriers of the Dream Wheel. Harper, 1975, p. 178.

1087. ________. "Exodus." In Niatum, Duane, ed., Carriers of the Dream Wheel. Harper, 1975, pp. 174-75.

1088. ________. "In the Flight of the Blue Heron..." In Niatum, Duane, ed., Carriers of the Dream Wheel. Harper, 1975, pp. 179-81.

1089. ________. "Learning the Spells..." In Niatum, Duane, ed., Carriers of the Dream Wheel. Harper, 1975, pp. 170-71.

1090. ________. "Manifest Destiny." In Niatum, Duane, ed., Carriers of the Dream Wheel. Harper, 1975, p. 163.

1091. ________. "Notes from an Analyst's Couch." In Niatum, Duane, ed., Carriers of the Dream Wheel. Harper, 1975, p. 172.

1092. ________. "Red Rock Ceremonies." In Niatum, Duane, ed., Carriers of the Dream Wheel. Harper, 1975, pp. 164-65.

1093. ________. "The Stripper." In Niatum, Duane, ed., Carriers of the Dream Wheel. Harper, 1975, pp. 168-69.

1094. ________. "The Truth about My Sister and Me." In Niatum, Duane, ed., Carriers of the Dream Wheel. Harper, 1975, pp. 166-67.

1095. Qoyawayma, Polingaysi. (Hopi) "The Select in the Desert." New Mexico Quarterly. v. 36 (Summer 1966) 143.

1096. Quartz, Susan. (Paiute) "The Dog." In Allen,

T. D., ed., Arrow III. U.S. Bureau Indian Affairs, Creative Writing Project, 1971, p. 15.

1097. A Quechan (unknown). "An Oration." Akwesasne Notes. v. 7 (Late Summer, 1975) 48.

1098. Ransom, W. M. (Cheyenne-Arapaho) "Catechism, 1958." In Niatum, Duane, ed., Carriers of the Dream Wheel. Harper, 1975, p. 202.

1099. ________. "Critter." In Niatum, Duane, ed., Carriers of the Dream Wheel. Harper, 1975, pp. 185-96.

1100. ________. Finding True North. Copper Canyon Press, 1973.

1101. ________. "Grandpa." In Lowenfels, Walter, ed., From the Belly of the Shark. Vintage, 1973, pp. 51-2.

1102. ________. "Grandpa's .45." In Niatum, Duane, ed., Carriers of the Dream Wheel. Harper, 1975, p. 201.

1103. ________. "Indian Summer: Montana, 1956." In Niatum, Duane, ed., Carriers of the Dream Wheel. Harper, 1975, p. 199.

1104. ________. "Message from Ohanapecosh Glacier." In Niatum, Duane, ed., Carriers of the Dream Wheel. Harper, 1975, p. 197.

1105. ________. "On the Morning of the Third Night..." In Niatum, Duane, ed., Carriers of the Dream Wheel. Harper, 1975, p. 200.

1106. ________. "Statement on Our Higher Education." In Niatum, Duane, ed., Carriers of the Dream Wheel. Harper, 1975, p. 198.

1107. Ravensblood. (Nootka) "Invocation." Sun Tracks. v. 1 (Fall, 1971) 20.

1108. Raymond, Art. "Cry to the Wind." Wassaja. v. 3 (August, 1975) 13.

1109. Redbird, Duke. (Ojibway) "Banff Indian Seminar." In Waubageshig, ed., The Only Good Indian. New Pr., 1970, p. 142.

1110. ______. "The Beaver." In Gooderham, Kent, ed., I Am an Indian. Toronto, Dent, 1969, pp. 97-9.

1111. ______. "The Dance." In Waubageshig, ed., The Only Good Indian. New Pr., 1970, p. 125.

1112. ______. "The Distant Lonely Soul of Me." In Waubageshig, ed., The Only Good Indian. New Pr., 1970, p. 51.

1113. ______. "I Am a Redman." In Waubageshig, ed., The Only Good Indian. New Pr., 1970, p. 61.

1114. ______. "Language of the Soul." In Waubageshig, ed., The Only Good Indian. New Pr., 1970, p. 161.

1115. ______. "Littleleaf." In Waubageshig, ed., The Only Good Indian. New Pr., 1970, p. 4.

1116. ______. "The Marriage." In Waubageshig, ed., The Only Good Indian. New Pr., 1970, p. 73.

1117. ______. "My Lodge." In Waubageshig, ed., The Only Good Indian. New Pr., 1970, p. 110.

1118. ______. "My Moccasins." In Waubageshig, ed., The Only Good Indian. New Pr., 1970, p. 103.

1119. ______. "My Way." In Waubageshig, ed., The Only Good Indian. New Pr., 1970, p. 41.

1120. ______. "Old Woman." In Waubageshig, ed., The Only Good Indian. New Pr., 1970, pp. 181-3.

1121. ______. "The Small Drum." In Waubageshig, ed., The Only Good Indian. New Pr., 1970, p. 156.

1122. ______. "Tobacco Burns." In Waubageshig, ed., The Only Good Indian. New Pr., 1970, p. 1.

1123. Red Cloud, Fred. (Seneca) "Five Days I Fasted." Prairie Schooner. v. 45 (Fall, 1971) 198.

1124. Red Cloud, Fred. (Seneca) "I Came to the Foothills. Akwesasne Notes. v. 6 (Early Autumn, 1974) 48.

1125. ______. "Machu Picchu, Peru." In Dodge, Robert K. & Joseph B. McCullough, eds., Voices from Wah'kon-tah. International Publishers, 1974, p. 88.

1126. ______. "The Sky Was..." Akwesasne Notes. v. 5 (Early Winter, 1973) 48.

1127. ______. "A Story of Coyote Man." Prairie Schooner. v. 45 (Fall, 1971) 197.

1128. ______. "A Tale of Last Stands." In Dodge, Robert K. & Joseph B. McCullough, eds., Voices from Wah'kon-tah. International Publishers, 1974, p. 86.

1129. ______. "A Tale of Last Stands." Prairie Schooner. v. 44 (Spring, 1970) 21-2.

1130. ______. "What Did You Leave Me, White Man?" Akwesasne Notes. v. 3 (May, 1971) 48.

1131. ______. "White Man Says to Me." Akwesasne Notes. v. 4 (Late Winter, 1972) 48.

1132. ______. "White Man Says to Me." In Lowenfels, Walter, ed., From the Belly of the Shark. Vintage, 1973, p. 53.

1133. ______. "White Man Says to Me, Save." In Levitas, Gloria, Frank Robert & Jacqueline J. Vivelo, eds., American Indian Prose & Poetry. Putnam, 1974, p. 291.

1134. Reeves, David. (Navajo) "Loser." In Allen, T. D., ed., Arrow I. U.S. Bureau of Indian Affairs, Creative Writing Project, 1969, p. 12.

1135. ______. "Loser." In Witt, Shirley H., comp., The Way; an Anthology of American Indian Literature. Knopf, 1972, p. 149.

1136. Reyna, Juan. "For Native People." Akwesasne Notes. v. 7 (Late Summer, 1975) 48.

1137. Reyna, Juan. "know all those roads" [first line]. Akwesasne Notes. v. 7 (Early Winter, 1975) 48.

1138. Rice, Joe (Tahca isnala). "Great Spirit..." [first line]. Akwesasne Notes. v. 7 (Early Winter, 1975) 48.

1139. Richey, C. C. "Owl Power." Akwesasne Notes. v. 4 (Early Spring, 1972).

1140. Rickards, Montana H. (Cherokee) "The American Indian." In Rickards, M. H., Literature for the Native American. Atlanta, Natl. Council of Teachers of English, Nov. 1970, p. 14.

1141. Rivas, Ophelia. (Papago) "Indians." In Allen, T. D., ed., Arrow III. U.S. Bureau of Indian Affairs, Creative Writing Project, 1971, p. 16.

1142. Rivers, Mike. "Above..." Akwesasne Notes. v. 7 (Early Autumn, 1975) 48.

1143. _______. "Dream Poem." Akwesasne Notes. v. 6 (Early Autumn, 1974) 48.

1144. Roanhorse, Jefferson. (Navajo) "The Docks Are Quiet" [first line]. In Allen, T. D., ed., Arrow IV. U.S. Bureau of Indian Affairs, Creative Writing Project, 1972, p. 12.

1145. Roberts, Earleen. "Love: Washington Style." In Henry, Jeannette, ed., The American Indian Reader: Literature. Indian Historian Pr., 1973, p. 53.

1146. _______. "People through My Eyes." In Henry, Jeannette, ed., The American Indian Reader: Literature. Indian Historian Pr., 1973, p. 54.

1147. Roecker, William H. "Private Chant of a Young Apache." Sun Tracks. v. 1 (June, 1971) 8.

1148. Rogers, Ronald. (Cherokee) "Adjustments." Akwesasne Notes. v. 1, sec. 3 (Nov., 1969) 9.

1149. _______. "The Crimson Door." The Indian Historian. v. 4 (Sept., 1968) 26.

1150. Rogers, Ronald. (Cherokee) "The Crimson Door." In Henry, Jeannette, ed., The American Indian Reader: Literature. Indian Historian Pr., 1973, p. 51.

1151. _______. "The Jewelry Store." In Henry, Jeannette, ed., The American Indian Reader: Literature. Indian Historian Pr., 1973, p. 59.

1152. _______. "The Jewelry Store." The Indian Historian. v. 1 (Sept., 1968) 27.

1153. _______. "Kindergarten." In Allen, Terry, ed., The Whispering Wind; Poetry by Young American Indians. Doubleday, 1972, pp 87-8.

1154. _______. "Kindergarten." In Dodge, Robert K. & Joseph B. McCullough, eds., Voices from Wah'kontah. International Publishers, 1974, p. 91.

1155. _______. "Sioux City: January--Very Late." In Allen, Terry, ed., The Whispering Wind; Poetry by Young American Indians. Doubleday, 1972, p. 89.

1156. _______. "Sioux City: January--Very Late." In Milton, John R., comp., The American Indian Speaks. Vermillion: U. of S. Dak., 1969, p. 105.

1157. _______. "Taking Off." In Allen, Terry, ed., The Whispering Wind; Poetry by Young American Indians. Doubleday, 1972, pp. 85-6.

1158. _______. "Taking Off." In Dodge, Robert K. & Joseph B. McCullough, eds., Voices from Wah'kon-tah. International Publishers, 1974, p. 89.

1159. _______. "Taking Off." In Milton, John R., comp., The American Indian Speaks. Vermillion: U. of S. Dak., 1969, pp. 103-4.

1160. Rokwaho. "Moon Dance Music." Akwesasne Notes. v. 8 (Early Summer, 1976) 48.

1161. Romero, Johnny. (Taos) "Reach Out" Sun Tracks. v. 1 (Fall, 1971) 18.

1162. Romero, Johnny. (Taos) "Wild." Sun Tracks. v. 1 (Fall, 1971) 18.

1163. Rose, Wendy, or Chiron Khanshendel. (Hopi) "America." In Niatum, Duane, ed., Carriers of the Dream Wheel. Harper, 1975, p. 213.

1164. ________. "Celebration for My Mother." In Niatum, Duane, ed., Carriers of the Dream Wheel. Harper, 1975, p. 208.

1165. ________. "Epitaph." In Niatum, Duane, ed., Carriers of the Dream Wheel. Harper, 1975, p. 219.

1166. ________. "For My People." In Niatum, Duane, ed., Carriers of the Dream Wheel. Harper, 1975, p. 217.

1167. ________. "For Steph." In Niatum, Duane, ed., Carriers of the Dream Wheel. Harper, 1975, pp. 214-15.

1168. ________. "For Walter Lowenfels." In Niatum, Duane, ed., Carriers of the Dream Wheel. Harper, 1975, p. 207.

1169. ________. "Grunion." In Niatum, Duane, ed., Carriers of the Dream Wheel. Harper, 1975, p. 218.

1170. ________. Hopi Roadrunner Dancing. Greenfield Center, N.Y.: The Greenfield Review Pr., 1973.

1171. ________. "Oh Father." In Niatum, Duane, ed., Carriers of the Dream Wheel. Harper, 1975, p. 206.

1172. ________. "Oh My People I Remember." In Niatum, Duane, ed., Carriers of the Dream Wheel. Harper, 1975, p. 211.

1173. ________. "Poem to a Redskin." In Niatum, Duane, ed., Carriers of the Dream Wheel. Harper, 1975, p. 205.

1174. ________. "Saint Patrick's Day, 1973." In Niatum, Duane, ed., Carriers of the Dream Wheel. Harper, 1975, p. 210.

1175. Rose, Wendy, or Chiron Khanshendel. (Hopi) "Self Dirge." In Niatum, Duane, ed., Carriers of the Dream Wheel. Harper, 1975, p. 212.

1176. ______. They Sometimes Call Me." In Niatum, Duane, ed., Carriers of the Dream Wheel. Harper, 1975, p. 216.

1177. ______. "To an Imaginary Father." In Niatum, Duane, ed., Carriers of the Dream Wheel. Harper, 1975, p. 209.

1178. Roshey, Barbara. "Leaves." Angwamas Minesowag Anishinabeg. (Poets in the Schools Program) St. Paul Council of Arts and Sciences, Winter, 1973-74.

1179. Rowland, V. (Mrs.). (Sioux) "The Spirit Trail." In Gooderham, Kent, ed., I Am an Indian. Toronto, Dent, 1969, p. 80.

1180. Roy, Steve. "The Blue Deer Flew" [first line]. Angwamas Minosewag Anishinabeg. (Poets in the Schools Program) St. Paul Council of Arts and Sciences, Winter, 1973-74.

1181. Russell, Norman H. (Cherokee) "After the Night of Sweats." South Dakota Review. v. 10 (Winter 1972-73) 90.

1182. ______. "All My Dreams." South Dakota Review. v. 10 (Winter 1972-73) 89.

1183. ______. "All the White Night." Prairie Schooner. v. 45 (Spring, 1972) 35.

1184. ______. "Anna Wauneka Comes to My Hogan." In Lowenfels, Walter, ed., From the Belly of the Shark. Vintage, 1973, p. 54.

1185. ______. "Because This Is the Way Things Are." Little Square Review. Nos. 5&6 (Spring & Summer, 1968) 39-40.

1186. ______. "Charles Darwin 1832 the Jungle." South Dakota Review. v. 6 (Autumn 1968) 78.

1187. Russell, Norman H. (Cherokee) "Charles Darwin 1832 Tierra del Fuego." South Dakota Review. v. 6 (Autumn 1968) 77.

1188. ________. "Clerk's Song II." In Dodge, Robert K. & Joseph B. McCullough, eds., Voices from Wah'kon-tah. International Publishers, 1974, p. 95.

1189. ________. "Clerk's Song II." South Dakota Review. v. 9 (Autumn 1971) 29.

1190. ________. "Each Night Is a Long Winter." South Dakota Review. v. 9 (Autumn 1971) 28.

1191. ________. "The Earth Always Lies on His Back." In Lourie, Dick, ed., Come to Power. The Crossing Press, 1974, p. 39.

1192. ________. Ecosystem of Love. Umbilical Cord Pr., 1972.

1193. ________. "The Eyes of the Child Do Not See Me." In Dodge, Robert K. & Joseph B. McCullough, eds., Voices from Wah'kon-tah. International Publishers, 1974, p. 92.

1194. ________. "The Great Way of the Man." In Dodge, Robert K. & Joseph B. McCullough, eds., Voices from Wah'kon-tah. International Publishers, 1974, p. 94.

1195. ________. "The Great Way of the Man." In Milton, John R., comp., The American Indian Speaks. Vermillion: U. of S. Dak., 1969, p. 21.

1196. ________. "His Howling Voyage." In Lourie, Dick, ed., Come to Power. The Crossing Press, 1974, p. 34.

1197. ________. "How Many Days?" Prairie Schooner. v. 46 (Spring 1972) 37.

1198. ________. "I Am a Warrior." Pembroke Magazine. no. 3 (1972) 53.

1199. ________. "I Have Many Friends." In Milton,

John R., comp., The American Indian Speaks. Vermillion: U. of S. Dak., 1969, p. 18.

1200. Russell, Norman H. (Cherokee) "I Have Many Friends." In Sanders, Thomas E. & Walter W. Peek, Literature of the American Indian. Glencoe Pr., 1973, p. 468.

1201. ______. "I Kill Her Enemies." In Lourie, Dick, ed., Come to Power. The Crossing Press, 1974, p. 35.

1202. ______. "I Laughed, I Listen." Prairie Schooner. v. 46 (Spring, 1972) 36.

1203. ______. "I See a White Flower Dancing." Quetzal. v. 2 (Winter-Spring, 1972) 32.

1204. ______. "I See Many Ants." Little Square Review. Nos. 5&6 (Spring & Summer, 1968) 40-41.

1205. ______. "I Took His Scalp." In Lourie, Dick, ed., Come to Power. The Crossing Press, 1974, p. 38.

1206. ______. "I Who Have No Name." Many Smokes. v. 6 (Spring, 1972) 10.

1207. ______. "In the Bush of Thorns." Little Square Review. Nos. 5&6 (Spring & Summer, 1968) 41.

1208. ______. "In the Mouths of Birds." Pembroke Magazine. no. 3 (1972) 53.

1209. ______. "In the White Man's Town." Little Square Review. Nos. 5&6 (Spring & Summer, 1968) 41-2.

1210. ______. "Indian School." Little Square Review. Nos. 5&6 (Spring & Summer, 1968) 42.

1211. ______. Indian Thoughts: the Small Songs of God. Juniper Pr., 1972.

1212. ______. "The Juniper." In Lourie, Dick, ed., Come to Power. The Crossing Press, 1974, p. 36.

1213. Russell, Norman H. (Cherokee) "The Kingfisher." Pembroke Magazine. no. 3 (1972) 54.

1214. ________. "The Messenger." In Milton, John R., comp., The American Indian Speaks. Vermillion: U. of S. Dak., 1969, p. 19.

1215. ________. "More Colors than the Rainbow." South Dakota Review. v. 6 (Winter 1968-69) 41.

1216. ________. "The most beautiful thing." Akwesasne Notes. v. 3 (May, 1971) 48.

1217. ________. "My Fathers Hands Held Mine." Little Square Review. Nos. 5 & 6 (Spring & Summer, 1968) 43.

1218. ________. "My Only Wisdom." Quetzal. v. 2 (Winter-Spring, 1972) 32.

1219. ________. "Old Men Climbing." South Dakota Review. v. 6 (Winter, 1968-69) 42.

1220. ________. "Only I, an Old Woman." Pembroke Magazine. no. 2 (1971) 43.

1221. ________. "Singing Wolf Speaks." In Lourie, Dick, ed., Come to Power. The Crossing Press, 1974, p. 40.

1222. ________. "Snow Likely." Prairie Schooner. v. 46 (Spring, 1972) 35-6.

1223. ________. "That Bird Sings." Pembroke Magazine. no. 3 (1972) 54.

1224. ________. "There Is a Hungry Watching." In Lourie, Dick, ed., Come to Power. The Crossing Press, 1974, p. 37.

1225. ________. "This Great Cloud." Akwesasne Notes. v. 3 (June, 1971) 48.

1226. ________. "This Is a Sign." In Milton, John R., comp., The American Indian Speaks. Vermillion: U. of S. Dak., 1969, p. 20.

1227. Russell, Norman H. (Cherokee) "This Is a Sign." In Sanders, Thomas E. & Walter W. Peek, Literature of the American Indian. Glencoe Pr., 1973, pp. 468-9.

1228. _______. "A Time of War." Little Square Review. Nos. 5&6 (Spring & Summer, 1968) 39.

1229. _______. "The Tree Sleeps in the Winter." In Lourie, Dick, ed., Come to Power. The Crossing Press, 1974, p. 33.

1230. _______. "Way Down Pembroke Way." Quetzal. v. 2 (Winter-Spring, 1972) 32.

1231. _______. "What Is the Wind?" South Dakota Review. v. 6 (Winter, 1968-69) 40.

1232. _______. "The White Dog." Little Square Review. Nos. 5&6 (Spring & Summer, 1968) 43.

1233. _______. "The White Man's Whiskey." Akwesasne Notes. v. 3 (Sept., 1971) 48.

1234. _______. "The World Has Many Places Many Ways." In Dodge, Robert K. & Joseph B. McCullough, eds., Voices from Wah'kon-tah. International Publishers, 1974, p. 93.

1235. _______. "Your Fathers and Your Children." Pembroke Magazine. no. 2 (1971) 44.

1236. Saindon, Carolyn. (Karok) "The Taming of Fire." Indian Historian. v. 1 (Spring, 1968) 19-20.

1237. St. Clair, Darrel Daniel. (Tlingit) "Only in Silence." In Lowenfels, Walter, ed., From the Belly of the Shark. Vintage, 1973, pp. 55-7.

1238. Sainte-Marie, Buffy. (Cree) "The Beauty Way." Wassaja. v. 3 (June, 1975) 19.

1239. _______. The Buffy Sainte-Marie Songbook. Music ed. & arr. by Peter Greenwood. Grosset, 1971.

1240. _______. "The Civilized People." Wassaja. v. 3 (June, 1975) 19.

1241. Sainte-Marie, Buffy. (Cree) I'm Gonna be a Country Girl Again. Vanguard, 1968.

1242. ________. My Country 'Tis of Thy People You're Dying. Gypsy Boy Music, Inc., 1966.

1243. ________. "My Country 'Tis of Thy People You're Dying." Blue Cloud Quarterly. v. 14, no. 3.

1244. ________. [from] "My Country, 'Tis of Thy People You're Dying." In Lowenfels, Walter, ed., From the Belly of the Shark. Vintage, 1973, pp. 58-9.

1245. ________. Now that the Buffalo's Gone. Gypsy Boy Music, Inc., 1965.

1246. ________. "Now that the Buffalo's Gone." Blue Cloud Quarterly. v. 14, no. 3.

1247. ________. "Now that the Buffalo's Gone." In Gross, Theodore L., ed., A Nation of Nations. Macmillan, 1971, pp. 329-30.

1248. ________. "Seeds of Brotherhood." Blue Cloud Quarterly. v. 14, no. 3.

1249. ________. "Universal Soldier." In Gooderham, Kent, ed., I Am an Indian. Toronto, Dent, 1969, pp. 86-7.

1250. Sampson, Elliott V. "Singing a Song" [first line]. Akwesasne Notes. v. 4 (Early Spring, 1972) 48.

1251. ________. "We Are Now a Show." Akwesasne Notes. v. 3 (Dec., 1971) 48.

1252. Sanders, Thomas E. (Nippawanock-Cherokee) "The Museum of Manitou." The Indian Historian. v. 5 (Fall, 1972) 7-12, 22.

1253. Sanderville, Sandra. (Blackfoot) "Big, Green Speckled Frog" [first line]. In Allen, T. D., ed., Arrow IV. U.S. Bureau of Indian Affairs, Creative Writing Project, 1972, p. 11.

1254. Sandoval, S. Roberto. (Genizaro) "Going to the Place Where" [first line]. In Lourie, Dick, ed.,

Come to Power. The Crossing Press, 1974, p. 125.

1255. Sandoval, S. Roberto. (Genizaro) "Old Friends I Haven't Seen" [first line]. In Lourie, Dick, ed., Come to Power. The Crossing Press, 1974, p. 122.

1256. ______. "Pots." In Lourie, Dick, ed., Come to Power. The Crossing Press, 1974, p. 119.

1257. ______. "Speaks a Tongue" [first line]. In Lourie, Dick, ed., Come to Power. The Crossing Press, 1974, p. 127.

1258. ______. "Touching on a Mountain Top." In Lourie, Dick, ed., Come to Power. The Crossing Press, 1974, p. 126.

1259. ______. "Twin Apples Sitting on a White" [first line]. In Lourie, Dick, ed., Come to Power. The Crossing Press, 1974, p. 121.

1260. ______. "The Wind Never Stops Here in the Fall." In Lourie, Dick, ed., Come to Power. The Crossing Press, 1974, p. 123.

1261. ______. "Windless Night with Clear Stars" [first line]. In Lourie, Dick, ed., Come to Power. The Crossing Press, 1974, p. 120.

1262. Sandoval, Sandy. "Tight Mouth." In Lowenfels, Walter, ed., From the Belly of the Shark. Vintage, 1973, p. 59.

1263. Saubel, Catherine Siva. "Adventures of Konvaxmal, a Cahuilla Story." The Indian Historian. v. 1 (Sept., 1968) 28.

1264. Saunders, Jeff. (Navajo) "Black Wind." In Milton, John R., ed., Four Indian Poets. Dakota Press, 1974, p. 65.

1265. ______. "I Came Far Today." In Milton, John R., ed., Four Indian Poets. Dakota Press, 1974, p. 61.

1266. Saunders, Jeff. (Navajo) "Painted Land." In Milton, John R., ed., Four Indian Poets. Dakota Press, 1974, p. 67.

1267. ________. "Poles of Smoke." In Milton, John R., ed., Four Indian Poets. Dakota Press, 1974, p. 62.

1268. ________. "Snow Came Easy." In Milton, John R., ed., Four Indian Poets. Dakota Press, 1974, p. 66.

1269. ________. "Summer Came Lightly." In Milton, John R., ed., Four Indian Poets. Dakota Press, 1974, p. 63.

1270. ________. "The Weekend." In Milton, John R., ed., Four Indian Poets. Dakota Press, 1974, p. 64.

1271. Sea-Flower. "I Am Happy" [first line]. Akwesasne Notes. v. 3 (July/Aug., 1971) 48.

1272. ________. "Reminiscence." Akwesasne Notes. v. 3 (Sept., 1971) 48.

1273. ________. "We Are Brothers." Akwesasne Notes. v. 3 (Oct./Nov., 1971) 48.

1274. ________. "We Are Brothers." In Levitas, Gloria, Frank Robert & Jacqueline J. Vivelo, eds., American Indian Prose & Poetry. Putnam, 1974, pp. 305-06.

1275. Selam, Leroy B., or Suwaptsa. (Yakima) "What Is This Upon My Land?" The Indian Historian. v. 4 (Spring, 1971) 19.

1276. ________. "What Is This Upon My Land?" In Rickards, Montana H., ed., Literature for the Native American. Atlanta, Nat'l. Council Teachers of English, Nov. 1970, pp. 7-10.

1277. Seota, Faithe. (Pima) "It Is Time." Sun Tracks. v. 1 (Fall, 1971) 31.

1278. Seven Buffaloes, or Art Cuelho. "Indian Burial." Blue Cloud Quarterly. v. 20, no. 4.

1279. Severy, Bruce. "Deserted Farms Poem." In Dodge, Robert K. & Joseph B. McCullough, eds., Voices from Wah'kon-tah. International Publishers, 1974, p. 98.

1280. ________. "First and Last." In Dodge, Robert K. & Joseph B. McCullough, eds., Voices from Wah'kon-tah. International Publishers, 1974, p. 100.

1281. ________. "Opening Day." In Dodge, Robert K. & Joseph B. McCullough, eds., Voices from Wah'kon-tah. International Publishers, 1974, p. 97.

1282. ________. "Poems." In Dodge, Robert K. & Joseph B. McCullough, eds., Voices from Wah'kon-tah. International Publishers, 1974, p. 96.

1283. ________. "Struggle for the Roads." In Dodge, Robert K. & Joseph B. McCullough, eds., Voices from Wah'kon-tah. International Publishers, 1974, p. 99.

1284. Shearer, Tony. (Sioux) Lord of the Dawn; Quetzalcoatl, the Plumed Serpent of Mexico. Illus. by the author. Naturegraph, 1971.

1285. Shegonee, Loyal. (Potawatomi) "Loneliness." In Dodge, Robert K. & Joseph B. McCullough, eds., Voices from Wah'kon-tah. International Publishers, 1974, p. 101.

1286. ________. "Loneliness." In Milton, John R., comp., The American Indian Speaks. Vermillion: U. of S. Dak., 1969, p. 152.

1287. Shelby, Eva. "Grey Sky." Akwesasne Notes. v. 8 (Early Summer, 1976) 48.

1288. Shepard, Joanne. (Navajo) "Death & Life." In Allen, T. D., ed., Arrow IV. U.S. Bureau of Indian Affairs, Creative Writing Project, 1972, p. 26.

1289. Shield, Verdell Thunder. (Sioux) "From My Very Inner Self" [first line]. In Allen, T. D., ed.,

Arrow III. U.S. Bureau of Indian Affairs, Creative Writing Project, 1971, p. 2.

1290. Shotley, Dan. "I Am Ready for an End" [first line]. Angwamas Minosewag Anishinabeg. (Poets in the Schools Program) St. Paul Council of Arts and Sciences, Winter, 1973-74.

1291. Shotley, Mark. "I'm 53 Years Old" [first line]. Angwamas Minosewag Anishinabeg. (Poets in the Schools Program) St. Paul Council of Arts and Sciences, Winter, 1973-74.

1292. Shotley, Ted. "I Would Fly High in the Sky" [first line]. Angwamas Minosewag Anishinabeg. (Poets in the Schools Program) St. Paul Council of Arts and Sciences, Winter, 1973-74.

1293. Shown, Suzan. "I Am the Wind" [first line]. Akwesasne Notes. v. 4 (Late Winter, 1972) 48.

1294. ________. "i breathe as the night breathes" [first line]. In Lourie, Dick, ed., Come to Power. The Crossing Press, 1974, pp. 13-14.

1295. ________. "I Have Walked in the World of White Skin" [first line]. Akwesasne Notes. v. 4 (Early Spring, 1972) 48.

1296. ________. "rivers flow, where do they go." Akwesasne Notes. v. 5 (Late Summer, 1973) 48.

1297. ________. "Rodeo Kicks Off July 4 Holiday--Honors Indians." Akwesasne Notes. v. 3 (July/Aug., 1971) 48.

1298. Silko, Leslie. (Laguna Pueblo) "Indian Song: Survival." In Niatum, Duane, ed., Carriers of the Dream Wheel. Harper, 1975, pp. 229-31.

1299. ________. "Indian Song: Survival." In Lourie, Dick, ed., Come to Power. The Crossing Press, 1974, pp. 95-6.

1300. ________. "Love Poem." In Lourie, Dick, ed., Come to Power. The Crossing Press, 1974, p. 100.

1301. Silko, Leslie. (Laguna Pueblo) "Poem for Ben Barney." In Niatum, Duane, ed., *Carriers of the Dream Wheel*. Harper, 1975, p. 228.

1302. ________. "Prayer to Pacific Ocean." In Lourie, Dick, ed., *Come to Power*. The Crossing Press, 1974, p. 98.

1303. ________. "Prayer to the Pacific." In Niatum, Duane, ed., *Carriers of the Dream Wheel*. Harper, 1975, pp. 226-27.

1304. ________. "Slim Man Canyon." In Lourie, Dick, ed., *Come to Power*. The Crossing Press, 1974, p. 101.

1305. ________. "Snow Elk." *Quetzal*. v. 2 (Summer, 1972) 46.

1306. ________. "Sun Children." *Quetzal*. v. 2 (Summer, 1972) 47.

1307. ________. "The Time We Climbed Snake Mountain." In Lourie, Dick, ed., *Come to Power*. The Crossing Press, 1974, p. 97.

1308. ________. "Toe'osh: A Laguna Coyote Story." In Niatum, Duane, ed., *Carriers of the Dream Wheel*. Harper, 1975, pp. 223-25.

1309. Sindon, Carolyn. (Karok) "The Taming of Fire." *The Indian Historian*. v. 1 (Spring, 1968) 19-20.

1310. Sioux Indian Museum and Crafts Center, Rapid City, S. Dak. *Photographs, Poems by Sioux Children*. From Porcupine Day School, Pine Ridge Indian Res., S. Dak., 1970.

1311. Sireech, Boots. (Ute) "My Son." *Blue Cloud Quarterly*. v. 15, no. 3.

1312. ________. "My Son." In *Dance with Indian Children*. Washington, D.C.: Center for the Arts of Indian Children, 1972, p. 12.

1313. ________. "My Son." In Lowenfels, Walter, ed., *From the Belly of the Shark*. Vintage, 1973, p. 60.

1314. Sitting Up, Arlene. "Summer Sister." In Henry, Jeannette, ed., The American Indian Reader: Literature. Indian Historian Pr., 1973, pp. 41-2.

1315. ________. "Summer Sister." The Indian Historian. v. 4 (Winter, 1971) 47.

1316. Skaroniate. "To the Indian Women of all Ages." Akwesasne Notes. v. 5 (Early Autumn, 1973) 48.

1317. Smith, Elizabeth. "My Brother." Akwesasne Notes. v. 7 (Early Winter, 1975) 48.

1318. Smith, Hugh. "Black Moon, Red Cloud" [first line]. Akwesasne Notes. v. 4 (Late Autumn, 1972) 48.

1319. Smith, Jeffrey Keith. "The Drums of Freedom." Wassaja. v. 1 (January, 1973) 18.

1320. Smith, Kate W. (Cherokee-Delaware) "The Grandfather People." In Henry, Jeannette, ed., The American Indian Reader: Literature. Indian Historian Pr., 1973, pp. 47-48.

1321. ________. "The Grandfather People." The Indian Historian. v. 2 (Spring, 1969) 34.

1322. Smith, Richard. "Till Forever and More." Akwesasne Notes. v. 4 (Late Autumn, 1972) 42.

1323. ________. "Till Forever and More." In Lowenfels, Walter, ed., From the Belly of the Shark. Vintage, 1973, pp. 61-2.

1324. Smith, Tommy. (Navaho) "Gonna Ride a Bull." In Gooderham, Kent, ed., I Am an Indian. Toronto, Dent, 1969, pp. 59-60.

1325. Smohalla. (Nez Perce) "Speech." In David, Jay, ed., The American Indian, the First Victim. Morrow, 1972, pp. 85-6.

1326. Snake, Reuben. "Being Indian Is..." Akwesasne Notes. v. 3 (Sept., 1971) 42.

1327. Snyder, Leo T. (Eskimo) "Cactus." In Allen,

T. D., ed., Arrow I. U.S. Bureau of Indian Affairs, Creative Writing Project, 1969, p. 9.

1328. Sohappy, Liz, or Om-na-ma. (Yakima) "Behold My World." In Allen, Terry, ed., The Whispering Wind; Poetry by Young American Indians. Doubleday, 1972, pp. 18-19.

1329. ________. "Boston Shoes at I.A.I.A." In Future Directions in Native American Art. Santa Fe, N.M.: The Institute of American Indian Arts, [1973], p. 7.

1330. ________. "Farewell." In Dance with Indian Children. Washington, D.C.: Center for the Arts of Indian Children, 1972, p. 7.

1331. ________. "Farewell." In Future Directions in Native American Art. Santa Fe, N.M.: The Institute of American Indian Arts, [1973], p. 22.

1332. ________. "The Indian Market." In Allen, Terry, ed., The Whispering Wind; Poetry by Young American Indians. Doubleday, 1972, p. 15.

1333. ________. "Once Again." In Allen, Terry, ed., The Whispering Wind; Poetry by Young American Indians. Doubleday, 1972, p. 17.

1334. ________. "Once Again." In Dodge, Robert K. & Joseph B. McCullough, eds., Voices from Wah'kon-tah. International Publishers, 1974, p. 102.

1335. ________. "Once Again." In Henry, Jeannette, ed., The American Indian Reader: Literature. Indian Historian Pr., 1973, pp. 57-8.

1336. ________. "Once Again." In Milton, John R., comp., The American Indian Speaks. Vermillion: U. of S. Dak., 1969, pp. 131-2.

1337. ________. "Once Again." Sun Tracks. v. 1 (June, 1971) 3.

1338. ________. "The Parade." In Allen, Terry, ed., The Whispering Wind; Poetry by Young American Indians. Doubleday, 1972, p. 16.

1339. Sohappy, Liz, or Om-na-ma. (Yakima) "The Parade." In Dodge, Robert K. & Joseph B. McCullough, eds., Voices from Wah'kon-tah. International Publishers, 1974, p. 103.

1340. ________. "Traditional War Dancer." Sun Tracks. v. 1 (June, 1971) 16-17.

1341. Southerland, Clev B., or Red Bird. (Potawatami) "Legend of the Coyote." Sun Tracks. v. 1 (Spring, 1972) 6-7.

1342. Stabber, Larry. "Just Take a Look." In Henry, Jeannette, ed., The American Indian Reader: Literature. Indian Historian Pr., 1973, p. 33.

1343. ________. "Just Take a Look." The Indian Historian. v. 2 (Fall, 1969) 33.

1344. Stalker, Leonard. "Behind the City, in Mountains" [first line]. Akwesasne Notes. v. 4 (Late Spring, 1972).

1345. Starr, John. (Choctaw) "Death of a Rain." In Allen, T. D., ed., Arrow II. U.S. Bureau of Indian Affairs, Creative Writing Project, 1970, p. 16.

1346. ________. "One Indian Nation." In Allen, T. D., ed., Arrow III. U.S. Bureau of Indian Affairs, Creative Writing Project, 1971, p. 17.

1347. Sterling, Mary Jane. (Thompson River Indian) "Thoughts on Silence." In Gooderham, Kent, ed., I Am an Indian. Toronto, Dent, 1969, pp. 37-8.

1348. Stoeckel, Carl. "Simulated War-Dance Tourist Attraction at the St. Croix Indian Reservation." Akwesasne Notes. v. 3 (April, 1971) 48.

1349. Storm, Hyemeyohsts, David and Sandy Storm. The Magnifying Glass. Pembroke, N.C.: Quetzal-Vihio Pr., 1971.

1350. Strong, Connie. (Chippewa) "The Eyes of the Eagle Are in Me" [first line]. Angwamas Minosewag

Anishinabeg. (Poets in the Schools Program) St. Paul Council of Arts and Sciences, Winter, 1973-74.

1351. Strother, Garland. "Washakie." Akwesasne Notes. v. 7 (Early Summer, 1975) 48.

1352. Stump, Sarain. (Shoshone-Cree-Salish) There Is My People Sleeping. Sidney, B.C.: Gray's Pub. Ltd., 1971.

1353. Sullateskee, Greta. (Cherokee) "Daydreams." In Allen, T. D., ed., Arrow II. U.S. Bureau of Indian Affairs, Creative Writing Project, 1970, pp. 21-2.

1354. _______. "Daydreams." Sun Tracks. v. 1 (Winter, 1971/72) 27.

1355. Sultz, Philip. "I Know, I Know." Akwesasne Notes. v. 3 (Jan./Feb., 1971) 48.

1356. _______. "Sophie Many Deeds." Akwesasne Notes. v. 2 (Nov./Dec., 1970) 48.

1357. Sun-ka-ku, Isnala. "The Lonely One." Akwesasne Notes. v. 5 (Early Summer, 1973) 48.

1358. Swanson, R. A. (Chippewa) "Come Unto Me Oh My Children." Akwesasne Notes. v. 5 (Early Autumn, 1973) 3.

1359. _______. "Little Warrior." Many Smokes. v. 6 (Fall, 1972) 8.

1360. _______. "Lonely Warriors." Akwesasne Notes. v. 1, sec. 3 (Nov., 1969) 9.

1361. _______. Solemn Spirits; American Indian Poetry. Harrah, Washington, [n.d.].

1362. _______. "Solemn Spirits." Many Smokes. v. 6 (Fall, 1972) 8.

1363. _______. "We Are the Warrior Spirits." Many Smokes. v. 6 (Fall, 1972) 8.

1364. Tahdooahnippah, George. (Comanche) "Little Red Birds." In Allen, T. D., ed., Arrow III. U.S. Bureau of Indian Affairs, Creative Writing Project, 1971, p. 15.

1365. Tajinita. "Occupied Territory." Akwesasne Notes. v. 4 (Early Autumn, 1972) 48.

1366. Taos Pueblo. "I Have Killed the Deer." In Levitas, Gloria, Frank Robert & Jacqueline J. Vivelo, eds., American Indian Prose & Poetry. Putnam, 1974, p. 294.

1367. _______. "The World Out There Called." In Levitas, Gloria, Frank Robert & Jacqueline J. Vivelo, eds., American Indian Prose & Poetry. Putnam, 1974, pp. 292-93.

1368. _______. "You Tell Us Times Are Changing." In Levitas, Gloria, Frank Robert & Jacqueline J. Vivelo, eds., American Indian Prose & Poetry. Putnam, 1974, p. 293.

1369. Tayah, Sam. (Navajo) [Ft. Wingate H.S.] "In the Cold of Morning" [first line]. Sun Tracks. v. 1 (June, 1971) 14.

1370. _______. "Recalling." In Allen, T. D., ed., Arrow I. U.S. Bureau of Indian Affairs, Creative Writing Project, 1969, p. 8.

1371. Teeseteskie, Raymond. (Cherokee) "My Kind of School." Blue Cloud Quarterly. v. 15, no. 3.

1372. _______. "My Kind of School." In Henry, Jeannette, ed., The American Indian Reader: Literature. Indian Historian Pr., 1973, p. 55.

1373. _______. "My Kind of School." In Lowenfels, Walter, ed., From the Belly of the Shark. Vintage, 1973, p. 63.

1374. _______. "My Kind of School." Wassaja. v. 3 (August, 1975) 13.

1375. Tekahionwake. (Mohawk) "The Cattle Thief." In Lowenfels, Walter, ed., From the Belly of the Shark. Vintage, 1973, pp. 64-6.

1376. Thaylor, Richard. "The Wisdom of an Old Man of Our Village." Sun Tracks. v. 1 (Spring, 1972) 24.

1377. Thompson, Maurena. "Prayerful People." Akwesasne Notes. v. 7 (Early Autumn, 1975) 48.

1378. Tollerud, James. (Makah) "Belief." Quetzal. v. 2 (Winter-Spring, 1972) 33.

1379. ________. "Clouds of Laura C." Quetzal. v. 2 (Winter-Spring, 1972) 33.

1380. Tollerud, Jim. "Bird of Power." Akwesasne Notes. v. 6 (Early Spring, 1974) 48.

1381. ________. "Earth." Akwesasne Notes. v. 8 (Early Summer, 1976) 48.

1382. ________. "Eye of God." Akwesasne Notes. v. 5 (Early Autumn, 1973) 3.

1383. Tompkins, Richard. "Solitary." Akwesasne Notes. v. 4 (Early Autumn, 1972) 48.

1384. Tonka, Chante (Frank L. Woods). "A Thousand Lives Beyond." Akwesasne Notes. v. 7 (Early Winter, 1975) 48.

1385. Track, Soge. (Sioux-Pueblo from Taos) "Butterflies." In Dance with Indian Children. Washington, D.C.: Center for the Arts of Indian America, 1972, p. 7.

1386. ________. "Indian Love Letter." In David, Jay, ed., The American Indian, the First Victim. Morrow, 1972, pp. 142-43.

1387. ________. "Indian Love Letter." In Dodge, Robert K. & Joseph B. McCullough, eds., Voices from Wah'kon-tah. International Publishers, 1974, p. 104.

1388. ________. "Indian Love Letter." In Milton, John R., comp., The American Indian Speaks. Vermillion: U. of S. Dak., 1969, p. 136.

1389. ________. "Indian Love Letter." In Sanders,

Thomas E. & Walter W. Peek, Literature of the American Indian. Glencoe Pr., 1973, p. 463.

1390. Tse-waa. "Mountain Spirit." Akwesasne Notes. v. 7 (Early Spring, 1975) 48.

1391. ________. "People of the Earth" [first line]. Akwesasne Notes. v. 7 (Early Spring, 1975) 48.

1392. ________. "Tree of Life." Akwesasne Notes. v. 7 (Early Spring, 1975) 48.

1393. Tso, Eugene. "I Am Hungry." Akwesasne Notes. v. 3 (April, 1971) 48.

1394. ________. "I Am Hungry." In Lowenfels, Walter, ed., From the Belly of the Shark. Vintage, 1973, pp. 66-7.

1395. Tsosie, Tom Nakai. (Navajo) "Cross and Rusty Medals." In Allen, T. D., ed., Arrow I. U.S. Bureau of Indian Affairs, Creative Writing Project, 1969, p. 10.

1396. Tsosie, Tony. (Navajo) "December's Child." Sun Tracks. v. 1 (Spring, 1972) 28.

1397. ________. "The Old Leupp Station." In Allen, T. D., ed., Arrow I. U.S. Bureau of Indian Affairs, Creative Writing Project, 1969, p. 7.

1398. ________. "The Old Leupp Station." Sun Tracks. v. 1 (Spring, 1972) 29.

1399. Turtle's Son. "Pyramid Lake 1970." In Lowenfels, Walter, ed., From the Belly of the Shark. Vintage, 1973, pp. 68-9.

1400. Twiss, Eldean. (Sioux) "Stone." In Allen, T. D., ed., Arrow IV. U.S. Bureau of Indian Affairs, Creative Writing Project, 1972, p. 28.

1401. V., Jackie. "Wolf." Angwamas Minosewag Anishinabeg. (Poets in the Schools Program) St. Paul Council of Arts and Sciences, Winter, 1973-74.

1402. Vgl. "Jethro." Akwesasne Notes. v. 7 (Early Summer, 1975) 48.

1403. Vandall, Donna Whitewing. (Winnebago-Sioux) "Laughing Bowl." In Future Directions in Native American Art. Santa Fe, N.M.: The Institute of American Indian Arts, [1973], p. 30.

1404. Vigil, Vickie. "Native Tongue." Akwesasne Notes. v. 5 (January, 1973) 48.

1405. ________. "Native Tongue." In Lowenfels, Walter, ed., From the Belly of the Shark. Vintage, 1973, p. 62.

1406. ________. "Our Meeting." Akwesasne Notes. v. 5 (Early Winter, 1973) 48.

1407. Villebrun, Carol. "I Feel Like the Earth." In Angwamas Minosewag Anishinabeg. (Poets in the Schools Program) St. Paul Council of Arts and Sciences, Winter, 1973-74.

1408. Vizenor, Gerald Robert. (Anishinabe) Anishinabe Nagamon; Songs of the People. Interpreted and re-expressed from the original Anishinabe song transcriptions. Nodin Pr., 1970 [1965].

1409. ________. Empty Swings; Haiku in English. Minneapolis: Nodin Pr., 1967.

1410. ________. "Fathers of My Breath." In Tvedten, Benet, comp., An American Indian Anthology. Marvin, S. D.: Blue Cloud Abbey, 1971, p. 45.

1411. ________. "Haiku." In Lowenfels, Walter, ed., From the Belly of the Shark. Vintage, 1973, pp. 69-70.

1412. ________. "Long After the Rivers Change." In Tvedten, Benet, comp., An American Indian Anthology. Marvin, S. D.: Blue Cloud Abbey, 1971, p. 46.

1413. ________. "Love Poems and Spring Poems, and Dream Poems and War Poems" [from the Anishinabe]. In Witt, Shirley H., The Way; an Anthology of American Indian Literature. Knopf, 1972, pp. 134-6.

1414. ________. "The Moon Upon a Face Again." In

Tvedten, Benet, comp., An American Indian Anthology. Marvin, S. D.: Blue Cloud Abbey, 1971, p. 47.

1415. Vizenor, Gerald R. (Anishinabe) The Old Park Sleepers; a Poem. Copyright by the author, 1961.

1416. ________. "An Old Spider Web." In Tvedten, Benet, comp., An American Indian Anthology. Marvin, S. D.: Blue Cloud Abbey, 1971, p. 48.

1417. ________. Poems Born in the Wind. Copyright by the author, 1960.

1418. ________. "Poems: The Sky Clears; Concerning a Brave Woman; Mide Initiation Song; Song of Spring." Sun Tracks. v. 1 (June, 1971) 10-11.

1419. ________. Raising the Moon Vines. Nodin Pr., 1968. [1964]

1420. ________. Seventeen Chirps; Haiku in English. Nodin Press, 1964.

1421. ________. South of the Painted Stones. Minneapolis, 1963.

1422. ________. Summer in the Spring; Lyric Poems of the Ojibway. Nodin Pr., 1965.

1423. Vlahos, George. "Jemez River." Pembroke Magazine. no. 2 (1971) 21.

1424. Wah-zin-ak. "Loneliness." Akwesasne Notes. v. 6 (Early Summer, 1974) 48.

1425. ________. "Loneliness." Native Nevadan. v. 9 (December, 1973) 10.

1426. ________. "My Blood." Native Nevadan. v. 9 (December, 1973) 11.

1427. ________. "Straighten Up." Akwesasne Notes. v. 6 (Early Summer, 1974) 48.

1428. ________. "A Time to be Strong." Native Nevadan. v. 9 (December, 1973) 10.

1429. Walking Behind. "For America." Akwesasne Notes. v. 6 (Late Spring, 1974) 48.

1430. ______. "it is finished." Akwesasne Notes. v. 6 (Early Summer, 1974) 48.

1431. ______. "little sioux woman." Akwesasne Notes. v. 7 (Early Winter, 1975) 48.

1432. Wall, Stephen. "For 14 Days..." Sun Tracks. v. 1 (June, 1971) 13.

1433. Wallace, Laurie. "from the animal liberation front." Akwesasne Notes. v. 3 (Dec., 1971) 48.

1434. Walsh, Marnie. (Dakota) "Bessie Dreaming Bear Rosebud, So. Dak. 1960." In Dodge, Robert K. & Joseph B. McCullough, eds., Voices from Wah'kon-tah. International Publishers, 1974, p. 118.

1435. ______. "Charlie Two-Head, White Shield, No. Dak. 1968." In Dodge, Robert K. & Joseph B. McCullough, eds., Voices from Wah'kon-tah. International Publishers, 1974, p. 116.

1436. ______. "Emmet Kills-Warrior Turtle Mountain Reservation." In Dodge, Robert K. & Joseph B. McCullough, eds., Voices from Wah'kon-tah. International Publishers, 1974, p. 106.

1437. ______. "John Knew-the-Crow." In Lowenfels, Walter, ed., From the Belly of the Shark. Vintage, 1973.

1438. ______. "Seth Dismounts Thrice Rapid City, So. Dak. 1967." In Dodge, Robert K. & Joseph B. McCullough, eds., Voices from Wah'kon-tah. International Publishers, 1974, p. 114.

1439. ______. "Thomas Iron-Eyes, Born Circa 1840, Died 1919 Rosebud Agency, So. Dak." In Dodge, Robert K. & Joseph B. McCullough, eds., Voices from Wah'kon-tah. International Publishers, 1974, p. 108.

1440. ______. "Vickie, Fort Yates, No. Dak. 1970."

In Dodge, Robert K. & Joseph B. McCullough, eds., Voices from Wah'kon-tah. International Publishers, 1974, p. 111.

1441. Walters, Winifred Fields. (Choctaw) "Navajo Signs." In Dodge, Robert K. & Joseph B. McCullough, eds., Voices from Wah'kon-tah. International Publishers, 1974, p. 119.

1442. Wapp, Josephine. (Comanche) "Strange and Difficult Are the Rituals of My Brothers" [first line]. In Dance with Indian Children. Washington, D.C.: Center for the Arts of Indian Children, 1972, p. 26.

1443. ________. "To Stretch." In Dance with Indian Children. Washington, D.C.: Center for the Arts of Indian Children, 1972, p. 14.

1444. Washburn, Archie. (Navajo) "Almshouse." In Milton, John R., comp., American Indian II. Vermillion: U. of S. Dak., 1971, p. 157.

1445. ________. "Aunt Annie." Akwesasne Notes. v. 2 (May, 1970) 48.

1446. ________. "Aunt Annie's Prayer Letter." In Milton, John R., comp., American Indian II. Vermillion: U. of S. Dak., 1971, p. 156.

1447. ________. Desert Flower." In Milton, John R., comp., American Indian II. Vermillion: U. of S. Dak., 1971, p. 155.

1448. ________. "Hogan." In Dodge, Robert K. & Joseph B. McCullough, eds., Voices from Wah'kon-tah. International Publishers, 1974, p. 121.

1449. ________. "Hogan." In Milton, John R., comp., American Indian II. Vermillion: U. of S. Dak., 1971, p. 155.

1450. ________. "Listen." Akwesasne Notes. v. 2 (May, 1970) 48.

1451. ________. "Loneliness." In Milton, John R., comp., American Indian II. Vermillion: U. of S. Dak., 1971, p. 154.

1452. Washburn, Archie. (Navajo) "My Dear Grandmother" [first line]. Akwesasne Notes. v. 2 (May, 1970) 48.

1453. ________. "Unknown Smoke." In Dodge, Robert K. & Joseph B. McCullough, eds., Voices from Wah'kon-tah. International Publishers, 1974, p. 122.

1454. ________. "Unknown Smoke." In Milton, John R., comp., American Indian II. Vermillion: U. of S. Dak., 1971, p. 153.

1455. Welch, James. (Blackfoot-Gros Vendre) "Across to the Peloponnese." In Niatum, Duane, ed., Carriers of the Dream Wheel. Harper, 1975, p. 237.

1456. ________. "Arizona Highways." In Niatum, Duane, ed., Carriers of the Dream Wheel. Harper, 1975, pp. 240-41.

1457. ________. "Birth on Range 18." In Milton, John R., comp., The American Indian Speaks. Vermillion: U. of S. Dak., 1969, p. 30.

1458. ________. "Blackfeet, Blood and Piegan Hunters." In Carroll, Paul, ed., Young American Poets. Big Table Pub. Co., 1968, pp. 499-500.

1459. ________. "Blue Like Death." In Niatum, Duane, ed., Carriers of the Dream Wheel. Harper, 1975, p. 235.

1460. ________. "Christmas Comes to Moccasin Flat." In Carroll, Paul, ed., Young American Poets. Big Table Pub. Co., 1968, pp. 495-6.

1461. ________. Christmas Comes to Moccasin Flat." In David, Jay, ed., The American Indian, the First Victim. Morrow, 1972, pp. 150-1.

1462. ________. "Christmas Comes to Moccasin Flat." In Niatum, Duane, ed., Carriers of the Dream Wheel. Harper, 1975, p. 247.

1463. ________. "Christmas Comes to Moccasin Flat." Poetry Northwest. v. 8 (Spring, 1967) 34-5.

1464. Welch, James. (Blackfoot) "Christmas Comes to Moccasin Flat." In Turner, Frederick W., III, The Portable North American Reader. Viking, 1974, pp. 597-8.

1465. ______. "D-Y Bar." In Carroll, Paul, ed., Young American Poets. Big Table Pub. Co., 1968, pp. 496-7.

1466. ______. "D-Y Bar." In Niatum, Duane, ed., Carriers of the Dream Wheel. Harper, 1975, p. 250.

1467. ______. "Dancing Man." Harper's Bazaar. v. 103 (August, 1970) 156.

1468. ______. "Directions to the Nomad." In Niatum, Duane, ed., Carriers of the Dream Wheel. Harper, 1975, p. 253.

1469. ______. "Dreaming Winter." In Dodge, Robert K. & Joseph B. McCullough, eds., Voices from Wah'kon-tah. International Publishers, 1974, p. 125.

1470. ______. "Dreaming Winter." Poetry. v. 112 (April, 1968) 16.

1471. ______. "Getting Things Straight." In Lowenfels, Walter, ed., From the Belly of the Shark. Vintage, 1973, p. 70.

1472. ______. "Going to Remake This World." In Niatum, Duane, ed., Carriers of the Dream Wheel. Harper, 1975, p. 246.

1473. ______. "Grandma's Man." In Haslam, Gerald W., ed., Forgotten Pages of American Literature. Houghton, 1970, pp. 48-9.

1474. ______. "Grandma's Man." In Milton, John R., comp., The American Indian Speaks. Vermillion: U. of S. Dak., 1969, p. 33.

1475. ______. "Harlem, Montana: Just Off the Reservation." In Dodge, Robert K. & Joseph B. McCullough, eds., Voices from Wah'kon-tah. International Publishers, 1974, p. 126.

1476. Welch, James. (Blackfoot-Gros Vendre) "Harlem, Montana..." In Niatum, Duane, ed., Carriers of the Dream Wheel. Harper, 1975, p. 242.

1477. ________. "Harlem, Montana: Just Off the Reservation." Poetry. v. 112 (April, 1968) 17-18.

1478. ________. "In My First Hard Springtime." In Carroll, Paul, ed., Young American Poets. Big Table Pub. Co., 1968, p. 495.

1479. ________. "In My First Hard Springtime." In Niatum, Duane, ed., Carriers of the Dream Wheel. Harper, 1975, p. 238.

1480. ________. "In My First Hard Springtime." Poetry Northwest. v. 8 (Spring, 1967) 34.

1481. ________. "In My Lifetime." In Turner, Frederick W., III, The Portable North American Reader. Viking, 1974, p. 598.

1482. ________. "In My Lifetime." In Sanders, Thomas E. & Walter W. Peek, Literature of the American Indian. Glencoe Pr., 1973, p. 469.

1483. ________. "Legends Like This." In Milton, John R., comp., The American Indian Speaks. Vermillion: U. of S. Dak., 1969, p. 31.

1484. ________. "Magic Fox." In Niatum, Duane, ed., Carriers of the Dream Wheel. Harper, 1975, p. 251.

1485. ________. "The Man from Washington." In Dodge, Robert K. & Joseph B. McCullough, eds., Voices from Wah'kon-tah. International Publishers, 1974, p. 123.

1486. ________. "The Man from Washington." In Milton, John R., comp., The American Indian Speaks. Vermillion: U. of S. Dak., 1969, p. 27.

1487. ________. "The Man from Washington." In Momaday, Natachee Scott, ed., American Indian Authors. Houghton, 1972, p. 132.

1488. ________. "The Man from Washington." In Niatum,

Duane, ed., Carriers of the Dream Wheel. Harper, 1975, p. 248.

1489. Welch, James. (Blackfoot-Gros Vendre) "The Man from Washington." In Tvedten, Benet, comp., An American Indian Anthology. Marvin, S.D.: Blue Cloud Abbey, 1971, p. 38.

1490. ______. "The Man from Washington." In Witt, Shirley H., comp., The Way; an Anthology of American Literature. Knopf, 1972, p. 139.

1491. ______. "Montana, Nothing like Boston." In Carroll, Paul, ed., Young American Poets. Big Table Publ. Co., 1968, p. 498.

1492. ______. "One More Time." In Dodge, Robert K. & Joseph B. McCullough, eds., Voices from Wah'kon-tah. International Publishers, 1974, p. 124.

1493. ______. "One More Time." In Milton, John R., comp., The American Indian Speaks. Vermillion: U. of S.D., 1969, p. 29.

1494. ______. "The Only Bar in Dixon." New Yorker. v. 46 (Oct. 10, 1970) 48.

1495. ______. "Please Forward." In Niatum, Duane, ed., Carriers of the Dream Wheel. Harper, 1975, pp. 242-43.

1496. ______. "The Renegade Wants Words." In Niatum, Duane, ed., Carriers of the Dream Wheel. Harper, 1975, p. 236.

1497. ______. Riding the Earthboy; 40 Contemporary Poems. World, 1971.

1498. ______. "Snow Country Weavers." In Haslam, Gerald W., Forgotten Pages of American Literature. Houghton, 1970, p. 48.

1499. ______. "Snow Country Weavers." In Milton, John R., comp., The American Indian Speaks. Vermillion: U. of S. Dak., 1969, p. 28.

1500. Welch, James. (Blackfoot-Gros Vendre) "Snow Country Weavers." In Niatum, Duane, ed., Carriers of the Dream Wheel. Harper, 1975, p. 249.

1501. ________. "Snow Country Weavers." In Sanders, Thomas E. & Walter W. Peek, Literature of the American Indian. Glencoe Pr., 1973, p. 470.

1502. ________. "Spring for All Seasons." In Carroll, Paul, ed., Young American Poets. Big Table Publ. Co., 1968, p. 497.

1503. ________. "Surviving." In Haslam, Gerald W., Forgotten Pages of American Literature. Houghton, 1970, p. 48.

1504. ________. "Surviving." In Milton, John R., comp., The American Indian Speaks. Vermillion: U. of S. Dak., 1969, p. 32.

1505. ________. "Surviving." In Niatum, Duane, ed., Carriers of the Dream Wheel. Harper, 1975, p. 239.

1506. ________. "Surviving." In Turner, Frederick W., III, The Portable North American Indian Reader. Viking, 1974, p. 597.

1507. ________. "Verifying the Dead." In Niatum, Duane, ed., Carriers of the Dream Wheel. Harper, 1975, p. 254.

1508. ________. "The Versatile Historian." In Sanders, Thomas E. & Walter W. Peek, Literature of the American Indian. Glencoe Pr., 1973, p. 470.

1509. ________. "Why I Didn't Go to Delphi." In Niatum, Duane, ed., Carriers of the Dream Wheel. Harper, 1975, p. 252.

1510. ________. "Winter Indian." In Carroll, Paul, ed., Young American Poets. Big Table Pub. Co., 1968, pp. 498-9.

1511. ________. "Wolf Song, the Rain." In Carroll, Paul, ed., Young American Poets. Big Table Pub. Co., 1968, p. 50.

1512. Welch, James. (Blackfoot-Gros Vendre) "The Wrath of Lester Lame Bull." In Carroll, Paul, ed., Young American Poets. Big Table Publ. Co., 1968, p. 500.

1513. Werito, George. "Place in the Sun." Akwesasne Notes. v. 2 (May, 1970) 48.

1514. West, Martha. "Metis." Akwesasne Notes. v. 3 (June, 1971) 48.

1515. ______. "Sounds." Akwesasne Notes. v. 3 (March, 1971) 48.

1516. ______. "Sounds." Akwesasne Notes. v. 3 (July/Aug., 1971).

1517. Westrum, Dexter. "Prayer for Mitch." Akwesasne Notes. v. 3 (Oct./Nov., 1971) 48.

1518. White, Gary. "Boom the Explosion." In Henry, Jeannette, ed., The American Indian Reader: Literature. Indian Historian Pr., 1973, p. 31.

1519. ______. "Boom, the Explosion." The Indian Historian. v. 2 (Fall, 1969) 34.

1520. White, Glenn. "He-e-e and Chakwaina; Kachinas." American Indian Crafts and Culture. v. 5 (Nov., 1971) 14-15.

1521. White, John. "Listen to the Songs." Wassaja. v. 2 (June, 1974) 2.

1522. ______. "Three Poems. [March 2, 1973]." The Indian Historian. v. 6 (Spring, 1973) 31-2.

1523. White, Robert C. "Prayer to the Light in the East." Akwesasne Notes. v. 4 (Early Autumn, 1972) 48.

1524. White, Roy Lyle. "Lament." Akwesasne Notes. v. 4 (Late Winter, 1972) 48.

1525. Whitecloud, Tom. "An Indian Prayer." Akwesasne Notes. v. 1, sec. 3 (Nov., 1969) 9.

1526. ______. "Thief." Akwesasne Notes. v. 3 (May, 1971) 48.

1527. Whitecloud, Tom. "Thief." In Levitas, Gloria, Frank Robert & Jacqueline J. Vivelo, American Indian Prose & Poetry. Putnam, 1974, pp. 296-97.

1528. ________. "Thief." In Lowenfels, Walter, ed., From the Belly of the Shark. Vintage, 1973, p. 71.

1529. Whitewing, Donna. (Sioux-Winnebago) "August 24, 1963--1:00 A.M.--Omaha." In Allen, Terry, ed., The Whispering Wind; Poetry by Young American Indians. Doubleday, 1972, p. 57.

1530. ________. "August 24, 1963--1:00 A.M.--Omaha." In Dodge, Robert K. & Joseph B. McCullough, eds., Voices from Wah'kon-tah. International Publishers, 1974, p. 128.

1531. ________. "August 24, 1963--1:00 A.M.--Omaha." In Milton, John R., comp., The American Indian Speaks. Vermillion: U. of S. Dak., 1969, p. 106.

1532. ________. "Can You Can't." In Allen, Terry, ed., The Whispering Wind; Poetry by Young American Indians. Doubleday, 1972, p. 57.

1533. ________. "Cry Silent." In Allen, Terry, ed., The Whispering Wind; Poetry by Young American Indians. Doubleday, 1972, p. 56.

1534. ________. "The Gathering Time." In Allen, Terry, ed., The Whispering Wind; Poetry by Young American Indians. Doubleday, 1972, pp. 52-3.

1535. ________. "Love Song." In Allen, Terry, ed., The Whispering Wind; Poetry by Young American Indians. Doubleday, 1972, p. 51.

1536. ________. "A Vegetable, I Will Not Be." In Allen, Terry, ed., The Whispering Wind; Poetry by Young American Indians. Doubleday, 1972, pp. 54-5.

1537. ________. "A Vegetable I Will Not Be." In Dodge, Robert K. & Joseph B. McCullough, eds., Voices from Wah'kon-tah. International Publishers, 1974, p. 129.

1538. Whitewing, Donna. (Sioux-Winnebago) "Why Is Happy?" In Allen, Terry, ed., The Whispering Wind; Poetry by Young American Indians. Doubleday, 1972, p. 56.

1539. Wiede, Donald J. "When I Was Lost, the Moon Showed Me Home" [first line]. Akwesasne Notes. v. 3 (Dec., 1971) 48.

1540. Williams, Dan. (Maidu) "Earthmaker." In Henry, Jeannetee, ed., The American Indian Reader: Literature. Indian Historian Pr., 1973, p. 12.

1541. ________. "Earthmaker." The Indian Historian. v. 1 (Spring, 1968) 8.

1542. Williams, Gordon. (Okanagan-Shuswap) "The Last Crackle." In Gooderham, Kent, ed., I Am an Indian. Toronto, Dent, 1969, pp. 35-6.

1543. Wilson. "As the Rain Begins to Fall" [first line]. Akwesasne Notes. v. 4 (Late Winter, 1972) 48.

1544. Wilson, Julie. "I Traveled to the West." In Levitas, Gloria, Frank Robert & Jacqueline J. Vivelo, eds., American Indian Prose & Poetry. Putnam, 1974, p. 296.

1545. Wilson, Sherman G. "Right." Akwesasne Notes. v. 3 (Dec., 1971) 48.

1546. ________. "The Supposedly Minute Effects (i.e., interruptions in Daily Routine, inconveniences, etc.) created by excessive anthropology studies of a supposedly unsophisticated and unwordly-wise backward race, e.g., The American Indian." Akwesasne Notes. v. 3 (Oct./Nov., 1971) 48.

1547. Win, Wicahpi Wiyakpa. "I Love You" [first line]. Akwesasne Notes. v. 4 (Early Spring, 1972) 48.

1548. Winters, Ray. "False Pride." Akwesasne Notes. v. 3 (Dec., 1971) 48.

1549. Woody, Shirley. (Navajo) "Navajo Was His Name." Sun Tracks. v. 1 (Winter, 1971/72) 20.

1550. ________. "One Sultry Summer" [first line]. In Allen, T. D., ed., Arrow III. U.S. Bureau of Indian Affairs, Creative Writing Project, 1971, pp. 3-4.

1551. Wright, Brenda. "As I Walked" [first line]. Angwamas Minosewag Anishinabeg. 1st issue. (Poets in the Schools Program) St. Paul Council of Arts and Sciences, [1972].

1552. ________. "Before the Sun Sleeps" [first line]. Angwamas Minosewag Anishinabeg. 1st issue. (Poets in the Schools Program) St. Paul Council of Arts and Sciences, [1973].

1553. ________. "Before the Sun Sleeps" [first line]. Angwamas Minosewag Anishinabeg. (Poets in the Schools Program) St. Paul Council of Arts and Sciences. Winter, 1973-74.

1554. ________. "Don't Intrude" [first line]. Angwamas Minosewag Anishinabeg. (Poets in the Schools Program) St. Paul Council of Arts and Sciences, Winter, 1973-74.

1555. ________. "Feeling Naked Like I Lost My Soul" [first line]. Angwamas Minosewag Anishinabeg. 1st issue. (Poets in the Schools Program) St. Paul Council of Arts and Sciences, [1972].

1556. ________. "Flowers that Blossom." Angwamas Minosewag Anishinabeg. 1st issue. (Poets in the Schools Program) St. Paul Council of Arts and Sciences, [1973].

1557. ________. "The Hall Found Its Way to My Mind." Angwamas Minosewag Anishinabeg. 1st issue. (Poets in the Schools Program) St. Paul Council of Arts and Sciences, [1972].

1558. ________. "I'm an Indian..." [first line]. Angwamas Minosewag Anishinabeg. 1st issue. (Poets in the Schools Program) St. Paul Council of Arts and Sciences, [1973].

1559. Wright, Brenda. "I'm Giving You a License" [first line]. Angwamas Minosewag Anishinabeg. 1st issue. (Poets in the Schools Program) St. Paul Council of Arts and Sciences, [1973].

1560. ________. "Look at My Big Man" [first line]. Angwamas Minosewag Anishinabeg. 1st issue. (Poets in the Schools Program) St. Paul Council of Arts and Sciences, [1973].

1561. ________. "My Eyes Search the Room" [first line]. Angwamas Minosewag Anishinabeg. 1st issue. (Poets in the Schools Program) St. Paul Council of Arts and Sciences, [1972].

1562. ________. "My Son... My Light..." [first line]. Angwamas Minosewag Anishinabeg. 1st issue. (Poets in the Schools Program) St. Paul Council of Arts and Sciences, [1973].

1563. ________. "Sex invented by Angels" [first line]. Angwamas Minosewag Anishinabeg. (Poets in the Schools Program) St. Paul Council of Arts and Sciences, Winter, 1973-74.

1564. ________. "Shine on Me" [first line]. Angwamas Minosewag Anishinabeg. (Poets in the Schools Program) St. Paul Council of Arts and Sciences, Winter, 1973-74.

1565. ________. "Trees and Trees and Open Fire" [first line]. Angwamas Minosewag Anishinabeg. 1st issue. (Poets in the Schools Program) St. Paul Council of Arts and Sciences, [1972].

1566. ________. "Try Me?" [first line]. Angwamas Minosewag Anishinabeg. (Poets in the Schools Program) St. Paul Council of Arts and Sciences, Winter, 1973-74.

1567. ________. "When Dark Becomes a Form" [first line]. Angwamas Minosewag Anishinabeg. 1st issue. (Poets in the Schools Program) St. Paul Council of Arts and Sciences, [1973].

1568. ________. "Would If I Should Die?" [first line]. Angwamas Minosewag Anishinabeg. 1st issue.

(Poets in the Schools Program) St. Paul Council of Arts and Sciences, [1972].

1569. Wright, Sandy. "The Flames Flicker" [first line]. Angwamas Minosewag Anishinabeg. (Poets in the Schools Program) St. Paul Council of Arts and Sciences, Winter, 1973-74.

1570. ________. "They Must Feel Like I Feel" [first line]. Angwamas Minosewag Anishinabeg. (Poets in the Schools Program) St. Paul Council of Arts and Sciences, Winter, 1973-74.

1571. Wyman, Barb. "I Wonder about Many Things" [first line]. Angwamas Minosewag Anishinabeg. (Poets in the Schools Program) St. Paul Council of Arts and Sciences, Winter, 1973-74.

1572. Wynne, Annette. "Indian Children." Akwesasne Notes. v. 3 (Sept., 1971) 42.

1573. Yazzie, Bessie. "Home." Akwesasne Notes. v. 2 (May, 1970) 48.

1574. Yeagley, Joan. "The Water Carrier." Akwesasne Notes. v. 5 (Early Autumn, 1973) 48.

1575. Yellowbird, Lydia. (Cree) "To Be Young, and Indian." In Waubageshig, ed., The Only Good Indian. New Pr., 1970, pp. 104-9.

1576. Yellowfly, Donnie. [Native Brotherhood of Indians and Metis, Saskatchewan Penitentiary.] "A Living Breathing Soul" [first line]. Sun Tracks. v. 1 (Spring, 1972) 25.

1577. Yellowman, Tom. "Class Hour." Akwesasne Notes. v. 2 (May, 1970) 48.

1578. York, Mildred. (Choctaw) "A Sudden Discovery." In Allen, T. D., ed., Arrow III. U.S. Bureau of Indian Affairs, Creative Writing Project, 1971, p. 21.

1579. Young Bear, Ray A. (Mesquaki/Sauk & Fox) "Another Face." In Lourie, Dick, ed., Come to Power. The Crossing Press, 1974, p. 17.

1580. Young Bear, Ray A. (Mesquaki/Sauk & Fox) "Another Face." In Niatum, Duane, ed., Carriers of the Dream Wheel. Harper, 1975, p. 274.

1581. ________. "Behind." Pembroke Magazine. no. 3 (1972) 59.

1582. ________. "Birds with Tears in their Bones." In Milton, John R., comp., American Indian II. Vermillion: U. of S. Dak., 1971, pp. 41-2.

1583. ________. "Black Dog." In Niatum, Duane, ed., Carriers of the Dream Wheel. Harper, 1975, pp. 294-95.

1584. ________. "Catching the Distance." In Milton, John R., comp., American Indian II. Vermillion: U. of S. Dak., 1971, pp. 27-28.

1585. ________. "Celebration." In Niatum, Duane, ed., Carriers of the Dream Wheel. Harper, 1975, pp. 275-77.

1586. ________. "Challenge Glancing Off the Sun-train." In Milton, John R., comp., American Indian II. Vermillion: U. of S. Dak., 1971, pp. 46-7.

1587. ________. "Coming Back Home." In Milton, John R., comp., American Indian II. Vermillion: U. of S. Dak., 1971, pp. 29-30.

1588. ________. "Coming Back Home." In Niatum, Duane, ed., Carriers of the Dream Wheel. Harper, 1975, pp. 280-81.

1589. ________. "The Cook." In Niatum, Duane, ed., Carriers of the Dream Wheel. Harper, 1975, pp. 288-89.

1590. ________. "The Crow-Children Walk..." In Niatum, Duane, ed., Carriers of the Dream Wheel. Harper, 1975, pp. 286-87.

1591. ________. "Differences." Pembroke Magazine. no. 2 (1971) 6.

1592. ________. "Empty Streams of Autumn." In Dodge,

Robert K. & Joseph B. McCullough, eds., Voices from Wah'kon-tah. International Publishers, 1974, p. 134.

1593. Young Bear, Ray. (Mesquaki/Sauk & Fox) "February Children." In Levitas, Gloria, Frank Robert & Jacqueline J. Vivelo, eds., American Indian Prose & Poetry. Putnam, 1974, pp. 295-96.

1594. ________. "February Children." In Milton, John R., comp., American Indian II. Vermillion: U. of S. Dak., 1971, p. 34.

1595. ________. "For 100 Poems." Pembroke Magazine. no. 2 (1971) 8.

1596. ________. "Four Songs of Life." In Lourie, Dick, ed., Come to Power. The Crossing Press, 1974, pp. 20-1.

1597. ________. "Four Songs of Life." In Turner, Frederick W., III, The Portable North American Reader. Viking, 1974, pp. 610-2.

1598. ________. "Four Songs of Life: 1) A Young Man." In Milton, John R., comp., American Indian II. Vermillion: U. of S. Dak., 1971, p. 36.

1599. ________. "Four Songs of Life: 2) An Old Man Alone." In Milton, John R., comp., American Indian II. Vermillion: U. of S. Dak., 1971, p. 36.

1600. ________. "Four Songs of Life: 3) One Who Realized." In Milton, John R., comp., American Indian II. Vermillion: U. of S. Dak., 1971, p. 37.

1601. ________. "Four Songs of Life: 4) He was Approached." In Milton, John R., comp., American Indian II. Vermillion: U. of S. Dak., 1971, p. 37.

1602. ________. "Grandmother." Pembroke Magazine. no. 2 (1971) 5.

1603. ________. "A Growing Trust." In Milton, John R.,

comp., American Indian II. Vermillion: U. of S. Dak., 1971, p. 48.

1604. Young Bear, Ray A. (Mesquaki/Sauk & Fox) "In Dream: The Privacy of Sequence." In Niatum, Duane, ed., Carriers of the Dream Wheel. Harper, 1975, pp. 264-68.

1605. ________. "In Missing." In Niatum, Duane, ed., Carriers of the Dream Wheel. Harper, 1975, pp. 278-79.

1606. ________. "The Listening Rock." In Dodge, Robert K. & Joseph B. McCullough, eds., Voices from Wah'kon-tah. International Publishers, 1974, p. 136.

1607. ________. "The Listening Rock." Pembroke Magazine. no. 2 (1971) 9.

1608. ________. "Mix These Eyes with Bone and Rain." In Milton, John R., comp., American Indian II. Vermillion: U. of S. Dak., 1971, pp. 31-32.

1609. ________. "Morning-Talking Mother." In Milton, John R., comp., American Indian II. Vermillion: U. of S. Dak., 1971, p. 38.

1610. ________. "Morning-Talking Mother." In Turner, Frederick W., III, The Portable North American Indian Reader. Viking, 1974, pp. 612-3.

1611. ________. "Morning-water Train Woman." In Milton, John R., comp., American Indian II. Vermillion: U. of S. Dak., 1971, pp. 45-6.

1612. ________. "Now that It Has Passed." In Milton, John R., comp., American Indian II. Vermillion: U. of S. Dak., 1971, p. 35.

1613. ________. "Of Poems and Poets." Pembroke Magazine. no. 2 (1971) 6.

1614. ________. "One Chip of Human Bone." In Dodge, Robert K. & Joseph B. McCullough, eds., Voices from Wah'kon-tah. International Publishers, 1974, p. 133.

1615. Young Bear, Ray. (Mesquaki/Sauk & Fox) "One Chip of Human Bone." Pembroke Magazine. no. 2 (1971) 5.

1616. ________. "One Chip of Human Bone." In Witt, Shirley N., The Way; An Anthology of American Literature. Knopf, 1972, p. 139.

1617. ________. "One Day of Meanings." In Milton, John R., comp., American Indian II. Vermillion: U. of S. Dak., 1971, pp. 43-4.

1618. ________. "One Who Cries Alone." In Tvedten, Benet, comp., An American Indian Anthology. Marvin, S. D.: Blue Cloud Abbey, 1971, p. 38.

1619. ________. "One Winter Thought." In Milton, John R., comp., American Indian II. Vermillion: U. of S. Dak., 1971, p. 33.

1620. ________. "A Poem for Diane Wakoski." In Niatum, Duane, ed., Carriers of the Dream Wheel. Harper, 1975, p. 297.

1621. ________. A Poem for Diane Wakoski." Pembroke Magazine. no. 2 (1971) 6.

1622. ________. "Poem for Vietnam." Pembroke Magazine. no. 2 (1971) 7-8.

1623. ________. "Poem for Vietnam." In Witt, Shirley H., The Way; an Anthology of American Indian Literature. Knopf, 1972, pp. 147-9.

1624. ________. "The Rain Sings." Pembroke Magazine. no. 3 (1972) 59.

1625. ________. "Regretting." Pembroke Magazine. no. 2 (1971) 6.

1626. ________. "A Remembrance of a Color..." In Niatum, Duane, ed., Carriers of the Dream Wheel. Harper, 1975, pp. 290-91.

1627. ________. "Rushing." In Niatum, Duane, ed., Carriers of the Dream Wheel. Harper, 1975, pp. 284-85.

1628. Young Bear, Ray. (Mesquaki/Sauk & Fox) "Rushing." _Pembroke Magazine_. no. 2 (1971) 5.

1629. ________. "Star Blanket." In Niatum, Duane, ed., _Carriers of the Dream Wheel_. Harper, 1975, pp. 258-60.

1630. ________. "These Horses Came." In Lourie, Dick, ed., _Come to Power_. The Crossing Press, 1974, p. 19.

1631. ________. "These Horses Came." In Niatum, Duane, ed., _Carriers of the Dream Wheel_. Harper, 1975, p. 257.

1632. ________. "This." In Tvedten, Benet, comp., _An American Indian Anthology_. Marvin, S. D.: Blue Cloud Abbey, 1971, p. 39.

1633. ________. "This House." In Niatum, Duane, ed., _Carriers of the Dream Wheel_. Harper, 1975, pp. 292-93.

1634. ________. "Through Lifetime." In Lowenfels, Walter, ed., _From the Belly of the Shark_. Vintage, 1973, pp. 72-3.

1635. ________. "Through Lifetime." In Milton, John R., comp., _American Indian II_. Vermillion: U. of S. Dak., 1971, pp. 39-40.

1636. ________. "Through Lifetime." In Turner, Frederick W., III, _The Portable North American Indian Reader_. Viking, 1974, pp. 613-4.

1637. ________. "Trains Made of Stone." In Milton, John R., comp., _American Indian II_. Vermillion: U. of S. Dak., 1971, pp. 25-6.

1638. ________. "Trains Made of Stone." In Niatum, Duane, ed., _Carriers of the Dream Wheel_. Harper, 1975, pp. 282-83.

1639. ________. "Ulysses Returned." _Pembroke Magazine_. no. 3 (1972) 68.

1640. ________. "Waiting to Be Fed." In Niatum, Duane,

ed., Carriers of the Dream Wheel. Harper, 1975, pp. 269-73.

1641. Young Bear, Ray. (Mesquaki/Sauk & Fox) "War Walking Near." In Lourie, Dick, ed., Come to Power. The Crossing Press, 1974, p. 18.

1642. ________. "War Walking Near." In Niatum, Duane, ed., Carriers of the Dream Wheel. Harper, 1975, p. 296.

1643. ________. "Warrior Dreams." In Dodge, Robert K. & Joseph B. McCullough, eds., Voices from Wah'kon-tah. International Publishers, 1974, p. 132.

1644. ________. "Warrior Dreams." Pembroke Magazine. no. 2 (1971) 5.

1645. ________. "The Way the Bird Sat." In Niatum, Duane, ed., Carriers of the Dream Wheel. Harper, 1975, pp. 261-63.

1646. ________. "World War Three." Pembroke Magazine. no. 2 (1971) 6.

1647. ________. "Wrong Kind of Love." In Dodge, Robert K. & Joseph B. McCullough, eds., Voices from Wah'kon-tah. International Publiishers, 1974, p. 131.

1648. ________. "Wrong Kind of Love." Pembroke Magazine. no. 2 (1971) 8.

1649. Zonge, Harry. "I Don't Know When I'm Thinking Good or Bad" [first line]. Akwesasne Notes. v. 5 (Early Winter, 1973) 48.

Part 3

NATIVE AMERICAN SPIRITUAL HERITAGE
Including a Selection of Traditional Narratives

1650. Alexander, Hartley B., ed. The World's Rim; Great Mysteries of the North American Indians. Foreword by Clyde Kluckhohn. U. of Neb. Pr., 1953.
    Traditional rites and ceremonies illustrate how the gifts of nature from Earthmaker to man symbolize man's relationship to the Great Spirit.

1651. Anon. "Some People Call Him Waynahbozho" [first line]. Angwamas Minosewag Anishinabeg. 1st issue. (Poets in the School Program) St. Paul Council of Arts and Sciences, [1972].
    The story of the bet between the giant and Waynahbozho, on who could eat the most.

1652. Azbill, Henry. (Maidu) "How Death Came to the People." [legend]. In Henry, Jeannette, ed., The American Indian Reader: Literature. The Indian Historian Pr., 1973, pp. 162-6.
    Death came as a result of disobedience to the command of the Two Old Men from the Northland, who would restore the people in their worship and their way to manhood.

1653. ________. "Maidu Dances." [legend]. In Henry, Jeannette, ed., The American Indian Reader: Literature. Indian Historian Pr., 1973, pp. 166-8.
    Seasonal events and observances in the life cycle of a person and people were celebrated and ritualized by dance forms and ceremonials.

1654. ________. "World Maker." [legend]. In Henry, Jeannette, ed., The American Indian Reader: Literature. The Indian Historian Pr., 1973, pp. 161-2.

A creation story: a time of no sickness or death, but an evil force came, and "they began fighting and killing for no reason." A "big water" filled the valley; only two people escaped.

1655. Baker, Betty. At the Center of the World; based on Papago and Pima Myths. Macmillan, 1973.
How Earth Magician, Coyote, Buzzard and Eetoi, each with his own special powers, attempted to create the world and people. By trial and error, Eetoi finally succeeded, and subdued the other three. The author's purpose is to preserve the truths expressed in the earliest versions of Papago and Pima myths.

1656. Barney, Randy. "Waynahbozho and the Wolves." Angwamas Minosewag Anishinabeg. 1st issue. (Poets in the Schools Program) St. Paul Council of Arts and Sciences, [1973].
Tells the story of why there is red brush, and why there are countless twigs in the forests.

1657. Beardy, Jackson. (Cree) "Wesakachak and the Beaver." In Gooderham, Kent, ed., I Am an Indian. Dent, 1969, pp. 124-6.
Beaver outwits Wesakachak, the trickster.

1658. ________, collector. "Wesakachak and the Geese." In Gooderham, Kent, ed., I Am an Indian. Dent, 1969, pp. 62-4.
How Wesakachak tricked the geese, and the part loon played.

1659. Big White Owl, or Jasper Hill. (Lennie-Lenape) "Native Religion." The Blue Cloud Quarterly. v. 18, no. 2.
He concludes that the White man has not tried to understand the religious beliefs of the Red man.

1660. Black Elk. (Sioux) The Sacred Pipe: Black Elk's Account of the Seven Rites of the Oglala Sioux. Ed. by Joseph Epes Brown. Norman: U. of Okla. Pr., 1953.
Purpose of the account was to demonstrate a harmony of living together for all people, creatures and Nature.

1661. Bright, William, tr. "Karok Coyote Stories." In Henry, Jeannette, ed., The American Indian Reader: Literature. Indian Historian Pr., 1973, pp. 79-91.

Several Coyote stories compared with translator's own version. He does it by episode rather than by complete story.

1662. Brown, William. (Crow) "Messiah." [prose] In Tvedten, Benet, comp., An American Indian Anthology. Marvin, S. D.: Blue Cloud Abbey, 1971, pp. 69-70.

1663. Chafetz, Henry. Thunderbird and other Stories. illus. by Ronnie Solbert. Pantheon, 1971 [1964].

Legends retold by the author.

1664. Clark, Ella E., collector. "Coyote and the Monster of the Columbia." In Gooderham, Kent, ed., I Am an Indian. Dent, 1969, pp. 26-9.

The tale of Coyote's plan to destroy the monster who was killing the animal people.

1665. ________. Indian Legends from the Northern Rockies. U. of Okla. Pr., 1966.

Includes myths, legends, personal narratives and traditions. Information received directly from the oral literature of the Northwest Natives.

1666. ________. Indian Legends of Canada. Toronto: McClelland and Stewart, 1960.

Stories that reveal the every day life, beliefs, and customs of the natives; and from them discover their basic philosophies of life.

1667. ________, ed. Indian Legends of the Pacific Northwest. Berkeley: U. of Calif. Pr., 1969.

Interesting and true tales about the natural formations in Oregon and Washington.

1668. Clutesi, George. (Tse-shaht) "Ko-Ishin-Mit Takes a Partner" [a fable told by George Clutesi]. In Gooderham, Kent, ed., I Am an Indian. Dent, 1969, pp. 2-4.

The "greedy-glutton" sees the mote in his brother's eye but not the beam in his own.

1669. Clutesi, George. (Tse-shaht) "Laughter Behind the Trees." In Gooderham, Kent, ed., I Am an Indian. Dent, 1969, pp. 7-9.
Describes the performance of the "laughing sirens," one of the most beautiful dances of the Tloo-qwah-nah.

1670. ______. Potlatch. illus. by the Author. Sidney, B. C.: Gray's Pub. Ltd., 1969.
A participant gives an account of the last Tloo-quah-nah (a feast, or potlatch).

1671. ______. Son of Raven, Son of Deer; Fables of the Tse-shaht People. Gray's Publ. Ltd., 1967.
The wonders of nature, man's relationship and dependence on the gifts from the Great Spirit presented through Nature were passed on from generation to generation by means of the story. The minute and seemingly insignificant creatures are all akin in the Earthmaker's plan.

1672. Coffin, Tristram P., ed. Indian Tales of North America; an Anthology for the Adult Reader. Am. Folklore Soc., 1961.
Tales are arranged under the following themes: 1) The way the world is; 2) What man must know and learn; 3) The excitement of living.

1673. Cohoe, Grey. (Navajo) "Grandfather Tells the Cat Story." Pembroke Magazine. no. 4 (1973) 5-8.
Nishoni, the cat, occupied a special place. In a dream she had saved grandfather from evil spirits, and from death during a blizzard.

1674. ______. "Great Spirit Protect Us" [legend]. In Milton, John R., comp., American Indian II. Vermillion: U. of S. D., 1971, pp. 163-7.
Destruction of the monster relieved the fears of the land, but not the sorrow for a lost sister.

1675. Coleman, Sister Bernard, Ellen Frogner and Estelle Eich. Ojibwa Myths and Legends. Minneapolis: Ross, 1971 [1962].
Reviews and encourages the custom of storytelling at present among Northern Minnesota Ojibwas by bringing together a new collection.

1676. Concha, Carl. (Pueblo at Taos) "The Spirit Dreams." [prose]. In Milton, John R., comp., The American Indian Speaks. Vermillion: U. of S.D., 1969, p. 140.
The spirits acting within you can "forever tune you in" and keep you "vibrating."

1677. Cornplanter, Jesse J. (Seneca) Legends of the Longhouse. Told to Sah-Nee-Weh, the White Sister. Port Washington, N.Y.: Friedman, 1963 [1938].
The legend's concerns are numerous: creation, good and evil, love, a horned serpent, and the little people, of which there are many tribes. One tribe paints the flowers and the fruits when they are in season.

1678. Courlander, Harold, collector. People of the Short Blue Corn. Harcourt, 1970.
Seventeen stories of the Hopi world and how they arrived there. Background information supports the tales; also there are notes on oral literature.

1679. Curry, Jane L. Down from the Lonely Mountain; California Indian Tales. Harcourt, 1965.
Stories on the beginnings of the world, how light was obtained, the theft of dawn, and others.

1680. Delorme, Jerry. (Sioux-Klamath) "Origin of Crater Lake." [story] In Allen, T. D., ed., Arrow IV. U.S. Bureau of Indian Affairs. Creative Writing Project, 1972, pp. 27-8.

1681. Dempsey, Hugh A. Blackfoot Ghost Dance. Calgary: Glenbow-Alberta Inst., 1968. (Glenbow Foundation Occasional Paper 3)
Describes the recording of the modern version of the ghost dance. The purification acts and the ritual are detailed.

1682. Dockstader, John, or Hia-Yon-Os. (Seneca) "The World on the Turtle's Back." In Gooderham, Kent, ed., I Am an Indian. Dent, 1969, pp. 148-50.
Turtle's back proved to be strong enough to hold the mud where Sky-woman was placed. A legend of world beginnings.

1683. Eastman, Charles A., or Ohiyesa. (Sioux) Soul of an Indian: An Interpretation. Houghton, 1911.
Mr. Eastman believed that the understanding of the Red man's religion is central to the White man's understanding of the Indian, but he had little hope of it ever happening.

1684. ________. "The Soul of the Indian." [excerpt] In Grass, Theodore H., ed., A Nation of Nations. Macmillan, 1971, pp. 278-83.

1685. ________. Wigwam Evenings. Co-authored by Elaine G. Eastman. Little, 1930 [1909].

1686. Feldmann, Susan, ed. The Storytelling Stone; Myths and Tales of the American Indians. Dell, 1965.
Creation stories, trickster stories and tales of heroes from the Zuni, Seneca, Iroquois, Mono, Wintun, Blackfoot, Winnebago, Eskimo, Tlingit, Micmac, Comanche, Modoc and others.

1687. Fletcher, Alice C. Indian Games and Dances with Native Songs. Arr. from Am. Indian Ceremonials and Sports. N.Y.: AMS Pr., 1971 [1915].
Miss Fletcher's enjoyment of nature increased after living with Native Americans.

1688. Fredericks, Oswald White Bear. (Hopi) Book of the Hopi, as told to Frank Waters. Viking, 1963.
Presents the Hopi's Road to Life from their emergence through three worlds and into the fourth, or the present. Encompasses their physical migrations from the West, across the sea by "stepping stones" and by a long, round-about route to Oraibi. Annual ceremonies reveal their secular and sacred Cycle of Life intimately related, and not separable.

1689. George, Phil. (Nez Percé) "As I Dance." In Tvedten, Benet, comp., An American Indian Anthology. Marvin, S. D.: Blue Cloud Abbey, 1971, pp. 56-62.

1690. Grey, Herman, or Shul-ya of Beaver Clan. (Mohave) Tales from the Mohaves. Foreword by Alice Marriott. Norman: U. of Okla. Pr., 1969.
Written to preserve Mohave culture. Two mythological heroes: Red Hand and Swift Lance.

1691. Grey, Herman, or Shul-ya. (Mohave) Tales from the Mohaves. U. of Okla. Pr., 1971.
Seldom are the great myths of a people written by one of the people. These tales were written primarily for his children.

1692. Gringhuis, Richard H. Lore of the Great Turtle; Indian Legends of Mackinac Retold. Mackinac Island State Park Commission, 1970.
Mackinac Island was held in awe by the Natives from East and West. Here the Great Spirit, Gitchi Manitou, dwelt alone except for the Giant in the rocks.

1693. Hail, Raven. (Cherokee) "The Green Corn Dance." In Tvedten, Benet, comp., An American Indian Anthology. Marvin, S. D.: Blue Cloud Abbey, 1971, pp. 63-5.
Recounts the details and significance of the Green Corn Dance, which has not been observed for one hundred years. Today the whole world shares in the gifts of the Corn Mother, but does not share in the festival of Thanksgiving.

1694. Haloo, Delbert. (Zuni) "The Loneliness of the Coyote." [prose] In Allen, T. D., ed., Arrow IV. U.S. Bureau of Indian Affairs, Creative Writing Project, 1972, pp. 13-14.

1695. Herman, Jake. (Sioux) "The Seven Camp Fires." [stories]. In Henry, Jeannette, ed., The American Indian Reader: Literature. The Indian Historian Pr., 1973, pp. 142-6.
Legend says that Seven Camp Fires represent the seven stars of the Great Dipper. The teller continues with seven codes of life and other tales supporting their philosophy of life.

1696. Hillerman, Tony. The Boy Who Made Dragonfly. Harper, 1975.
A tribal story of the Zuni.

1697. Holterman, Jack. "Seven Blackfeet Stories." In Henry, Jeannette, ed., The American Indian Reader: Literature. Indian Historian Pr., 1973, pp. 92-100.
Seven stories in versions which have not been

published until this time: the Woman of Stone; the Pleiades; the Frog and the Rain; Old Man and the Rock; the Ghost Wife; the Half Man; and Sacrifice.

1698. Holterman, Jack. "Seven Blackfeet Stories." The Indian Historian. v. 3 (Fall, 1970) 39-43.

1699. Hum-ishu-ma, or Mourning Dove. (Okanagan) Coyote Stories. Ed. by Heister Dean Guie. Caldwell, Idaho: Caxton, 1933.

1700. Hunt, Irvin. (Pueblo) "Among the Pueblos" [at Christmas]. In Henry, Jeannette, ed., The American Indian Reader: Literature. The Indian Historian Pr., 1973, pp. 124-6.

Native Americans often blend Christian customs and their own rituals. Christmas Day is a day of worship and feasting. The three following days are celebrated with dancing and tribal elections.

1701. Jacobs, Melville, ed. Nehalem, Tillamook Tales. Eugene: U. of Oregon Bks., 1956.

These tales traditionally told by Tillamook Indians during winter. Told to Elizabeth D. Jacobs by a full-blood.

1702. Jenness, Diamond. The Corn Goddess & other Tales from Indian Canada. Illus. by Winifred K. Bentley. 2nd ed. 1960. National Museum of Canada Bulletin 141, Anthropological Series no. 37.

Tales of literary merit chosen from each part of Canada, to gain Indian's outlook on the universe.

1703. Kelly, Peter R. (Haida) "My People the Haida." In Gooderham, Kent, ed., I Am an Indian. Dent, 1969, pp. 12-5.

The traditional houses were built of red cedar. In front of each house a totem pole of red cedar was erected. It was not an idol to be worshipped. It represented a coat of arms and could only be erected upon accession to the family title.

1704. Kilpatrick, Anna Gritts. (Oklahoma Cherokee) Friends of Thunder, Folktales of the Oklahoma

Cherokees. S.M.U. Pr., 1964.

Contains tales of humor besides bird, animal and monster stories; also Uk'ten, Tseg'sgin narratives. Ethnographic data and historical sketches included.

1705. Kilpatrick, Jack F. (Cherokee), and Anna G. Kilpatrick. "A Cherokee Conjuration to Cure a Horse." Southern Folklore Quarterly. v. 28 (Sept., 1964) 216-18.

Contains two Cherokee texts in Cherokee with English translation. One was discovered in 1962, the other dates from the nineteenth century. Includes instructions on how to implement the conjuring ceremony.

1706. ________. ________. "Cherokee Rituals Pertaining to Medicinal Roots." Southern Indian Studies. v. 16 (1964) 24-28.

Records the translation of three chants used by medicine men while collecting medicinal roots and preparing medicine.

1707. ________. ________. "The Foundation of Life: the Cherokee National Ritual." American Anthropologist. v. 66 (1964) 1386-91.

Details about when ritual observed and intricacies of the ritual itself. An interlinear and also a free translation is included.

1708. ________. ________. Muskogean Charm Songs among the Oklahoma Cherokees. Smithsonian Contributions to Anthropology, v. 2, no. 3. Washington, 1967.

Words of songs are in native language, with explanations. Examples of subjects: to make a woman lovesick; for luck in hunting.

1709. ________. ________. "A Note on Wind-Controlling Magic." Southern Folklore Quarterly. v. 29 (1965) 204-6.

Wind-lore is common in the hill country of Eastern Oklahoma where tornadoes frequently occur.

1710. ________. ________, eds. Run Toward the Nightland: Magic of the Oklahoma Cherokees. Dallas:

Southern Methodist Univ. Pr., 1967.
Songs related to magic intersperse the accounts of charms and occasions for their use.

1711. Kilpatrick, Jack Frederick, and Anna G. Kilpatrick. (Cherokee) The Shadow of Sequoyah: Social Documents of the Cherokees, 1862-1964. Tr. and ed. by the Kilpatricks. Norman: U. of Okla. Pr., 1965.
Includes myths, letters, incantations, records of epidemics, etc.

1712. Kingbird, Jeff. "The Man." [prose]. In Angwamas Minosewag Anishinabeg. (Poets in the Schools Program) St. Paul Council of Arts and Sciences, Winter, 1973-74.
A story of how a frog turned into a man.

1713. Landes, Ruth. Ojibwa Religion and the Midewiwin. U. of Wis. Pr., 1968.
Detailed record of the Ojibwa Midewiwin ritual and organization.

1714. Leekley, Thomas B. The World of Manabozho; Tales of the Chippewa Indians. Vanguard, 1965.
These stories are retold primarily by contemporary Chippewa and Ottawa Indians for American boys and girls. Originally these tales were told around the lodge fires of the Algonquins.

1715. Link, Margaret S. Beautiful on the Earth. Santa Fe, N.M.: Hazel Dreis Editions, 1947.
Includes songs, chants, and illustrations of sandpaintings. A beautiful book!

1716. Livingston, John. "If They Are Going about Our Religion..." [prose]. In Angwamas Minosewag Anishinabeg. 1st issue. (Poets in the Schools Program) St. Paul Council of Arts and Sciences, [1972].
Religion represents life. Learning continues --even if you get to be 92.

1717. Lone Dog, Louise. (Mohawk-Delaware) Strange Journey: The Vision Life of a Psychic Indian Woman. Healdsburg, Calif.: Naturegraph Co., 1964.

1718. McClintock, Walter. The Blackfoot Beaver Bundle. Southwest Museum, Highland Park, Los Angeles, Calif. (Leaflet nos. 2 & 3)

The legend of Round-Cut-Robe, a very modest young man, and how the first beaver bundle was obtained, including the dance, songs and prayers.

1719. ________. Blackfoot Medicine-Pipe Ceremony. Southwest Museum, Highland Park, Los Angeles, Calif. (Leaflet no. 21)

Describes the procedure for the "purchasing" of the Medicine-Pipe and the ceremonies which follow. Responsibilities of the office are numerous and detailed.

1720. MacFarlan, Allan A., ed. American Indian Legends. Illus. by Everett G. Jackson. Heritage Pr., 1968.

Legends included which were "most interesting, varied and representative." Legends reveal Indian way of life, beliefs.

1721. Marriott, Alice and Carol K. Rachlin, comps. American Indian Mythology. Crowell, 1968.

Each story is preceded by information about its origin, and its significance in the life of the tribe. At the end of each tale, the name and tribe of the person who told the tale to Alice Marriott is noted.

1722. Miller, David H. Ghost Dance. Duell, Sloan, 1959.

Miller, adopted by Black Elk in 1939, promised to tell the white man the true story of the Indian Ghost Dance. It is based on interviews with Indians who participated in the preliminary ceremonies, the dance, and survived the Wounded Knee Massacre (1890).

1723. Momaday, N. Scott. (Kiowa) "Two Tales from 'The Journey of Tai-Me': The Beginning; the Arrow." Little Square Review. Nos. 5&6 (Spring & Summer, 1968) 30-31.

The Beginning explains why the Kiowas are a small tribe. The Arrow describes the well-made arrow, and how and why a certain man sent it "straight to his enemy's heart."

1724. Momaday, N. Scott. (Kiowa) The Way to Rainy Mountain. Albuquerque: U. of N.M. Pr., 1969.

A personal pilgrimage into the past: reminiscences of his childhood lived with his grandmother; after her death he returned to her home, and to her grave. She had lived in the shadow of Rainy Mountain. He relates legends of his people, reviews their historical setting, and gives his own reactions and their significance to him as he has lived in their mystery and reality. Interestingly arranged and illustrated--a spiritual treasure.

1725. Moriarty, James R. Chingchinx; an Indigenous California Indian Religion. Southwest Museum, 1969.

A book of rites: initiation, leadership, taboo, and ceremonial.

1726. Morriseau, Norval. (Ojibway) Legends of My People, the Great Ojibway. Ryerson, 1965.

Tales of the Ojibways who lived in the Lake Nipigon and Thunder Bay area.

1727. ________. "My People the Great Ojibway." In Gooderham, Kent, ed., I Am an Indian. Dent, 1969, pp. 136-8.

Compares religious beliefs of Ojibway and Christian--"and where is heaven!"

1728. ________. Windigo; and other Tales of the Ojibway. Retold by Herbert T. Schwarz. Toronto: McClelland and Stewart, 1969.

Windigo was the evil spirit who ate human flesh and grew to a great height.

1729. Mountain, Chief. (Tsimshian) "The Totem Pole of Sakau'wan." As told to Marius Barbeau. In Gooderham, Kent, ed., I Am an Indian. Dent, 1969, pp. 21-4.

The story of the tallest totem pole.

1730. Nequatewa, Edmund. (Hopi) Truth of a Hopi: Stories Relating to the Origin, Myths, and Clan Histories of the Hopi. (Museum of Northern Arizona Bulletin No. 8) Flagstaff: Arizona Northland Pr., 1967.

1731. Nieberding, Velma. "Shawnee Indian Festival: the Bread Dance." Chronicles of Oklahoma. v. 42 (August, 1964) 253-261.

1732. Nowell, Charles J. (Kwakiutl) "A Cannibal Loose in St. Louis." In Gooderham, Kent, ed., I Am an Indian. Dent, 1969, pp. 5-7.

Describes a performance of the Hamatsa (Cannibal) Society in which a "magical" dance scares the audience.

1733. Nye, Wilbur S. Bad Medicine and Good; Tales of the Kiowas. Norman: U. of Oklahoma Pr., 1962.

Recounting of actual events of the Kiowa people, by Kiowans during 1933-37, interspersed with historical background. Included are exploits of bravery, performance of the medicine dance (sun dance), power of superstition, consequences of a person's "medicine": favor with the Great Spirit, ability to heal, or what can happen if "medicine" goes bad.

1734. Oaks, Abel. (Cree) "The Boy and the Buffalo." In Henry, Jeannette, ed., The American Indian Reader: Literature. Indian Historian Pr., 1973, pp. 61-2.

This collection represents the type of traditional story in which animals came to a human in his need. In this case a buffalo saved a boy from desertion by his parents. The question arises: Was this "desertion" or a part of the Great Spirit's plan for the child?

1735. O'John, Calvin. (Ute-Navaho) "Basket Lady." [story] In Tvedten, Benet, comp., An American Indian Anthology. Marvin, S.D.: Blue Cloud Abbey, 1971, pp. 66-8.

A story of how the Basket Lady was outwitted, deprived of her prey and destroyed.

1736. Paige, Harry W. Songs of the Teton Sioux. Westernlore, 1970.

Gives background of people and settings for individual and ceremonial songs. Excerpts of songs are included.

1737. Palmanteer, Ted. (Chinook) "Chinook Dance." [prose] In Henry, Jeanette, ed., The American Indian Reader: Literature. The Indian Historian Pr., 1973, pp. 109-112.
By morning the Chinook winds have returned and Spring has arrived.

1738. Palmer, Wm. R. Why the North Star Stands Still and other Indian Legends. Prentice, 1957.
Legends and stories of the Paiute Indians (Utah).

1739. Pietroforte, Alfred. Songs of the Yokuts and Paiutes. Healdsburg, Calif.: Naturegraph, 1965.
To understand Indian music, one must be able to place one's self as far as possible in the setting of the Native American.

1740. Platero, Dillon and Robert A. Roessel, comps. Coyote Stories of the Navaho People. Illus. by Geo. Mitchell. Rough Rock, Arizona: Navaho Curriculum Center, 1968.
Prepared primarily for Navaho boys and girls. Coyote stories were connected with various ceremonies and retold when they were performed.

1741. Rafaël, Simon. (Lake St. John Band) "Me'jo Talks to Himself." In Gooderham, Kent, ed., I Am an Indian. Dent, 1969, pp. 106-7.
The use of the sweat lodge in killing bear.

1742. Reid, Dorothy M. Tales of Nanabozho. Henry Z. Walck, Inc., 1963.
Reid has written her own versions of the tales, which are true to the spirit of the original. Nanabozho was a great magician and trickster whose foolish mistakes appealed to the Ojibway Indians' sense of humor.

1743. Reilly, P. T. "The Disappearing Havasupai Corn-Planting Ceremony." Masterkey. 44 (Jan.-Mar., 1970) p. 30-4.

1744. Roberts, Helen H., and Morris Swadesh. Songs of the Nootka Indians of Western Vancouver Island.

Based on Phono Records, Linguistic, and other Field Notes made by Edward Sapir. Phila.: Am. Philos. Soc., 1955. (New Series, v. 45, pt. 3, 1955)

1745. Schorer, C. E. "Indian Tales of C. C. Trowbridge: The Ornamented Head." Southern Folklore Quarterly. v. 33 (1969) 317-32.

Tale of a bachelor and his nephew. The nephew needed moccasins to protect his feet, he said. He really wanted to find a wife, and he did. The uncle saw through his ruse. When he returned with his wife, the uncle had all preparations completed. He knew his nephew would be a great man. Variants of the tale are listed.

1746. Seelatsee, Julia. (Yakima) "Among the Yakima" [at Christmas]. In Henry, Jeannette, ed., The American Indian Reader: Literature. The Indian Historian Pr., 1973, pp. 126-7.

Those who have not adopted white man's religion hold a feast. Dances and religious Indian songs continue for two weeks.

1747. Seton, Ernest Thompson. The Gospel of the Red Man; an Indian Bible. Doubleday, 1936.

The product of a life-long mission: to give the Red Man's message to the White Man. He was assisted by Natives in organizing these fundamental truths. White denominational leaders acknowledged their universality.

1748. Shaw, Anna Moore. Pima Indian Legends. U. of Ariz. Pr., 1968.

A rewriting of their legends for contemporary Pima Indians who employ English rather than their native language. Anna Shaw states that "whole elements are no longer appropriate and have been either re-worded or dropped."

1749. Slickpoo, Allen P., Sr., Leroy L. Seth and Deward E. Walker, Jr. Nu Mee Poom Tit Wah Tit; Nez Percé Legends. Nez Percé Tribe of Idaho, 1972.

A Nez Percé Tribal project of writing and editing their legends.

1750. Smith, George. (Winnebago) "About the Happy

Hunting Ground" [interview]. In Cash, J. H., & H. T. Hoover, eds., To Be an Indian. Holt, 1971, pp. 17-18.

1751. ________. "How a Dog Saved Lone Wolf" [interview]. In Cash, J. H. & H. T. Hoover, eds., To Be an Indian. Holt, 1971, pp. 19-21.

1752. Snake, Sterling. (Winnebago) "Native American Church Practices" [interview]. In Cash, J. H. & H. T. Hoover, eds., To Be an Indian. Holt, 1971, pp. 35-38.

1753. Sohappy, Liz. (Yakima Tribal Group) "White Bluffs." [prose] In Milton, John R., comp., The American Indian Speaks. Vermillion: U. of S. Dak., 1969, p. 139.

The cleansing waters grant forgiveness and renewal after she had broken the dance rhythm.

1754. Sun Bear. (Chippewa) Buffalo Hearts. Healdsburg, Calif., Naturegraph, 1971.

He views his own culture: history and religion, which each Native American needs today to survive with pride and respect.

1755. Tetlaneetsa. (Thompson Chief) ["The Twin Bear Song that Saved His Life."] In Gooderham, Kent, ed., I Am an Indian. Dent, 1969, pp. 31-4.

An incident from his Personal Reminiscences.

1756. Thomas, Lorna Jamieson. (Six Nations Reserve) "The Hideous One." In Gooderham, Kent, ed., I Am an Indian. Dent, 1969, pp. 155-7.

The Great Spirit and the Hideous One meet to decide who has been responsible for the "splendor of creation."

1757. Thomas, Mary A. "A Lad Who Doesn't Like Work: A Huasteca Nahuatl Tale." Tlalocan. v. 6 (1970) 146-58.

A tale in which a boy discovers magical qualities of a horse and carpenter, and capitalizes on them in his day's work.

1758. Thompson, Stith. Tales of the North American Indians. Harvard U. Pr., 1929.

Folklore specialist Thompson's purpose in this collection was to correct the erroneous impressions of Indian traditions as retold by Schoolcraft. The collection is arranged under nine categories: mythological stories, mythical incidents, trickster tales, hero tales, journeys to the other world, animal wives and husbands, miscellaneous tales, tales borrowed from Europeans, and Bible stories. The source of each tale is indicated: tribe, and first recording. There are extensive comparative notes; list of motifs; authorities by culture area and tribes; also a bibliography of original collections. The 1966 copyright of this title is a reprint.

1759. Towendolly, Grant. (Wintu) A Bag of Bones; Legends of the Wintu Indians. Ed. by Marcelle Masson. Healdsburg, Calif.: Naturegraph Publ., 1966.

Towendolly was the last of the Wintu Indian shamans. This collection of his stories is recorded as he told them: a mixture of native and contemporary English. The stories concern the mean giant Supchet; the two powerful brothers Norwanchakas and Keriha, who destroyed Supchet; Nordalmunoko, short but very powerful, who outwits all his adversaries; Tolchuharas, who with his magic cap forced Old Man Sun to "stay up there," and his daughters to the Moon; the escapades of Pine Squirrel and his uncle Old Badger; and the travels of Sedit, the coyote, and Torraharsh, the sandhill crane.

1760. Traveller Bird. (Cherokee) The Path to Snowbird Mountain; Cherokee Legends. Farrar, 1972.

Traveller Bird revisits the scene of his childhood and recalls the precepts and traditions of his people via the stories his grandfather told. "How the earth was formed," "the vanity of man," "how the animals outwitted each other," are subjects of the tales.

1761. Trejo, Judy. (Paiute) "Coyote Tales." Journal of American Folklore. v. 87 (Jan.-Mar., 1974) 66-71.

Grandfather's coyote tales which he told around the wood-burning stove and the mellow light of the kerosene lamp are especially memorable to the author. She retells four of them.

1762. Vaudrin, Bill. (Chippewa) Tanaina Tales from Alaska. Norman: U. of Okla. Pr., 1969.
Portrays picture of life through legends: customs, events and humor.

1763. Velarde, Pablita. (Santa Clara Pueblo) Old Father, the Story Teller. Globe, Ariz.: Dale Stuart King, 1960.
Author has simplified the stories of her grandfather, especially for the non-Indian. The six stories: The Stars, Sad Eyes, Enchanted Hunter, Turkey Girl, Butterfly Boy, and First Twins.

1764. Villasenor, David. (Otomi) Tapestries in Sand; the Spirit of Indian Sandpainting. Healdsburg, Calif.: Naturegraph Co., 1963.
The sand painting was created by the medicine man as a visible element in the healing ceremony. Colored plates of a number of paintings are reproduced within the text, together with the details of the ceremonies for which they were designed.

1765. Vizenor, Gerald R., ed. (Anishinabe) Anishinabe Adisokan. Minneapolis: The Nodin Pr., 1970.
Anishinabe Adisokan (the People's Stories) were originally told by two members of the Midewiwin in their own language to convey to the people their religious heritage. They were originally printed in The Progress, 1887-88, a weekly newspaper published on the White Earth Reservation in northern Minnesota. The illustrations are photographs or original Anishinabe pictomyths first published by the American Bureau of Ethnology. The collection includes tales of exploits credited to Manabozho, the "compassionate trickster."

1766. Wanica, Anpetu Olhanke, or Jeffrey Zelitch. (Dakota) "The Lakota Sun Dance." Expedition. v. 13 (Fall, 1970) 17-23.
Author, as a participant in the ceremony of the Sun Dance, captures the essence and spirit of this ritual of sacrifice and thanksgiving: the

yielding of body and spirit to the Great Spirit. All seven steps, from preparatory details to final dispersion of personnel and equipment, are performed with a reverent sense of deep personal commitment.

1767. Warren, David. (Tewa) "In Beauty I Walk." National Wildlife. v. 12 (Jan., 1974) 4-11.

The Native American's indissoluble union with the world of nature and that of the Great Spirit was the first cause for continuous communion and frequent celebration in song and ceremony. Thus he would endure. Only once had a native culture met disaster, and that by a human invasion, when the Aztecs were crushed by the Spaniards. Today's Native fears destruction of life along with that of the white man, who has wasted the gifts of nature.

1768. Webb, George. (Pima) A Pima Remembers. U. of Ariz. Pr., 1959.

Webb has recorded the narratives of his people as he heard them told by his grandparents. His purpose is to preserve them for future generations.

1769. White, Noah. (Winnebago) ["Native American Church Worship"] [interview by Herbert Hoover]. South Dakota Review. v. 8 (Autumn, 1970) 171-7.

Describes a worship service which includes individually performed songs, prayers and meditations based on Biblical portions in addition to the sacramental use of peyote. The latter produces keener awareness and consciousness in the worshippers relation to God. Individual participation of all members is possible in an all-night devotion which is followed by breakfast.

1770. ________. "A Native American Church Service." [interview]. In Cash, J. H. & H. T. Hoover, eds., To Be an Indian. Holt, 1971, pp. 30-4.

Details of a Native American Church Service.

1771. Wicasa, Wambdi, narrator. (Sioux) "The Beginning of our People." The Blue Cloud Quarterly. v. 19, no. 1.

In Paha Sapa (the Black Hills), Wakantanka

walked. He was lonely, and needed love. Mother Earth sang her love, she needed a response of warmth--the South wind, who was gentle. A man, red as the sun, stood upright on a "high bare hill" and could say "Father" to Wakantanka.

1772. Wicasa, Wambdi, narrator. (Sioux) "Sica Hollow." The Blue Cloud Quarterly. v. 19, no. 1.

Another story of how Evil came among the people. A Flood from the clouds destroyed all, except the maiden Fawn. Her prayer song for a new people was heard by Wakantanka and "He sent a white cloud to cover her."

1773. Willoya, William. (Eskimo) Warriors of the Rainbow; Strange and Prophetic Dreams of the Indian People. Co-authored by Vinson Brown. Healdsburg, Calif.: Naturegraph, 1962.

Compares Messianic prophecies, dreams and visions: Hebrew, Christian, Native American and Oriental. Messiahs appeared to bring release from spiritual bondage rather than from physical or political oppression. The persecuted misread the prophets' symbolic language and suffered deprivation in soul and body.

1774. Wyman, Jerry. "My Name Is Blue Flying Deer." [prose]. In Angwamas Minosewag Anishinabeg. (Poets in the Schools Program) St. Paul Council of Arts and Sciences, Winter 1973-4.

Terse, perceptive description of the fast of a 13-yr.-old boy.

1775. The Zunis; Self Portrayals. By the Zuni People. Trans. by Alvina Quam. U. of N. Mex. Pr., 1972.

Governor of the pueblo of the Zuni, Robert E. Lewis, in his introduction compares this recording of Zuni oral history to the "first fruits of a harvest at which a family is gathered in a thanksgiving ritual." The collection is made up of six parts: Society; History; Fables; Fables of Moral Instruction; Religion; War and Defense.

Part 4

AUTOBIOGRAPHY, BIOGRAPHY, LETTERS AND PERSONAL NARRATIVES

1776. Antell, Will. (Chippewa) William Warren. Dillon Publishing, 1973.

A brief biography of an Ojibway born in 1825 on the west coast of Lake Superior. He was educated by an uncle in New York and at the age of 16 returned to his home in northern Minnesota Territory. His achievements during the remaining twelve years of his life included the recording of myths and stories of the Ojibway together with a fair start on the history of his people. An expert interpreter, he was adept at translating and communicating the needs and rights of his people to U.S. government officials. He served one year as a representative in the Legislative Assembly of Minnesota Territory where he also was active on behalf of his people. Written especially for young adults.

1777. Bedford, Denton R. (Minsee) Tsali. Illus. by Dan R. Timmons. (Cherokee) Indian Historian Pr., 1972.

True story of the man, Tsali, his family and nation: the Cherokee, who in 1838 were about to be removed to the West. Tsali, his family and at least 60 others escaped. In doing so and to protect his wife, he killed a white soldier. Isolation, hunger, separation and uncertainty became their way of life. Capture and the white officer's retaliation only perpetuated Tsali's heroism and fame.

1778. Bennett, Kay. (Navajo) Kaibah: Recollections of a Navajo Girlhood. Los Angeles: Western Lore Press, 1964.

This is the story of Mother Chischillie as well as that of Kaibah, her ten-year-old daughter. Mother C. radiates a warmth within her family which sustains them through the commonplace activities and brings satisfaction. She is the strong matriarch who with innate wisdom, love for her family and devotion to the Navajo tradition teaches her family by precept the unity of life: the relation between man and nature, the Navajo way. Increases in number of sheep and the drought years bring on a crisis between the government and the Navajo people.

1779. Betzinez, Jason, or Batsinas. (Apache) I Fought with Geronimo. Ed. by Wilber S. Nye. Bonanza Bks., 1959.

Jason's own story, from warring Apache to the "civilized" white man's way, spans almost a century. Descriptions of escape from San Carlos reservation, flight from one mountain hide-out to another are interspersed with skirmishes and raids for food and hostages. Submission to Gen'l Cook, followed by Geronimo's surrender, terminated in imprisonment at St. Augustine, Florida. Several years later he was among those chosen to be educated at Carlisle. He found contentment living at Ft. Sill, Okla., working at his trade, blacksmithing, and giving support and encouragement to his people. Romance came to him late in life.

1780. Black Elk. (Oglala Sioux) Black Elk Speaks; Being the Life Story of a Holy Man of the Oglala Sioux. As told to John G. Neihardt. Lincoln: U. of Nebr. Pr., 1961 [1932].

At nine years of age Black Elk received a vision through which he was granted powers to aid in relieving his people in their approaching difficulties. As a very old man he recalled the vision in all its solemnity. At the conclusion of the account he and John Neihardt return to the mountain peak on which the vision appeared. With his sacred bow he prayed that the Six Powers would continue to grant his people life. The response he received satisfied him.

1781. Buffalo Child Long Lance. (Blackfoot) Long Lance.

New York: Cosmopolitan Book Corporation, 1936 [1928].

1782. Buffalo Child Long Lance. (Blackfoot) *Redman Echoes: Comprising the Writings of Chief Buffalo Child Long Lance and Biographical Sketches by His Friends.* Los Angeles: Frank Wiggins Trade School, 1933.

1783. Cochise, Ciye Nino. (Apache) *The First Hundred Years of Nino Cochise.* By the grandson of the Legendary Chief Cochise. Pyramid, 1972.

Nino Cochise, grandson of the great chief Cochise, depicts dramatically the events and adventures of his long life, 1876-1970. As one of the "nameless ones," the "missing ones," he escaped with the Chiricahui of the Apaches, while they were herded to a reservation in Arizona Territory. Their refuge was an impregnable mountain in Mexico, where they sustained their way of life while testing the white man's word: distrusting General Torres and his *revolucionarios*, refusing Pres. Roosevelt's offers of scholarships, and negotiating with copper mining magnates. After a rich, full life with his clansmen, wife and mother, personal tragedy struck. He struggled to retain his fortune, and worked for the white man when necessary: in Hollywood and in World War II industry. When he became physically incapacitated and lost his fortune, he succumbed to the co-author's urgings to write his life story.

1784. Cohoe, William. (Cheyenne) *A Cheyenne Sketchbook.* Commentary by E. Adamson Hoebel and Karen Daniels Petersen. Norman: U. of Okla. Pr., 1964.

While a prisoner at St. Augustine, Florida after forcible removal from the Central Plains, the author drew sketches of the scenes, people, and things which he chose to remember. No scenes of war are included.

1785. Crashing Thunder, or Warudjarega, or Sam Blowsnake. (Winnebago) *Crashing Thunder: The Autobiography of a Winnebago.* Ed. by Paul Radin. Dover Publications, Inc., 1963 [1926].

At birth Crashing Thunder was considered "not an ordinary person." As he was growing up and preparing for his vision, he found it difficult to observe the required standards. Openly he professed that he had experienced the vision, but secretly he knew that he had not. After some years of dissipation, he was converted to the peyote religion, led an exemplary life and was married. A happy conclusion!

1786. Cuero, Delphina. (Southern Diegueno) The Autobiography of Delphina Cuero; A Diegueno Indian. As told to Florence C. Shipek. Los Angeles: Dawson's Book Shop, 1968.

The Diegueno Indian's homeland was the San Diego coastland. Their original independence of life and spirit disintegrated as a consequence of the degrading influences of the dominant modern society. Thus society as a whole suffers as well as the individual.

1787. Deloria, Vine V., Sr. (Sioux) "The Standing Rock Reservation--A Personal Reminiscence." In Milton, John R., comp., American Indian II. Vermillion: U. of S.D., 1971, pp. 175-195.

An Episcopal minister, a mixed-blood Indian, who had many contacts with white people during his early years, he is still an Indian at heart. Indians were among the first ecumenists: they could not understand denominational differences among Christians. They could understand Jesus but not St. Paul.

1788. Eastman, Charles A., or Ohiyesa. (Sioux) From the Deep Woods to Civilization: Chapters in the Autobiography of an Indian. Little, 1925 [1916].

After Ohiyesa's father was released from prison, he was converted to Christianity and the white man's way. Under the Homestead Act he secured a farm in South Dakota and operated it successfully. Then he set out for Canada to find his son, who was now 15. Ohiyesa, somewhat reluctant, returned with his father and started his education. Later he continued at Beloit, Knox and Dartmouth, and received his medical degree at Boston University. He was appointed government physician at the Pine Ridge Reservation.

He won the confidence of the people and found satisfaction in serving the needs of his people. The Ghost Dance craze of the late 1880's violated the government edict against "religious dances," and precipitated the tragic conflict at Wounded Knee (1890). Eastman's attempts to enlist the sympathies of the U.S. government only resulted in his being relieved of his position. Understanding friends and his faithful wife encouraged him to write of his experiences, and to accept speaking engagements. His contacts with literary, national and world-renowned persons were stimulating and gave publicity to his cause.

1789. Eastman, Charles, or Ohiyesa. (Sioux) Indian Boyhood. McClure, [1904] 1972.

A tribute to his grandmother, Uncheedah, who in her wisdom, love and devotion reared him in the traditions of the Sioux. An Indian child was taught that silence and reticence fostered the virtues of patience and self-control. Goodness and wisdom were required if one would be a medicine man. Possessions were not to be accumulated for their own sake, but to share with others. At eight years of age he made his first offering--his dearest possession. The Minnesota Massacre broke up his happy childhood. His father was taken prisoner, the others found exile in Canada.

1790. ________. Indian Heroes and Great Chieftains. Little, 1924 [1918].

Fifteen of the greatest chiefs are presented "in the light of native character." In making his last stand for freedom against the westward-moving white man, the Indian skillfully exercised physical prowess, strength of character, ingenuity and resourcefulness. Crazy Horse, Sitting Bull and Chief Joseph are among the renowned. Gall, Tamahay and Dull Knife also led their people proudly, unashamedly against great odds.

1791. Enriquez, Cathy. (Papago) "Someone I'll Never Forget." In Allen, T. D., ed., Arrow III. U.S. Bureau of Indian Affairs, Creative Writing Project, 1971, pp. 25-6.

1792. George, Phil. (Nez Perce) "My Indian Name."

[personal narrative] In Milton, John R., comp., The American Indian Speaks. Vermillion: U. of S.D., 1969, pp. 142-7.

The name ceremony in his eighth year was preceded by participation in the "ancient sweat bath purification." On Medicine Day, Seven Drum Services, a religious service, was conducted in a long lodge. Feasting, songs of thanksgiving and ritual dances followed. After all this his grandfather made introductions and explained the history of his name.

1793. Gridley, Marion E. American Indian Women. Hawthorn Books, 1974.

Chapter one tells the facts about the Native American woman's tribal status. She had a place of equality and respect which white American women are now fighting for. Eighteen women have been chosen for inclusion, ranging in time from Sacajawea to her great-great-granddaughter Esther Burnett Horne, organizer of the first Indian Girl Scout Troop in the U.S.A. and a distinguished teacher.

1794. ________. Contemporary American Indian Leaders. Dodd, 1972.

Chapters on 26 Native American men and women, most of whom are less well-known than Vine Deloria, Jr., N. Scott Momaday, Maria Martinez and LaDonna Harris.

1795. ________, ed. Indians of Today. 4th ed. Chicago: Indian Council Fire, 1971.

The editor's life-long interest in Indian culture and the years of her life lived among Indians qualify her to produce this work. The "personal accomplishment" of each individual is the criterion for inclusion in this biographical source. Eskimos have been included in this edition.

1796. Hart, Hazel. (Chippewa) "Ge Chi Maung Won; the Life Story of an Old Chippewa Woman." In Allen, T. D., ed., Arrow IV. U.S. Bureau of Indian Affairs, Creative Writing Project, 1972, pp. 31-37.

1797. Hastin, Biyo; or Son of Former Many Beads. The

Ramah Navahos [autobiography]. Navaho Historical Series, no. 1.

1798. Herman, Jake. (Sioux) "Pine Ridge." In Henry, Jeannette, ed., The American Indian Reader: Literature. The Indian Historian Pr., 1973, pp. 130-4.

Autobiographical sketch of his early attempts at education via the white man's way. His life as a cowboy in rodeo, with its many failures and few successes, is told candidly and with humor.

1799. Hoffman, Joseph. (Apache) "Personal Narrative of Joseph Hoffman." In Western Apache Raiding and Warfare. U. of Arizona Pr., 1971, pp. 73-91.

Recalls the raiding activities of Apache warriors when he was a boy. He describes preparations for attacks against the Navajo and Pima. In each case revenge for the death of tribal members was obtained.

1800. Holmes, Bill, or Tu-chill. (Cahuilla) "Qua-Quel and Tu-Chill." [prose]. In Henry, Jeannette, ed., The American Indian Reader: Literature. The Indian Historian Pr., 1973, pp. 114-5.

1801. Kaywaykla, James. (Apache) In the Days of Victorio; Recollections of a Warm Springs Apache. As told to Eve Ball. U. of Ariz. Pr., 1970.

Together with the titles by Nino Cochise and Jason Betzinez, this autobiography-history supports and adds to the information about the Apaches' struggles for their way of life in the late nineteenth century. Kaywaykla, as a child, experienced the horror, sadness, heroic feats of the warriors and women, and the utter degradation of defeat. He states that shooting would have been much less cruel than imprisonment at St. Augustine, Florida. The committed, consistent religious life of the Apaches is contrasted to the Christians' Sunday preachments and lack of everyday practice.

1802. Laflesche, Francis. (Omaha) The Middle Five: Indian Schoolboys of the Omaha Tribe. Madison: U. of Wisc. Pr., 1963 [1900].

Francis, one of the Middle Five, recalls with

humor and greater understanding of his white teachers than they had of the Native Americans, life in a mission school. Positive attitudes of native parents in regard to the education of their children is apparent. At the same time they maintain traditions in their home life.

1803. Lame Deer, or John Fire (Teton Sioux) and Richard Erdoes. Lame Deer, Seeker of Visions. Simon, 1972.

Opens with his vision experience at age sixteen. His greatest fear was that he would not receive a vision: he wanted to be a medicine man. In his vision he obtained his request: he would be a medicine man. And he received a new name: Lame Deer. His great grandfather had been the first Lame Deer, and his standard had been high. His encounters with the white man's civilization in school, reservation, Missions, bronco busting, and working as a hired hand had all been unhappy. These episodes were interspersed by intervals of tribal life to obtain more knowledge about "medicine" and the ancient ways. He "tried out" the peyote religion but regarded it as a dead end, and chose to go the way of the sacred pipe. After the Normandy invasion of France (World War II) the army discovered he was over 39 and released him. Then he settled down to the life of a "full-time" Indian.

1804. Left Handed. (Navajo) Son of Old Man Hat: A Navajo Autobiography. As told to Walter Dyk. Lincoln: U. of Nebr. Pr., 1967 [1938].

Left Handed records his own daily activities as a member of his family and clan. The life of a Navaho was one of continuous struggle for food. Navaho country is a land of little rain. Grazing sheep and goats in that region necessitated a nomadic life. During the summer the mountains gave relief from the burning sun for man, beast and corn. During the winter the canyons offered protection from the elements. Children were trained early for a life of physical endurance. Herding sheep and goats from sunrise to sunset was considered the daily task of a child of ten. Men, women and children all shared in the care of the herds: the wealth of the family.

The cultivation of corn, the staple food, required constant attention from planting to harvest. Left Handed's life was rather unspectacular. Although many women were attracted and attractive to him, his marriages were not successful.

1805. Longstreet, David. (Apache) "Personal Narrative of David Longstreet." In Western Apache Raiding and Warfare. U. of Arizona Pr., 1971, pp. 187-203.

Apache legends and customs are told; also the author's experiences as a government scout. Revenge was an inborn instinct and would send the natives on the warpath.

1806. Lowry, Annie. (Paiute) Karnee: A Paiute Narrative. Ed. by Lalla Scott. Reno: U. of Nevada Pr., 1966.

The story of Annie, half-blood, and her mother, Sau-tau-nee, full-blood, affords a contrasting picture in Indian-white relations. The time is the pre-reservation and pre-missionary era. The place is northwestern Nevada before the discovery of gold in California and silver in Nevada. Attending school with white children was not without its tensions. Her father's disloyalty to her mother influenced her in assessing the white man's way and deciding for the Native way of life.

1807. McCarty, Darlene. (Yakima) "A Day with Yaha" [personal narrative]. In Milton, John R., comp., The American Indian Speaks. Vermillion: U. of South Dakota Press, 1969, pp. 119-125.

Going to the cemetery with the family on Decoration Day to clean up the family graves brings to mind many happy times with Yaha (grandmother).

1808. Mathews, John Joseph. (Osage) Talking to the Moon. U. of Chicago Press, 1945.

Twelve beautifully written autobiographical nature essays based on life in the geographical area which the author locates "between the Great Plains and the Woodlands."

1809. Mitchell, Emerson Blackhorse. (Navajo) Miracle

Hill: The Story of a Navajo Boy. Assisted by T. D. Allen. Norman: U. of Okla. Pr., 1967.

Mitchell pours forth charm, beauty and joy as he writes his own story. As a small boy ambitious to learn English and curious about the rest of the world, going to school was not for him the traumatic experience of most Natives. He tells his story with detachment and humor as though he were observing someone else. His family relationships are typically Navaho: reared by his grandparents, tending sheep, assisting with activities about the hogan, indulging in escapades with his cousin Annie and his horse, Pinto. Mitchell employs the word "miracle" to account for, describe or analyze special events and happenings in his life. To him learning the English language was a miracle. It opened up for him a world of expression. One day at his home he sees a glow on the hill, and starts out to investigate; but he hesitates and does not go until some time later. He and his sister each see a stranger on the hill, but they find no evidence of him. Eventually he meets him, and he tells Mitchell that his life is just beginning. Then the stranger becomes a rock on a distant hill. He utters a prayer of Thanksgiving: he knows there will be other "Miracle Hills."

1810. Mitchell, Emerson B. (Navajo) "Miracle Hill" [excerpt]. In Faderman, Lillian & Barbara Bradshaw, eds., Speaking for Ourselves: American Ethnic Writing. Foresman, 1969, pp. 482-490.

1811. ________. "Miracle Hill" [story excerpt]. In Sanders, Thomas E. & Walter W. Peek, Literature of the American Indian. Glencoe Pr., 1973, pp. 482-91.

1812. Moises, Rosalio. (Yaqui) The Tall Candle; The Personal Chronicle of a Yaqui Indian. Joint authors: Jane Holden Kelley and Wm. Curry Holden. U. of Neb. Pr., 1971.

This extremely detailed account written by Moises himself in English (edited to the extent it is better organized and more easily read) portrays the life of the Yaqui Indian in the late nineteenth century and up to the 1950's in Northwest

Mexico. From time to time he worked in Arizona and California, but in spite of the higher wages, the call of the Rio Yaqui, home of his people, was stronger. Life there was a continuous struggle; the land suffered from drought or flood, with hunger, loss of property and life the expected consequences. Little help would come from a tyrannical Mexican government. In the final chapter he expresses a hope for the future of the Yaquis: irrigation projects and modern farming methods organized by the government. The fifty-six page introduction is extremely valuable in the understanding and appreciation of Yaqui culture. There is also a brief bibliography which includes Edw. Spicer's studies of the Yaqui.

1813. Momaday, Natachee Scott. (Cherokee) American Indian Authors. Houghton, 1972.

Includes biographical information about twenty Native American authors, from Chief Joseph to Patty Harjo, with an excerpt from each one's works. Discussion questions are added about each author's ideas.

1814. Monture, Ethel Brant. (Mohawk) Famous Indians: Brant, Crowfoot, and Oronhyatekha. Toronto: Clarke, Irwin, and Co., Ltd., 1960.

1815. ________. Joseph Brant: Mohawk. In collaboration with Harvey Chalmers. Michigan State U. Pr., 1955.

Brant's life was one of devotion to a fair land settlement from the British and Americans for his people following the Treaty of Paris, 1783. His objective was to maintain the Stanwix line, West and North of which had been declared as Indian territory. Problems arose from white settlers' infringements beyond this line, and Britain's failure to give the Indians clear title to Grand River, Quinte and other reservations. The book is a very detailed account of the strategy carried on between Brant on behalf of the Indian tribes, the British governors, generals and superintendents, in addition to American leaders: Washington and others. Explanatory footnotes are found at the end of each chapter. A bibliography of sources would have been useful. References are made within the text to journals and letters of individuals. It is assumed that Ethel Brant Monture provided the sources for facts about Brant. The study is scholarly in approach and discloses an intimate and thorough knowledge of the political history of the period: British, American and Indian.

1816. Mountain Wolf Woman. (Winnebago) Mountain Wolf Woman, Sister of Crashing Thunder: The Autobiography of a Winnebago Woman. Ed. by Nancy Oestreich Lurie. Ann Arbor: U. of Mich. Pr., 1961.

A delightful, spontaneous, warm-hearted recording of a Winnebago woman's life. As the sister of Crashing Thunder, her story complements his. His life was an unresolved conflict, whereas hers was a positive expression. Ms. Lurie, as an adopted Winnebago within Mountain Wolf Woman's clan, ably establishes a relationship of trust which frees Mountain Wolf Woman to detail effectively the events of her life. Her life was that of the traditional Native who moved about seasonally to take advantage of nature's produce: blueberries, cranberries, Indian potatoes, and deer hunting. She also experienced short periods of living in South Dakota and Nebraska in addition to her native Wisconsin home at Black River Falls. She was able to embrace and appropriate many of the white man's ways and found no insurmountable conflict between Christianity and Peyotism. She was also able to participate in Native rites and ceremonies with respect for their sacred aspects.

1817. Nowell, Charles James. (Kwakiutl) Smoke from Their Fires. As told to Clellan S. Ford. Archon, 1968 [1941].

Charles Nowell reveals intimate details of his life among his people, the Kwakiutl of North America's Northwest coast. In addition, Mr. Ford provides a forty-page introduction to Kwakiutl culture. Thus this is a source of first-hand information on their tribal life. The most significant and distinctive of their customs was the potlach. It was a give-away in honor of a family event, planned in advance. Blankets or coppers were the usual gifts: each recipient was given according to his status in the tribe. Charley's father advised him to continue the custom. It was a matter of honor, and in a sense an insurance policy.

1818. Nuligak. (Eskimo) I, Nuligak. Trans. from Eskimo by Maurice Melayer. Illus. by Ekootak. Peter Martin Associates, 1966.

Born in 1895 in the Canadian Arctic, Nuligak experienced changes in his 60+-year life from that time until mid-20th century comparable to those between Neolithic times and now.

1819. Old Mexican. (Navajo) Old Mexican, A Navajo Autobiography. As told to Walter Dyk. N.Y.: Viking, 1947. (Viking Fund Publication in Anthropology, No. 8).

His time and health were at the mercy of his drive to accumulate wealth and satisfy his personal ego. His inventive mind devised a method of building an irrigation dam and ditches to divert the precious rainfall to his fields of corn, oats, hay, melons and squash, with only a shovel for a tool. His life was disciplined and almost regimented. There was no time for gambling and drinking, nor did he attend squaw dances and sings, because his animals might be neglected. Through the customary bartering at the government agency, he acquired other tools and eventually a wagon which enabled him to haul freight from Winslow, Ft. Defiance and other points. Personal happiness was not his lot. His marriages, more or less forced upon him, were endured. His children did not play an important role in his life, but he did not neglect their needs.

1820. Oskison, John M. (Cherokee) Tecumseh and His Times; the Story of a Great Indian. Putnam, 1938.

Expresses the Native American viewpoint of American history, documented by letters of Jefferson, Harrison and others. The relationship between the Natives and the British and the French is clarified. The question is asked: Why remember Tecumseh? He was a man of honesty and fearlessness: two qualities required of those who would be leaders. Tecumseh hoped to regain for his people the land and life which they were losing to the white man. This hope still lives. The author speaks from his own soul as he depicts the man, Tecumseh.

1821. Pelletier, Milfred. (Odawa) "Childhood in an Indian Village." In David, Jay, ed., The American Indian, the First Victim. Morrow, 1972, pp. 56-69.

1822. Pitseolak. (Eskimo) Pictures out of My Life. Ed. from tape-recorded interviews by Dorothy Eber. Toronto: Oxford U. Pr., 1971.

Illustrated with colored pencil, felt pen and stone cuts--some in color.

1823. Plenty-Coups, or Aleek-chea-ahoosh. (Crow) Plenty-Coups, Chief of the Crows. Ed. by Frank Bird Linderman. Lincoln: U. of Nebr. Pr., 1962 [1930].

Many Native and White Americans had expressed an interest in the life-story of Plenty-Coups, a distinguished Crow Chief of extraordinary personal character and leadership qualities. Assured that Linderman's motives were to further a better understanding between Native and White American, he agreed to have his narration recorded. Rigorous physical training prepared a native boy for a life as hunter and warrior. His "medicine" [Spirit's power] was revealed to him by means of the sweat lodge fasting and dreams which culminated in the vision experience. The chickadee was divulged as the natural creature for Plenty-Coups to emulate as one who listens to learn. The chickadee became the model for the small Crow tribe. And thus they rationalized their scouting activities for the U.S. Army, and survived. He closes his account with the passing of the buffalo, and the beginning of degradation on reservations.

1824. Price, Anna, or Her Eyes Grey. (Apache) "Personal Narrative of Anna Price." In Western Apache Raiding and Warfare. Tucson: U. of Ariz. Pr., 1971, pp. 29-39.

The author, almost one hundred years of age, recalls her people's adventures: recovering stolen horses, a woman's miraculous escape from Mexicans, and war party victories and losses.

1825. Qoyawayma, Polingaysi, or Elizabeth Q. White. (Hopi) No Turning Back: A True Account of a Hopi Indian Girl's Struggle to Bridge the Gap Between the World of Her People and the World of the White Man. As told to Vada F. Carlson. Albuquerque: U. of N.M. Pr., 1964.

Polingaysi's spirit of independence and curiosity served her well throughout her life. As a child, in opposition to her parent's conservative attitude, but more because she wanted to find out for herself, she chose to attend the white missionary school. Little did she realize that she was embarking on a journey of learning and that she would make her greatest contribution to her people in the field of education.

1826. Relander, Click, or Now-tow Look. Drummers and Dreamers. Story of Smowhala, the Prophet, and His Nephew Puck Hyah Toot, the Last Prophet of the Nearly Extinct River People, the Last Wanapums. Caxton, 1956.

1827. Rogers, Will. (Cherokee) An Autobiography. Selected and edited by Donald Day. Houghton, 1949.

Excerpts from Will Rogers' writings selected by Donald Day, organized chronologically, form this autobiography. A master of understatement, he possessed the envied talent to view his own life and that of the nation and the world in perspective and with a judicious sense of humor. His observations are as pertinent today as they were forty years ago.

1828. Rope, John, or Black Rope. (Apache) "Personal Narrative of John Rope." In Western Apache Raiding and Warfare. U. of Ariz. Pr., 1971, pp. 93-185.

Rope introduces his narrative with recollections of childhood participation in the family's food-gathering activities: hunting rats and rabbits, picking acorns and juniper berries, as well as planting, caring for and harvesting corn. In the major portion of his account he refers to numerous customs, taboos, and characteristics of his people as he recounts his life as a scout with General Crook against the Chiricahua tribe. This is a valuable source of information on the times of Geronimo and Victorio.

1829. Sekaquaptewa, Helen. (Hopi) Me and Mine: The Life Story of Helen Sekaquaptewa. As told to Louise Udall. Tucson: U. of Ariz. Pr., 1969.

To Helen the government school proved to be enjoyable. Her eagerness to learn and her ability to appropriate the white man's education and religion, at the same time as she acknowledged the good in her own culture, enriched the pattern and quality of her life. Fortunately her husband, Emory, allied himself with her in these ideas. They both suffered the unfriendly and critical attitude of their Hopi neighbors. Encroached on all sides by Navahos, the Hopis and Navahos are traditional enemies. However, Helen and Emory bridged this chasm at least in one instance. In addition to their ten children they adopted two more--one a Navaho, who chose to live with them rather than his own family.

1830. Senungetuk, Joseph. (Eskimo) Give or Take a Century: The Story of an Eskimo Family. San Francisco: The Indian Historian Pr., 1970.

The anguish that was and is Alaska comes through in this autobiography with lacerating clarity. For over four centuries it was ravished by exploiters (explorers): Oriental, European, and finally American, the first of whom were either searching out a route to the Atlantic, or fishing the coastal waters, and later stripping the country of its fur-bearing animals. The title refers to this long period of endurance on the part of the natives: Eskimo; Indian and Aleut. Also embodied in the title is the continuing present-day conflict to settle the issues of Native Land Claims and the Alaskan Pipe Line. On these decisions hinge the shape and future of tomorrow's Eskimo generations, and their relationships with the white man. Specifically, this is the story of the Eskimos of Northwest Alaska at Wales, the author's ancestral village, where he lived until 1950. Then his father made the decision to move to Nome and live the life of an independent citizen with its responsibilities rather than remain in Wales under the Bureau of Indian Affairs.

1831. Sewid, James. (Kwakiutl) Guests Never Leave Hungry: The Autobiography of James Sewid, a Kwakiutl Indian. Ed. James P. Spradley. New Haven: Yale U. Press, 1969.

A Native American autobiography which was a source for an anthropological research project. James Sewid is unique in that he could adjust to two cultures. He maintained a full commitment to his native customs and became a successful businessman, active in local, state and national affairs. The title is taken from one of his Indian names, Poogleedee, which means "guests never leave his feasts hungry." This native trait of hospitality ran parallel in his personality with a magnanimous regard for individual and group welfare in family and clan, in the village, state and nation. All this he did without claims of power or privilege for himself. Commitment and involvement best characterize him in his responsibilities to family, clan, civic and religious affairs. He was instrumental in obtaining for his village, from the Canadian government, the privilege of an elected village council. This was a first in the progress of village government. He, as elected chief councillor, delegated the other three members as chairmen for local affairs: buildings, entertainment and recreation, and fire protection. He urged unity and opposed divisive elements, and encouraged a spirit of democracy.

1832. Shaw, Anna Moore. (Pima) A Pima Past. U. of Arizona Pr., 1974.

1833. Standing Bear, Chief Luther. (Sioux) Land of the Spotted Eagle. Houghton, 1933.

1834. ________. My Indian Boyhood. Houghton, 1928.

1835. ________. My People the Sioux. Ed. by E. A. Brininstool. Houghton, 1928.

During the latter part of the nineteenth century, a number of Native Americans were venturing to live the white man's way. The Anglo-American's wanton destruction of the buffalo completely altered the Native American's economic position. Forced to inhabit and extract an existence from unfarmable land, Luther volunteered to "go East" to the new Indian school at Carlisle, Pa. This occurred in 1879, the year of the school's opening. Shockingly inadequate physical facilities and deplorable teaching methods did not deter Luther from his determination to "make it" in a white world. Fortunately he possessed a sense of humor and physical stamina. After several years he became a teacher to his own people, and assisted his father in the agency store. His constant concern for his people's welfare culminated in his struggle to acquire citizenship for himself. For an Indian to be native born was not considered sufficient evidence. The U.S. government required triple proof: 1) He did not drink whiskey; 2) He was able to make a living off the reservation; 3) He had been educated. He traveled to Washington to attest to these facts and refused to leave until five weeks later when the document was forthcoming. In 1925 he gave up his business to write this book, which is a primary source of historical significance on his people, the Sioux.

1836. Stands in Timber, John (Cheyenne) and Margot Liberty. Cheyenne Memories, A Folk History. Assisted by Robert M. Utley. New Haven: Yale U. Pr., 1967.

Memories of a life as lived during the tragic years of a Native American tribe, the Cheyenne. Begins with creation stories, and the legend of their culture hero, Sweet Medicine. From these sources emerge the religious beliefs and philosophies which governed the Cheyenne way of life. Describes in considerable detail many of the ceremonies, the import of personal "medicine," historical events, and the continuing problems of "getting civilized," all of which the author experienced. The co-author has produced a documented study with a supportive bibliography and index.

1837. ________. "I Bid You Farewell." The Indian Historian. (Dec., 1967) 10-11.

He recalls learning to wake up to watch the sun rise. His mother said that the "sun had other things to do than to awaken him."

1838. Stanley, Mrs. Andrew. (Apache) "Personal Narrative of Mrs. Andrew Stanley." In Western Apache Raiding and Warfare. U. of Ariz. Pr., 1971, pp. 205-219.

Survival and escape from enemies in the Southwest desert regions required an intuitive nature, spirit of independence, boldness, daring and tenacity. Mrs. Stanley, a White Mountain Apache, eluded her captors, the Chiricahua, and matched her wits against nature, man and beast. All of this she recounts undramatically.

1839. Sweezy, Carl. (Arapaho) The Arapaho Way: A Memoir of an Indian Boyhood. As told to Althea Bass. N.Y.: Clarkson N. Potter, Inc., 1966.

1840. Talayesva, Don C. (Hopi) Sun Chief: The Autobiography of a Hopi Indian. Ed. by Leo W. Simmons. New Haven: Yale U. Pr., 1942.

A portion of a project for an anthropological study, originally written as a detailed diary by Don, Sun Chief contributes distinctively to information on Hopi culture. Don reveals himself as a person who exhibited extraordinary traits early in life, and was believed to have special powers. His account corroborates and complements that of other Hopi. While a student at Sherman Institute at Riverside, Calif., he contracted pneumonia. In his feverish state he had a vision which he regarded as the most significant event in his life. It was long and involved and he tells it in detail. He was led by his Guardian Spirit to the House of the Dead, and it was revealed to him that the Hopi road was the way for him to follow, rather than the Christian which he had encountered at the Riverside school. Later in life he did not regret having had a taste of white culture. It prepared him to meet the white man on an equal footing.

1841. Tetso, John. (Slavey) "Rabbit Hunting." In Gooderham, Kent, ed., I Am an Indian. Dent, 1969, pp. 112-13.

Tetso was a columnist for the Fort Simpson Catholic Voice. His writings were published after his death. The above is an excerpt from his book, Trapping Is My Life.

1842. Traveller Bird. (Cherokee) Tell Them They Lie; the Sequoyah Myth. Westernlore, 1971.

Claims that Sequoyah did not invent the Cherokee syllabary, but rather that he revived it. Its origin is ancient, and he, as a member of the Seven Scribe Society, was a keeper of its records. In 1795 he and other tribal members organized to teach their own people the 92 symbols of their original language, and prove to the white government that they were traditionally a literate people. Non-Indians refused to believe these facts and altered them, saying Sequoyah was a mixed-blood and therefore more intelligent than a Native. Thus they accounted for the language as an invention of Sequoyah, which until now has been accepted.

1843. Two Leggings. (Crow) Two Leggings: The Making of a Crow Warrior. Ed. by Peter Nabokov. Crowell, 1967.

Two Leggings' over-eagerness and impatience to attain the status of warrior, and get on with exploits which would secure for him a name among his people, pivoted his problems. He was reluctant to wait out the time until he received a vision of his life's goal from the Great Spirit. When a voice did speak he was apt to doubt its power. Also, he did not always consult with the elders in the interpretation of his dreams. Eventually he did win victories and returned to camp with captured horses and scalps which gave him the long-desired acclaim of his people.

1844. Valor, Palmer. (Apache) "Personal Narrative of Palmer Valor." In Western Apache Raiding and Warfare. U. of Ariz. Pr., 1971, pp. 41-71.

Concentrates on techniques and skills of horse raiding and warpathing, both of which brought him success and standing among his tribe; the White Mountain Apache horses were needed for food and transportation. Successful raids were followed by a feast and a victory dance.

1845. Vizenor, Gerald R. (Anishinabe) Thomas James White Hawk. Mound, Minn.: The Four Winds, 1968.

To all appearances, James White Hawk had

everything going for him. He was a credit to white education: mission, public and military schools, and finally a freshman in the pre-med program at the University of South Dakota. He had a girl friend; he wanted marriage. One night there was a gun, beer--and suddenly a dead jeweler. The rights of the accused to a speedy trial took no account of his medical or his personal history.

1846. Vogel, Virgil J. <u>This Country Was Ours; a Documentary History of the American Indian</u>. Harper, 1972.

Appendix 3: Famous Americans of Indian Descent, pages 310-50, furnishes an additional source of biographical information, especially about contemporary Native Americans.

1847. Waheenee, or Buffalo-Bird Woman. (Mandan-Hidatsa) <u>An Indian Girl's Story</u>. As told to Gilbert L. Wilson. Illus. by Frederick N. Wilson. St. Paul, Minn.: Webb Pub. Co., 1921. Also in: <u>North Dakota History</u>. v. 38 (Winter & Spring, 1971) 7-176.

Waheenee mirrors the significance and dignity of domestic life in Native American culture. It was a disciplined life in which man and woman, old and young, were infused by legend and example to identify themselves and each other as persons within a scheme for daily living in time of tranquility as well as in time of danger. She portrays minutely the intimate life of her family as integral to the Mandan-Hidatsa community on the Missouri River near the mouth of the Knife River in the late nineteenth century. Each child perceived his or her niche in the family and tribe, as a contributor to daily life as well as one in whom the hope of the future was entrusted. She treasures the memories of her growing-up years and early married life as she recalls them late in her life. The numerous clear, finely drawn illustrations enhance the text.

1848. White Bull, Joseph, or Pte-san-hunka. (Teton-Dakota) <u>The Warrior Who Killed Custer. The Personal Narrative of Chief Joseph White Bull</u>. U. of Nebr. Pr., 1969.

A personal account which establishes both White Bull and Custer as brave men. They met in hand-to-hand combat. White Bull says he never fought so hard, and credits Custer with being "strong and brave"--qualities much admired by Native Americans. White Bull also describes his other activities as Chief: successful hunting, raiding and warring expeditions. A typical Teton Dakota Winter Count which White Bull obtained from Hairy Hand forms a part of this personal history. Its first date is 1764/65 and White Bull brings it up to 1930/31. Thirty-nine plates are reproductions of White Bull's pictographs, which are valuable in themselves and as illustrations of the subject.

1849. Whitewolf, Jim. (Kiowa Apache) Jim Whitewolf: The Life of a Kiowa Apache Indian. Ed. by Charles S. Brant. Dover Bks., 1969.

Whitewolf's autobiography is another ethnographic study which enlarges our acquaintance with tribal cultures and preserves for the Kiowa Apache their traditions. His life bridges two cultures: native and white, and the demands of each engendered conflict within him. He describes himself as chiefly interested in "drinking, gambling and running around with women, like his father." Later in life he embraced the Native American Church with its ceremonial use of peyote. He also was baptized in the Baptist Church because all of his relatives were, and for a few years was an active member. The Native American experienced no conflict in being a member of both churches at the same time. Each one offered gifts from the Great Spirit.

1850. Winnie, Lucille "Jerry," or Sah-gan-de-oh. (Seneca-Cayuga) Sah-gan-de-oh, the Chief's Daughter. Vantage Pr., 1968.

Sah-gan-de-oh (Corn Blossom) achieved her life's ambition and carried on in her father's zealous spirit as a teacher to her people at reservation schools. Her warm, outgoing personality and adventuresome disposition were both valuable assets in her firm resolve to "see-the-world" and "earn-her-way" while doing so. Without completing a college degree, and in spite of a constant battle with health problems, she proved to her people (and others), with her pioneering spirit, resourcefulness, native organizational ability and dogged determination to surmount difficulties and demonstrate success, that the reviving of their heritage of arts and crafts was a spiritual as well as a material necessity. As Director of Arts and Crafts of the Northern Plains Indians, Browning, Montana, she surveyed the potential in arts and crafts on the Northern Cheyenne Reservations, searched out authentic patterns, set-up training programs and standards for quality workmanship, solved problems of quantity production, price standards, etc. The journalistic style of the author, her contagious spirit and practical ideas should occasion the reprinting of this title.

1851. Wooden Leg. (Cheyenne) Wooden Leg: A Warrior Who Fought Custer. As told to Thomas B. Marquis. Lincoln: U. of Nebr. Pr., 1962.

The Cheyenne were among the six bands and tribes of natives when Custer engaged them in battle at the Little Big Horn. Wooden Leg was a participant; therefore his account is source material for the historian. As Wooden Leg recounts it and as Thomas B. Marquis documents it, Custer's troops were young, inexperienced men from the east, unacquainted with Indian style of warfare. Actually they were not outnumbered. However, Indian ambush and tactics provoked panic, and rather than face the natives, Custer's men turned their guns upon themselves. Wooden Leg recounts this incident as a detail of his life, which was designed in the traditional way by his parents to develop in him the qualities of endurance and bravery through physical strength and religious precepts.

1852. Zitkala-sa, or Gertrude Bonin. (Dakota) "Impressions of an Indian Childhood." In Gross, Theodore L., ed., A Nation of Nations. Macmillan, 1971, pp. 160-2.

At age seven, Zitkala, disturbed by her mother's tears, questioned her about the "bad paleface." Her mother did not give details, but only said that the white man was more concerned about his own laws being obeyed than sustaining the life of Indian people.

1853. Zitkala-sa, or Gertrude Bonin. (Dakota) "Impressions of an Indian Childhood." Atlantic Monthly. v. 85 (January, 1900) 37-47.

This longer account of Impressions contains a group of delicately etched vignettes, which focus the beauty of relationships within her family.

Part 5

FICTION

1854. Bennett, Kay & Russ Bennett. Navajo Saga. Naylor, 1969.

The preface is devoted to imparting historical background, explicating the Navajo religion, and making some comparisons with world religions. The Saga is an historical novel depicting the life of the Navajos before, during and after their removal by U. S. government troops from their traditional homeland in present-day Northeast Arizona to Fort Sumner in Southwest New Mexico. It was a time of suffering, starvation, and death. The Federal government was lacking in knowledge of the Navajo people, of area geography, of the quantity of food, clothing, and numbers of horses and wagons needed to transport that number of people. The total unfitness of the area for agriculture and food production forced the U. S. to reverse its decision and return the people to their homeland. As a method of population decimation this procedure was extremely successful. One episode which contributes to the drama of the story is the retaliatory capture of Shebah, daughter of Grey Hat. After being a slave in a Mexican family for about 20 years, she escaped with her son, back to Navajo country.

1855. Eagle, Dallas. (Sioux) Winter Count. Denver: Golden Bell Press, 1968.

The story opens with preparations for and the marriage of Turtleheart and Evensigh (white captive who had known only the Indian way of life), who were one in heart and mind. As they were on the return journey from the traditional time Indian newlyweds spent together, they were attacked by three white men and a Santee Sioux.

Evensigh was taken captive and Turtleheart was left for dead. Before they were reunited a number of years later, Evensigh was adopted by a St. Louis white family. Turtleheart spent months in search of her before he returned to tribal life. Unhappiness sent him on a vision quest and participation in a Sun dance. He, together with Crazy Horse, Dull Knife and Gall, engaged in conflicts with other tribes and also skirmishes with the U.S. Army, including surrender at Wounded Knee (1890). The tale is one of deep love, bravery, loyalty and tragedy.

1856. Eagle Voice. (Sioux) When the Tree Flowered; the Fictional Autobiography of Eagle Voice, a Sioux Indian. As told to John G. Neihardt. U. of Nebr. Pr., 1970 [1952].

Eagle Voice recalls a better time for his people and himself: the history, legends, and outstanding personal events; the rigors of his vision quest, the satisfaction he found in being able to endure in the sun dance. There is a mutual understanding, a warmth of affection, kindness and a delicate sense of humor.

1857. Hale, Janet Campbell. (Coeur d'Alêne) The Owl's Song. Doubleday, 1974.

The owl sang its song for the passing of a person. That was what Waluwetsu (the Old One) had said, and soon it would sing for the end of the Red Man. To Billy in his 14th year this appeared as a possibility when he graduated from the village school where he never seemed to belong. This is another story which depicts the cry of the young Native American in his struggle with a white world which fails to see him as a human and a person; a world where he needs a courage grounded in his native religious heritage, which again a white world has all but succeeded in obliterating. During a year in a big-city school he suffers continual degradation. The one ray of hope, the discovery of his artistic talent, is soon extinguished when he is deprived of the opportunity of exhibiting his work. As he returns to his father, he senses an unexpected warmth and satisfaction in his home environment which sustains in him hope for the future. He is supported in this belief as he recalls a "vision" --his vision--but under unusual circumstances.

1858. Hum-ishu-Ma or Mourning Dove. (Okanagan) Co-ge-we-a, the Half-Blood: A Depiction of the Great Montana Cattle Range. As told to Sho-pow-tan. Boston: The Four Seas Co., 1927.

1859. McNickle, D'Arcy. (Flathead) Runner in the Sun; a Story of Indian Maize. Holt, 1954.

The corn was lacking in vitality; a new strain should be found, also a new source of water. Salt was 16, had received the turquoise ornament, and been admitted to the Kiva. Some of the elders were displeased with him for suggesting that corn be planted in the valley rather than in the upper fields. There was dissension in the tribe. His turquoise badge was removed, and his status of manhood. Humiliated at being called a child again, he visited Eldest Woman and the Holy One, who both gave hard advice but in love. He uncovered the secret route of the plotters, and the Holy One sent him on a mission to bring back a New Way, to the south, the Land of Fable: the source of their songs, dances and Mother Corn. If he is successful, the tribe will honor him as leader. Over a year later he returned. Even then he wasn't sure that he had been successful.

1860. ________. The Surrounded. Dodd, 1936.

Archilde was the youngest of the eleven children of Max Leon, non-Indian Spaniard, wealthy rancher, and Catharine, daughter of a Salish Chief. He was the first in his family to be educated through high school, and had just returned from Portland, where he had earned money playing the violin. On his arrival he was greeted with the news that his brother Louis had stolen fifty horses and that the Sheriff was out to get him. On a three-day hunting trip Catharine and Archilde encountered the hunted--Louis. The game warden unexpectedly walked into their camp. He fired at Louis and killed him. Catharine instinctively attacked and killed the warden. Archilde buried him and in Indian style concealed the grave. They brought the body of Louis home. The remainder of the story centers on the family and racial tensions aroused by the two killings. Whether or not justice was served is not indicated.

1861. Markoosie. (Eskimo) Harpoon of the Hunter. McGill-Queen's U. Pr., 1970.

Tragedy stalks the lives of the Eskimos. Hunting the polar bear and crossing open water on ice floes are all extremely dangerous. Skill and bravery are required. Kamik, son of Suluk and Ooramik, holds out against the rabid polar bear after other village hunters lose their lives. Crossing the bay on ice floes compounds tragedy in his life. It is more than he can endure.

1862. Mathews, John Joseph. (Osage) Sundown. Longmans, 1934.

Given the name Challenge by his father was not significant to Chal. He could have met the challenges of white society, even at the University, where he was "courted" as good football material. Also, he could have made it in the classroom. The money from the Osage oil would have paid for it all. Many of his friends joined the gin crowd, and he tried it out. When the boom years were over, the Depression years sifted out the real values. For Chal, his heart provided the answers. They had been there all the time, fostered by his mother and for the most part unspoken. He cherished the memories of his childhood: riding his horse on the prairie, dreaming under the blackjacks and fishing in the streams. And now, watching his childhood friend, Sun-on-His-Wings, dance in the tribal dances, he wanted to be a part of it. He sensed a spiritual exhilaration after the sweat lodge purification rite, and a feeling of completeness in the fellowship of the festival.

1863. Momaday, N. Scott. (Kiowa) House Made of Dawn. Harper, 1969.

An effective and objective portrayal of the contemporary Native American's dilemma. The locale is a Southwest Pueblo, rich in its own cultural and spiritual heritage and with a dutiful respect to feasts and ceremonies brought by Spanish priests. The time is the close of World War II. Abelito has fought honorably but now is overwhelmed by a great revulsion against the horrors of war. He expresses the revolt of his spirit by returning home to his well-loved grandfather in a drunken condition. Grandfather Francisco's deep love and understanding enable him to accept Abelito. The story emerges as a whole fabric by means of the author's weaving together flashbacks of Abelito's childhood in which he recalls his spiritual heritage in legend and myth. These are interspersed with unfortunate episodes in Abelito's struggle: six years in jail, on parole in the City and attempting to conform. His struggle seems controlled by sinister forces which leave him physically crushed. "Guardian Angels" who understand are Father Olguin, Angela, Milly, Tosomah, and Benally. Mentally and spiritually he finds release and reconciliation with himself as he catches the spirit of Benally's glimpse of the "House Made of Dawn." He returns to his dying grandfather, and spiritually joins the "Runners" in his own pursuit of the "House Made of Dawn"--where there is resurrection and new life. A story of great power and beauty, more fully appreciated if one has previously read <u>The Way to Rainy Mountain</u>, and Kiowan legends.

1864. Nasnaga. (Shawnee) <u>Indians' Summer</u>. Harper, 1975.

What might have happened on July 4, 1976 if the Navajo, Sioux, Mohawk, Apache and Pueblo nations had declared their independence from the U.S.A. On the New Mexico desert, Oklahoma and South Dakota plains, St. Regis on the New York-Quebec border, Indian sentries are stationed so many thousand feet apart; National Guard units are in full array; well-organized armed units approach the Posts. At the same time there is a hush, a quiet which is disconcerting. The Republic of India presents the new nation to the United Nations ... there are meetings in the Oval office ... meetings in the office of the Prime Minister of Canada. Congressman Small Wolf is asked by the President why he has let things go this far. The book reviews and presents the Native American cause in straightforward, clear-cut statements. And because the "President" was at the "last ditch" he had no choice; he acted favorably for the Native American. The Bi-Centennial celebration went on--celebrated together by white and Native Americans.

1865. Oskison, John M. (Cherokee) Brothers Three. Macmillan, 1935.

Francis and Janet O'Dell began their married life as Oklahoma pioneer farmers in 1873. Their three sons, Timothy, Roger and Henry, better known as Timmy, Bunny and Mister, are each represented as a characteristic symbol of white American culture. Timmy is the wide-awake, opportunistic small town merchant. Bunny, also called the herdsman by his mother, invests in cattle and purchases grazing land. The well-kept farm of Pa O'Dell becomes an unwiedly ranch. Mister, the young man who is compelled to "get away" from home, loves to read, obtains an education, and becomes a writer in New York City. The three brothers, their wives and children are a strongly knit unit, with deep sentiments about the farm. By the mid-1920's the three brothers had each reached the pinnacle of success and were reeling from the revenues. The novel is an excellent evocation of the spirit of the roaring 20's, without cynicism. Family love and loyalty comes through--deep and sincere.

1866. ________. Wild Harvest; Novel of Transition Days in Oklahoma. Chicago: White House Pub., 1925.

A more-or-less contrived story of life in the early days of white settlement in Oklahoma Indian country. Indians play a very minor role. Nancy Forest, age fifteen, is the unselfish, kind, loving heroine, who hoes corn, repairs fences, rakes hay, assists her uncle, Billy Dines, in the barn, and aunt Susan Dines with the cooking and housekeeping. She hoped to attend college and become an elocutionist in the big city, where she would earn money to help her father, Chester, who was impatient and experimental. Uncle Billy and Aunt Sue Dines are the lovable, understanding, salt-of-the-earth folks. Tom Winger--not the typical cowboy, but a cowboy nevertheless--is the hero. Ruby Engel, rough, drinking, the antithesis of Nan in appearance, style and manner, is out to get Tom away from Nan--and almost succeeds. Harvey Stokes, slow stodgy, obtuse, selfish, jealous, moneymaker, becomes engaged to Nan after Ruby succeeds in ensnaring Tom. There is sufficient shooting to maintain the Western atmosphere and dispose of characters as they prove dispensable.

1867. Pierre, Chief George. (Colville) Autumn's Bounty. Naylor, 1972.

A proper title for this satisfying heroic story. Alphonse, a chief for fifty years, poor in this world's goods, ill in health and bearing the wounds of World War I, suffers the reproach of the community and his granddaughter for his stand against the government policy of reservation termination. He is sustained by the love and devotion of his great grandson, and is respected by the hunters as a great hunter. It is time for the annual cougar hunt but he is delayed in joining it when he is attacked and injured by four children. But the spirit triumphs over the physical. As he rides his old horse into the mountains, the journey becomes in part a spiritual pilgrimage. In dream and reverie he reviews the past and comes to terms with himself, with life and with death. Warding off two packs of coyotes, he uses up his ammunition and loses his gun. A snare is his only weapon against the cougar, and the symbol of the tenacity of his will to live, and his desire for a better life for the boy.

1868. Sneve, Virginia Driving Hawk. (Brule Sioux) When Thunders Spoke. Holiday House, 1974.

Ten-year-old Norman Two Bulls discovers a Wakan (holy) coup stick on Thunder Butte, from which place the Plains Indians believed the Thunders spoke the message of the Great Spirit. Succeeding events, associated with the stick, bring an appreciation of the old Indian truths and values to him, his father and even his Christian mother and the white trader, and a better understanding between them and his grandfather, who lived in the Old Ways. When the white tourist wants to climb the Sacred Thunder Butte and dig for agates, they all agree that the answer is: "No."

1869. Tebbel, John. (Ojibwa) The Conqueror. Dutton, 1951.

A pre-French and Indian War story which takes place in what is now New York State. The reader's interest is easily sustained as the novel moves along over the early years of the career of William Johnson, Irish immigrant, nephew of Sir Peter Warren, a politically influential New York City businessman. William's Irish charm, strong ambition, rugged health, self-confidence, plus insight deepened and supported by his loyal assistant Mich, make him a worthy representative of his uncle in his dealings both with the chiefs of the Six Nations and with the Crown. He achieves great respect, wealth and power. However, his romances fail to give him the deep satisfaction he hopes to gain with Susannah, who seems to be always beyond his reach.

1870. Welch, James. (Blackfoot) Winter in the Blood. Harper, 1974.

He is thirty years old. There seems to be nothing for him on the reservation. He didn't want to be exploited by the city and its organizations to obtain its federal grants, so he returns home. There he was not satisfied, just as his father, First Raise, before him had not been satisfied. They found him frozen to death as he was returning from one of his city bouts. His brother Mose at 14 was killed in a highway accident during the return of the cattle from the mountains. Now he discovers they were the only two he loved. Around him and more especially within him there is only a feeling of distance from others, and from himself. He seems drawn at times to Yellow Calf, the supposed Gros Ventre, blind, aged one who lives three miles away in a rude log hut, among the willows. Yellow Calf's communication is with the creatures of nature and the elements. They "tell" him what is going on--and he knows that "things" are not right. And who was his grandfather? He recalls his grandmother's stories of her girlhood when she was a beauty, and Standing Bear's third wife for only a few years; how after his death she was deserted as the source of tribal ill luck and faced with starvation. After her death and another visit to Yellow Calf, he comes upon another meaningful link in his life. The hope for continuity exists.

1871. Williams, Ted C. (Tuscarora) The Reservation. Illus. by the author. Syracuse U. Press, 1976.

One needs to read large portions of this book at one sitting to see it as a whole. Each episode could be compared to a block in a quilted pattern. At the end one comes away with the feeling that a full rich life has been lived in which the traditions and wisdom of the Elders come through in an earthy humorous philosophy. The continuous encroachments of the white man these hundred years and more have left their imprint. He regrets not remembering more of the wisdom of the Elders. He asks the question: Will the generations coming carry on?

Part 6

PRESENT DAY REALITIES WHICH RECALL MEMORIES OF AN EARLIER AND BETTER TIME: Interviews, Letters, Stories, and Other Prose Selections

1872. Banyacya, Thomas [for Hopi Traditional Village Leaders]. "Letter to President Nixon to Protest Peabody Coal Company's Stripping Coal from 65,000 Acres Leased from Navajo-Hopi Tribes." In McLuhan, T. C., ed., Touch the Earth. New York: Outerbridge & Dienstfrey, 1970, pp. 170-71.

1873. Bennett, Kay. (Navajo) "Letter to the Editor." In Milton, John R., comp., The American Indian Speaks. Vermillion: U. of S.D., 1969, pp. 171-172.

Justifies her reason for writing: to preserve a dying culture, she tells her own story and that of her people's struggle against the invading white man and his culture.

1874. Big White Owl, or Jasper Hill. "The History of America Started with Us." Blue Cloud Quarterly. v. 16, no. 2.

1875. Carter, Caleb. (Nez Percé) "The Nez Percé" [at Christmas]. In Henry, Jeannette, ed., The American Indian Reader: Literature. The Indian Historian Pr., 1973, pp. 127-8.

The Christmas season is usually celebrated by both the "old time Indian" and the "Christian Indian." Many participate in both events, which are marked by the giving of gifts.

1876. Cohoe, Grey. (Navajo) "The Promised Visit." In Milton, John R., comp., The American Indian

Speaks. Vermillion: U. of S.D., 1969, pp. 45-56.

During a storm the storyteller offered a ride to a hitchhiker, Susan Billy. She promised to visit him. Later he found the sweater he had loaned her, and learned the legend about Susan Billy.

1877. Cohoe, Grey. (Navajo) "The Promised Visit." In Momaday, Natachee Scott, American Indian Authors. Houghton, 1972, pp. 106-116.

1878. Cook, Liz. (Crow-Creek-Sioux) "A Child's Story." Pembroke Magazine. no. 7 (1976) 225-6.

1879. Cox, Terry. "Run" [prose]. In Angwamas Minosewag Anishinabeg. (Poets in the Schools Program) St. Paul Council of Arts and Sciences, Winter, 1973-74.

Running is an expression of freedom and excitement. But one can't just run; there must be purpose and goal.

1880. Defender, Adelina, or Eagle Wing. "No Time for Tears" [story]. In Tvedten, Benet, comp., An American Indian Anthology. Blue Cloud Abbey, 1971, pp. 23-31.

A day in the life of a brother and sister, who must hoe grandmother's corn, while dreaming of new clothes they will have to attend their father's graduation from the University of New Mexico at Albuquerque.

1881. Downing, Linda. (Cherokee) "Day of Confusion" [story]. In Allen, T. D., ed., Arrow II. U.S. Bureau of Indian Affairs, Creative Writing Project, 1970, pp. 13-15.

1882. Flores, Chester. (Papago) "The Four Brothers" [story]. In Allen, T. D., ed., Arrow IV. U.S. Bureau of Indian Affairs, Creative Writing Project, 1972, pp. 29-30.

1883. Francisco, Bertha. (Navajo) "Barry" [a letter]. In Allen, T. D., ed., Arrow III. U.S. Bureau of Indian Affairs, Creative Writing Project, 1971, p. 38.

1884. George, Dan. (Salish) "Our Sad Winter Has Passed." In Gooderham, Kent, ed., I Am an Indian. Dent, 1969, pp. 17-19.

Recalls past tribal glories, days of struggle and transition, and today's indication of personal achievement.

1885. Gerard, Mary Ann. (Blackfoot) "It's My Rock" [story]. In Allen, T. D., ed., Arrow I. U.S. Bureau of Indian Affairs, Creative Writing Project, 1969, pp. 19-29.

1886. Gorman, R. C. (Navajo) "Nowhere to Go." In Rosen, Kenneth, ed., The Man to Send Rain Clouds. Viking Press, 1974, pp. 61-5.

1887. Green, Richard. (Oneida) "The Coming: a Short Story Based on an Iroquois Prophecy." Indian Voice. (April, 1973) 29.

1888. Harjo, Patty. (Seneca-Seminole) "Who Am I?" [prose]. In Henry, Jeannette, ed., The American Indian Reader: Literature. The Indian Historian Pr., 1973, p. 113.

Declared for all Native Americans a vibrant tribute to earlier generations and an assured hope for the future.

1889. ________. "Who Am I?" [prose]. The Indian Historian. v. 1 (Sept., 1968) 25.

1890. ________. "Who Am I?" [prose]. In Momaday, Natchee Scott, American Indian Authors. Houghton, 1972, pp. 79-80.

1891. ________. "Who Am I?" [prose]. In Milton, John R., comp., The American Indian Speaks. Vermillion: U. of South Dakota, 1969, p. 141.

1892. John, Martha. (Navajo) "Writing in the Wind" [prose]. In Allen, T. D., ed., Arrow IV. U.S. Bureau of Indian Affairs, Creative Writing Project, 1972, pp. 15-17.

1893. John, Richard Johnny. (Seneca) "Interview with a Seneca Songman," by Jerome Rothenberg. Alcheringa. v. 3 (Winter, 1971) 82-93.

Tells how as a 14-year-old he belonged to the Singing Society which sang the old songs and made up new ones. He goes into the technique of composing songs for social dances and also for Sacred dances upon request.

1894. Jumper, Laura Lee. (Eastern Cherokee) "A Child's First Tragedy" [story]. In Allen, T. D., ed., Arrow II. U.S. Bureau of Indian Affairs, Creative Writing Project, 1970, pp. 23-6.

1895. Kilpatrick, Jack F. (Cherokee) "An Adventure Story of the Arkansas Cherokees, 1829." Arkansas Historical Quarterly, v. 26 (1967) 40-7.

1896. ________. and Anna G. Kilpatrick. "Letter from an Arkansas Cherokee Chief (1828-29)." Great Plains Journal. v. 5 (1965) 26-34.

Letters which reflect life and living in Arkansas, Oklahoma and Texas and add character to the history of a period.

1897. Kingbird, Brenda. "My Grandfather" [prose]. Angwamas Minosewag Anishinabeg. (Poets in the Schools Program) St. Paul Council of Arts and Sciences, Winter, 1973-74.

Pleasant recollections of her grandfather.

1898. Kingbird, Joe. "Our Family" [prose]. Angwamas Minosewag Anishinabeg. (Poets in the Schools Program) St. Paul Council of Arts and Sciences, Winter, 1973-74.

A statement of pride in and understanding of his culture.

1899. LaPointe, Frank. (Rosebud Sioux) "Millie's Gift" [story]. In Tvedten, Benet, comp., An American Indian Anthology. Blue Cloud Abbey, Blue Cloud Quarterly, 1971, pp. 14-17.

Grandmother Millie takes in stride the white man's way while living her own way.

1900. Leith, Vincent. "The Difference Between the Res. and The City" [prose]. Angwamas Minosewag Anishinabeg. (Poets in the Schools Program) St. Paul Council of Arts and Sciences, Winter, 1973-74.

1901. Lewis, Edward. (Pima) " Cowboy's Last Ride" [prose]. In Allen, T. D., ed., Arrow IV. U.S. Bureau of Indian Affairs, Creative Writing Project, 1972, pp. 18-20.

1902. Link, Curtis. (Apache-Navajo) "The Turquoise Beads" [story]. In Milton, John R., comp., The American Indian Speaks. Vermillion: U. of South Dakota, 1969, pp. 126-9.

1903. Little, Joseph. (Mescalero Apache) "Impressions on Turning Wombward." In Rosen, Kenneth, ed., The Man to Send Rain Clouds. Viking Press, 1974, pp. 66-8.

1904. ______. "Whispers from a Dead World." In Rosen, Kenneth, ed., The Man to Send Rain Clouds. Viking Press, 1974, pp. 27-31.

1905. Littlebud, Larry & the Members of Circle Film. (Pueblo) "Saves a Leader." In Rosen, Kenneth, ed., The Man to Send Rain Clouds. Viking Press, 1974, pp. 155-60.

1906. Livingston, Katie. "I Am or Was a Leaf" [prose]. Angwamas Minosewag Anishinabeg. (Poets in the Schools Program) St. Paul Council of Arts and Sciences, Winter, 1973-74.

My end is the same, whether I survive or turn out badly.

1907. Lowry, Henry Berry. (Lumbee) "From Outlaw to Folk Hero" [an interview by Randall and Brenda Ackley]. Quetzal. v. 2 (Winter-Spring, 1972) 52-64.

1908. Lucero, Margaret. (Santo Domingo Pueblo) "A Necklace for Jason" [story]. In Allen, T. D., ed., Arrow II. U.S. Bureau of Indian Affairs, Creative Writing Project, 1971, pp. 1-4.

1909. McDaniel, Mary. (Hukpapa-Oglala) "Our Word for the White Man Is Wasi'Chu." In Levitas, Gloria, Frank Robert & Jacqueline J. Vivelo, eds., American Indian Prose & Poetry. Putnam, 1974, pp. 300-01.

1910. Many Children, Selena. (Navajo) "My Mother" [story]. In Allen, T. D., ed., Arrow II. U.S. Bureau of Indian Affairs, Creative Writing Project, 1970, pp. 7-10.

1911. Mendoza, Durango. (Creek) "Summer Water and Shirley" [story]. In Faderman, Lillian & Barbara Bradshaw, eds., Speaking for Ourselves; American Ethnic Writing. Foresman, 1969, pp. 492-98.

A boy is observing his sister Shirley who is dying from a sickness which no medicine doctor, nor white doctor could heal.

1912. ________. "Summer Water and Shirley." In Momaday, Natachee Scott, American Indian Authors. Houghton, 1972, pp. 96-105.

1913. ________. "Summer Water and Shirley." Prairie Schooner. (Fall, 1966) 219-28.

1914. ________. "Summer Water and Shirley." In Sanders, Thomas E. & Walter W. Peek, Literature of the American Indian. Glencoe Pr., 1973, pp. 498-505.

1915. Momaday, N. Scott. (Kiowa-Cherokee) "Flight on the Wind" [story]. In Sanders, Thomas E. & Walter W. Peek, Literature of the American Indian. Glencoe Pr., 1973, pp. 492-7.

A legendary episode from the author's House Made of Dawn, which is part of Abel's recall of happier times in his childhood. The beauty, grace and power of the soaring eagles in their mating rites or as they zoom down to attack their prey could very well be an inspiration and source of strength to one seeking security.

1916. ________. "A Vision Beyond Time and Place." Life Magazine. (July 2, 1971) 67.

Responds to his recollection of his grandfather's story describing "old-man Cheney's" greeting to the Dawn. Standing on the same spot himself, Momaday confirms the wonder and majesty of the Dawn. The only response can be prayer and praise.

1917. Momaday, N. Scott. (Kiowa-Cherokee) "The Well" [story]. In Gross, Theodore L., ed., A Nation of Nations. Macmillan, 1971, pp. 420-425.

He remembered her when he was tending sheep. She had been old--and drunk. He had grown to manhood, left home, and now returned. She was still old--and still drunk. At the Jicarilla fiesta they made fun of her. She wanted more whiskey. They told her to go the whiskey well, and laughed. Only Hobson tried to help her.

1918. ________. "The Well." Ramparts. v. 2 (May, 1963) 49-52.

1919. Montana, David. (Papago) "Day Dawns on an Old Night" [story]. In Tvedten, Benet, comp., An American Indian Anthology. Marvin, S. D.: Blue Cloud Abbey, 1971, pp. 32-37.

1920. Nez, Ella. (Navajo) "The Fox and the Stars" [prose]. In Allen, T. D., ed., Arrow IV. U.S. Bureau of Indian Affairs, Creative Writing Project, 1972, pp. 21-2.

1921. Ortiz, Simon J. (Acoma Pueblo) "The End of Old Horse." In Rosen, Kenneth, ed., The Man to Send Rain Clouds. Viking, 1974, pp. 145-8.

1922. ________. "Kaiser and the War" [story]. New Mexico Quarterly. v. 38 (Winter-Spring, 1969) 29-38.

1923. ________. "Kaiser and the War." In Rosen, Kenneth, ed., The Man to Send Rain Clouds. Viking, 1974, pp. 47-60.

1924. ________. "Kaiser and the War." In Turner, Frederick W., III, The Portable North American Indian Reader. Viking, 1974, pp. 615-25.

1925. ________. "The Killing of a State Cop." In Rosen, Kenneth, ed., The Man to Send Rain Clouds. Viking Press, 1974, pp. 101-8.

1926. ________. "The San Francisco Indians." In Rosen, Kenneth, ed., The Man to Send Rain Clouds. Viking Press, 1974, pp. 9-13.

1927. Ortiz, Simon J. (Acoma Pueblo) "A Story of Rios and Juan Jesus." In Rosen, Kenneth, ed., The Man to Send Rain Clouds. Viking Press, 1974, p. 79-81.

1928. ________. "Woman Singing" [story]. In Milton, John R., comp., The American Indian Speaks. Vermillion: U. of South Dakota, 1969, pp. 34-44.

He had heard the woman singing a song of the people, but after last night he knew she would not sing it again.

1929. ________. "Woman Singing." In Sanders, Thomas E. & Walter W. Peek, Literature of the American Indian. Glencoe Pr., 1973, pp. 506-14.

1930. ________. "Woman Singing." In Tvedten, Benet, comp., An American Indian Anthology. Marvin, S. D.: Blue Cloud Abbey, 1971, pp. 1-13.

1931. Patkotak, Ethel. (Eskimo) "Spring at Home" [story]. In Allen, T. D., ed., Arrow II. U.S. Bureau of Indian Affairs, Creative Writing Project, 1970, pp. 17-18.

1932. Platero, Jaunita (Navajo) and Siyowin Miller. "Chee's Daughter" [story]. Common Ground. v. 8 (Winter, 1948) 22-31.

In the end Chee saved his daughter's life. But tradition was not to be flaunted. Humanity and love brought joy and life.

1933. ________. ________. "Chee's Daughter." In Faderman, Lillian and Barbara Bradshaw, eds., Speaking for Ourselves: American Ethnic Writing. Scott, 1969.

1934. ________. ________. "Chee's Daughter" [story]. In Sanders, Thomas E. & Walter W. Peek, Literature of the American Indian. Glencoe Pr., 1973, pp. 471-81.

1935. Polacca, Vernida. (Tewa) "A Visit to Grandmother" [prose]. In Allen, T. D., ed., Arrow IV. U.S. Bureau of Indian Affairs, Creative Writing Project, 1972, pp. 23-4.

1936. Popkes, Opal Lee. (Choctaw) "Zuma Chowt's Cave." In Rosen, Kenneth, ed., The Man to Send Rain Clouds. Viking Press, 1974, pp. 109-27.

1937. Porter, Barry. "Kindergarten Dreams" [prose]. Angwamas Minosewag Anishinabeg. (Poets in the Schools Program) St. Paul Council of Arts and Sciences, Winter, 1973-74.
A typical child's dream, but they lived happily ever after.

1938. Powell, Tony. "As I Walk Along" [prose]. Angwamas Minosewag Anishinabeg. 1st issue. (Poets in the School Program) St. Paul Council of Arts and Sciences, [1972].
He talks to his forest friends as he walks along, and wonders.

1939. Rogers, Ronald. (Cherokee) "The Angry Truck" [prose]. In Milton, John R., comp., The American Indian Speaks. Vermillion: U. of S. Dak., 1969, pp. 114-118.
Could better be titled "Frustration when writer's mind is blank." The truck rumbling by in the street sounds angry.

1940. Sayers, Geraldine L. "Sometimes I Wish..." [prose]. Angwamas Minosewag Anishinabeg. 1st issue. (Poets in the Schools Program) St. Paul Council of Arts and Sciences, [1972].
Recalls the old ways and wishes she could teach them to her children.

1941. ________. "There's Something up in Northern Minnesota..." [prose]. Angwamas Minosewag Anishinabeg. 1st issue. (Poets in the Schools Program) St. Paul Council of Arts and Sciences, [1972].
Describes a night in Northern Minnesota.

1942. Scott, Ellen. (Mescalero Apache) "Mescalero Apache Mountain Spirit Dancers" [prose]. In Allen, T. D., ed., Arrow III. U.S. Bureau of Indian Affairs, Creative Writing Project, 1971, pp. 27-30.

1943. Self, Lydia. "If I Were a Rock" [prose]. Angwamas Minosewag Anishinabeg. (Poets in the Schools

Program) St. Paul Council of Arts and Sciences, Winter, 1973-74.

Interprets rock as part of nature, which blends its song.

1944. Shoemake, Ben. (Shawnee-Quapaw-Osage-Cherokee) "Dear Friends" [story]. In Tvedten, Benet, comp., An American Indian Anthology. Marvin, S.D.: Blue Cloud Abbey, 1971, pp. 18-22.

Walking at dawn to watch the ducks on the pond, he savors the wood smoke from his own hearth fire. Again, walking at dusk when the lights of a jet blink overhead, he muses fondly of his faithful team and wagon. Slowly but surely they serve him, and allow him time to enjoy nature.

1945. Shotley, Mark. "I'm 53 Years Old" [first line]. Angwamas Minosewag Anishinabeg. (Poets in the Schools Program) St. Paul Council of Arts and Sciences, Winter, 1973-74.

He imagines he is a Medicine Man, but he is "carried away" with his imagination.

1946. Silko, Leslie. (Laguna Pueblo) "Bravura." In Rosen, Kenneth, ed., The Man to Send Rain Clouds. Viking Press, 1974, pp. 149-54.

1947. ________. "A Geronimo Story." In Lourie, Dick, ed., Come to Power. The Crossing Press, 1974, pp. 81-94.

1948. ________. "A Geronimo Story." In Rosen, Kenneth, ed., The Man to Send Rain Clouds. Viking Press, 1974, pp. 128-44.

1949. ________. [from] "Humaweepi, the Warrior Priest." In Rosen, Kenneth, ed., The Man to Send Rain Clouds. Viking Press, 1974, pp. 161-8.

1950. ________. "Laughing and Laughing." In Lourie, Dick, ed., Come to Power. The Crossing Press, 1974, p. 99.

1951. ________. "The Man to Send Rain Clouds." In Rosen, Kenneth, ed., The Man to Send Rain Clouds; Contemporary Stories by American Indians. Viking Press, 1974, pp. 3-8.

1952. Silko, Leslie. (Laguna Pueblo) "Tony's Story." In Rosen, Kenneth, ed., The Man to Send Rain Clouds. Viking Press, 1974, pp. 69-78.

1953. ______. "Uncle Tony's Goat." In Rosen, Kenneth, ed., The Man to Send Rain Clouds. Viking Press, 1974, pp. 93-100.

1954. ______. "Yellow Woman." In Rosen, Kenneth, ed., The Man to Send Rain Clouds. Viking Press, 1974, pp. 33-45.

1955. Simpson, Wm. (Creek) "Stomp Dance Car" [prose]. In Allen, T. D., ed., Arrow III. U.S. Bureau of Indian Affairs, Creative Writing Project, 1971, pp. 23-4.

1956. Stands-in-Timber, John. "The Way the White Man Says Hello." In Levitas, Gloria, Frank Robert & Jacqueline J. Vivelo, eds., American Indian Prose & Poetry. Putnam, 1974, pp. 294-95.

1957. Stops, Roger. "My Father Learned to Be a Christian." In Levitas, Gloria, Frank Robert & Jacqueline J. Vivelo, eds., American Indian Prose & Poetry. Putnam, 1974, p. 302.

1958. Te-Ha-Ne-To-Rens. "We Hold in Our Hand Fourteen Strings..." In Levitas, Gloria, Frank Robert & Jacqueline J. Vivelo, eds., American Indian Prose & Poetry. Putnam, 1974, pp. 298-99.

1959. Track, Soge. (Sioux-Pueblo from Taos) "The Clearing in the Valley" [story]. In Henry, Jeannette, ed., The American Indian Reader: Literature. Indian Historian Pr., 1973, pp. 63-78.

On a wood-gathering trip to the valley with her grandparents, nine-year old granddaughter wanders away and meets Old Man, who tells her the story of crow, lizard and sparrow. Crow and lizard represent the spirit of selfishness. Sparrow represents the spirit of sharing and bringing joy and beauty with his song.

1960. ______. "The Clearing in the Valley." In Milton, John R., comp., The American Indian Speaks. Vermillion, U. of S. Dak., 1969, pp. 153-170.

1961. Walters, Anna Lee. (Pawnee-Otoe) "Chapter I." In Rosen, Kenneth, ed., The Man to Send Rain Clouds. Viking Press, 1974, pp. 82-92.

1962. ________. "Come My Sons." In Rosen, Kenneth, ed., The Man to Send Rain Clouds. Viking Press, 1974, pp. 15-26.

1963. Wright, Brenda. "Our Mother Was Made..." [prose]. Angwamas Minosewag Anishinabeg. 1st issue. (Poets in the Schools Program) St. Paul Council of Arts and Sciences, [1973].

A reverie on "making" our mother from everything that is finest.

1964. York, Lawrine. (Choctaw) "The Death of a Friend" [prose]. In Allen, T. D., ed., Arrow IV. U.S. Bureau of Indian Affairs, Creative Writing Project, 1972, pp. 25-6.

Part 7

HUMOR AND SATIRE

1965. Bibeau, Don, Carl Gawboy, and Naomi Lyme. Everything You Ever Wanted to Ask about Indians but Were Afraid to Find Out. Saint Cloud, Minn.: N. Star Pr., 1971.

In cartoon-format this title satirizes the smugness of the majority of white Americans who, these many years, have taken great pride in their prejudices, or in what they believe to be lack of prejudice. The cartoons are arranged under four "subjects": 1) Has Home on the Res' Really Changed? 2) Will Urbanization De-Indianize Joe Bad-Moccasin? 3) Can Indian Ed. Survive in the School? 4) Are Conferences Producing a New Tribe?

1966. Low Cloud, Charles Round. (Winnebago) Charles Round Low Cloud: Voice of the Winnebago. Edited by William L. Clark and Walker D. Wyman. Illus. by Helen B. Wyman. U. of Wis. at River Falls, 1973.

Low Cloud, Winnebago Indian from Black River Falls, Wisc., contributed a column during the years 1931-49 to the town's newspaper, Banner Journal. In his matter-of-fact, Indian-style English he reflects on the life of the Indian community, daily happenings, and its problems in relation to the immediate surroundings, the nation, and the world. His candid style and "pure Charley" form are both humorous and philosophic in tone. The editors have arranged his column by subject, and within each chapter, chronologically.

1967. Rogers, Will. (Cherokee) Ether and Me; or Just Relax. Putnam, 1935.

Will Rogers deals lightly and humorously with his "operation": Hospitalization and convalescence. He makes analogies with his experiences as a cowboy, actor, observer and commentator on the foibles of man in or out of the political scene, and without malice.

1968. Rogers, Will. (Cherokee) The Illiterate Digest. Boni, 1924.

At least two titles which bear Will Rogers' name as author are selections of his writings edited by Donald Day. Illiterate Digest is a Will Rogers "original." In his own inimitable style he expresses himself on weighty national issues and personal idiosyncrasies under chapter titles such as "Breaking into the Writing Game," "It's Time Somebody Said a Word for California," and "Mr. Ford and Other Political Self-Starters."

1969. ________. Letters of a Self-Made Diplomat to His President. Boni, 1926.

These letters were written when Will was an a 1926 tour in Europe as correspondent for the Saturday Evening Post and as President Coolidge's "ambassador of goodwill." His assumed naivete is convincing; his "assessment" of situations he finds in the various European capitals shows an uncanny wisdom, knowledge of historical facts, current events, and of humans in general--their strengths and weaknesses. All is told in the best traditions of humor.

1970. ________. Sanity Is Where You Find It; an Affectionate History of the United States in the 20's and 30's by America's Best-loved Comedian. Selected and edited by Donald Day. Houghton, 1955.

This is "history" by its most inclusive definition: economic, political, social, etc. The volume is a selection of materials chosen largely from Will Rogers' newspaper column, chronologically arranged. Chapter titles point up the similarity of the subject matter of that day's news to news of today; e.g., Political "Follies" of 1924, Trying to Tell What Russia Is, Restoring Confidence--Republican Style. He also makes "Senate Investigating observations" on committees.

1971. Tatsey, John. (Blackfoot) The Black Moccasin. Comp. and ed. by Paul T. DeVore. C. W. Hill, 1971.

John Tatsey, Blackfoot, tribal policeman, columnist for the weekly newspaper, Glacier Reporter, Browning, Montana, gained renown for his reportage on reservation life and Indian traditional customs. He does this with honesty, objectivity and some humor. His good friend, Senator Mike Mansfield has given him recognition in the Congressional Record. In addition to excerpts from his columns, a brief biography of John is included; also transcriptions of tape recordings John made about Blackfoot history and culture. Penline drawings by Albert Racine and colored photographs enhance the text.

Part 8

COLLECTIONS ANALYZED

1972. Allen, T. D., ed. Arrow. U.S. Dept. of Indian Affairs. Creative Writing Project, I-1969; II-1970; III-1971; IV-1972.
Each volume is small in size, but rich in content: the outstanding prose and poetry of each year's Creative Writing Project.

1973. ________. Arrows Four; Prose and Poetry by Young American Indians. Washington Square Press, 1974.
This title is a cumulation of the four separate Arrow titles in the above entry.

1974. ________. The Whispering Wind; Poetry by Young American Indians. Doubleday, 1972.
This collection is a product of the course in writing at the Institute of American Indian Arts, Santa Fe. It is a credit to the creative ability of the Native American in an art form other than painting, weaving and ceramics. The editor was the first teacher appointed to the position in Creative Writing. One-page biographical notes on each poet add interest to the collection.

1975. Angwamas Minosewag Anishinabeg. Poets in the Schools Program. St. Paul Council of Arts and Sciences, 1971- .
Perceptive prose-poems, and poems by children and young people.

1976. Carroll, Paul, ed. Young American Poets. Chicago: Big Table Pub. Co., 1968.
Ted Berrigan and James Welch are included in this general collection of Young American Poets published in 1968. Much has happened during the

last five years to bring out the American Indian voice. Today, a collection of this sort could include a substantial number of Native American poets.

1977. Dance with Indian Children. Wash., D.C.: Center for the Arts of Indian Children, 1972.
Brief, terse, descriptive, imaginative poems embellish this brochure on the dance as art. Photographs and drawings of American Indian dances with expressive detail make this a delight.

1978. David, Jay, ed. The American Indian, the First Victim. Morrow, 1972.
Essays and poems by Native Americans.

1979. Dodge, Robert K. & Joseph B. McCullough, eds. Voices from Wah'kon-tah: Contemporary Poetry of Native Americans. Foreword by Vine Deloria, Jr. International Publishers, 1974.

1980. Faderman, Lillian & Barbara Bradshaw, eds. Speaking for Ourselves: American Ethnic Writing. Scott, Foresman, 1969.

1981. Future Directions in Native American Art. Santa Fe, N.M.: The Institute of American Indian Arts, [1973].
Another brochure which describes in words, photographs and drawings the various art forms (including poetry) which are expressed by Native American students at the Institute of American Indian Arts, Santa Fe, New Mexico.

1982. Gooderham, Kent, ed. I Am an Indian. Toronto: Dent, 1969.
The first anthology of Indian literature published in Canada, written and illustrated by Indians.

1983. Gross, Theodore L., ed. A Nation of Nations. Macmillan, 1971.
Selections from the writings of American Indian authors.

1984. Haslam, Gerald W. Forgotten Pages of American Literature. Houghton Mifflin Co., 1970, pp. 1-70.

Includes Asian-American, Latin-American and African-American in addition to American Indian literature. Gives suggestions for more extensive reading.

1985. Henry, Jeannette, ed. The American Indian Reader: Literature. The Indian Historian Pr., 1973.

1986. Indian Arts and Crafts Board. Photographs and Poems by Sioux Children. An exhibition organized by the above board and the Dept. of Interior, 1971.
Perceptive, thought-provoking, 2-20 line poems, each related to a photograph on opposite page.

1987. Levitas, Gloria, Frank Robert & Jacqueline J. Vivelo, eds. American Indian Prose & Poetry: We Wait in the Darkness. Putnam, 1974.

1988. Lewis, Richard. I Breathe a New Song; Poems of the Eskimo. Simon, 1971.

1989. Lourie, Dick, ed. Come to Power; Eleven Contemporary American Indian Poets. Intro. by Joseph Bruchac. The Crossing Press, 1974.

1990. Lowenfels, Walter, ed. From the Belly of the Shark; a New Anthology of Native Americans. Vintage, 1973.

1991. Milton, John R., comp. The American Indian Speaks. Vermillion: U. of S. Dak. Pr., 1969.

1992. ________. American Indian II. Vermillion: U. of S. Dak., 1971.

1993. ________. Four Indian Poets. Dakota Press, 1974.

1994. Momaday, Natachee Scott, ed. (Cherokee) American Indian Authors. Houghton, 1971.
A representative cross-section of literature of the Native American, from Chief Joseph to Vine Deloria, Jr. Gives brief biographical information on each author in addition to an example or excerpt of his writing.

1995. Niatum, Duane, ed. Carriers of the Dream Wheel. Harper, 1975.

1996. Quasha, George, & Jerome Rothenberg, eds. America, a Prophecy: A New Reading of American Poetry from Pre-Columbian Times to the Present. Vintage Books, 1973.

1997. Rosen, Kenneth, ed. The Man to Send Rain Clouds; Contemporary Stories by American Indians. Viking Press, 1974.

1998. Sanders, Thomas E. (Cherokee) and Walter W. Peek. (Narragansett-Wampanoag) Literature of the American Indian. Glencoe Pr., 1973.

Designed to be used as a textbook. The eight chapters present, in a broad chronological fashion, the centrality of religion in the Native American's life; their unique relationship with nature; their oneness with it and dependence upon it; their great oral tradition, represented by the didactic tales, orations, songs and chants; and finally today's prose and poetry.

1999. Turner, Frederick W., III. The Portable North American Indian Reader. Viking, 1974.

2000. Tvedten, Benet, comp. An American Indian Anthology. Blue Cloud Abbey, Blue Cloud Quarterly, 1971.

To aid present-day Americans in the discovery of the prose and poetry produced by contemporary Native Americans and thereby obtain an appreciation of their culture and present day problems.

2001. Waubageshig, or Harvey McCue, ed. The Only Good Indian; Essays by Canadian Indians. New Pr., 1970.

2002. Western Apache Raiding and Warfare. From the notes of Grenville Goodwin. Ed. by Keith H. Basso, E. W. Jernigan, and W. B. Kessel. Tucson: U. of Ariz. Pr., 1971.

Six personal narratives make up Part I of this volume. Part II includes eleven chapters on topics Goodwin considered important on the general subject of raiding and warfare. These selections are also in the form of personal statements obtained from tribal members.

2003. Witt, Shirley H. (Iroquois) and Stan Steiner. The Way: An Anthology of American Indian Literature. Knopf, 1972.

Excerpts from traditional and contemporary Native American literature, which describe the path he has walked, the traditions and beliefs which have directed his life; the difficulties he has encountered, and the events which have brought him to this day.

Part 9

SOURCES: BIBLIOGRAPHIES AND INDEXES

2004. American Indian Index, no. 1, 1953. Chicago, Ill.: J. A. Huebner, 1953. [mimeo]

Comprehensive subject index including legends, music, religion, myths and mythology. Analyzes the U.S. Bureau of American Ethnology Bulletins.

2005. Blew, Carol Van Antwerp Holliday, and others. Current North American Indian Periodicals. Washington, D.C., Smithsonian Center for the Study of Man, 1972.

Includes approximately one hundred and fifty newsletters, newspapers and other periodicals, which are current sources of information about or of interest to North American Indians, including literary selections by native contributors.

2006. Bush, Alfred L. & Robert S. Fraser. American Indian Periodicals in the Princeton University Library; a Preliminary List. Princeton U. Pr., 1970.

A study of 271 contemporary newspapers, newsletters and journals produced by and for Native Americans. For a non-Indian audience, with content of interest and value to the American Indian community. [preface]

2007. Byler, Mary G., comp. (Cherokee) American Indian Authors for Young Readers. New York: Association on American Indian Affairs, 1973.

Foreword emphasizes the fact that only a Native American can really convey what it means to be Sioux, Cheyenne, Apache or other tribal member. Books for "young readers" includes a wide span of reading level, including "adult" books, briefly annotated. Includes a list of publishers with addresses.

2008. Freeman, John F. A Guide to Manuscripts Relating to the American Indian in the Library of the American Philosophical Society. Phila., 1966. Includes Recordings [p. 60-66] of songs, stories.

2009. Haywood, Charles. A Bibliography of North American Folklore and Folksong. 2nd rev. ed. Dover, 1961. 2v.

Arranged by culture areas, each divided into studies related to: 1) Folklore; 2) Music. An alphabetic arrangement by tribe follows and is subdivided into: Folklore, Myths, Beliefs-Customs, Folk Art--Speech, Games, Music. Could be extremely useful in the study of American Indian Culture. Few if any imprints as late as 1950.

2010. Hirschfelder, Arlene B., comp. American Indian Authors; A representative bibliography. New York: Association on American Indian Affairs, Inc., 1970.

Alphabetically arranged by name of Native American responsible for the narration. Many titles are reprints of older versions. Includes autobiography, biography, fiction, folktales, history. Supplements include lists of: 1) Anthologies of folk tales, traditional poetry, oratory; 2) Periodical publications of Native Americans.

2011. ______. American Indian and Eskimo Authors. New York: Association on American Indian Affairs, 1973.

The Foreword states that this revised and enlarged edition is more than double the size of the 1970 edition. Includes traditional and contemporary works of both fact and fiction. Other features are a Tribal Index of the authors included, and a list of publishers and their addresses.

2012. Hodge, William. A Bibliography of Contemporary North American Indians; Selected and Partially Annotated with Study Guide. New York: Interland Publishing Inc., 1976.

Represents a labor of love for and understanding of Native Americans who were childhood friends of the compiler. Section XIX--Music & Dance, and Section XX--Religion are the two parts most useful to the subject of my bibliography. Includes a list of "Current Newspapers, Newsletters, Magazines," and a Tribal Index.

2013. Index to Literature on the American Indian. Editorial board: Jeannette Henry, Helen Redbird-Selam, Mary Nelson, and Rupert Costo. Indian Historian Pr., Inc., 1970- .

Annual subject bibliography of books and periodicals by and about the Native American. Intensively classified. Includes poetry, literature, music and religion.

2014. Kluckhohn, Clyde and Katherine Spencer. A Bibliography of the Navaho Indians. J. J. Augustin, 1940.

Primarily for the anthropologist. Portions on Ceremonialism and Mythology, Music and Poetry, and Ceremonies.

2015. Murdock, George P. Ethnographic Bibliography of North America. 3rd ed. Human Relations Files, 1960.

By geographic region, and tribe within region. Includes traditional literature: ceremonial, legends, poetry. Imprint dates as late as 1958.

2016. National Indian Training Center. Indian Bibliography. 2nd ed. Brigham City, Utah, 1972.

Titles by and about American Indians, including autobiographies and collections of traditional narratives and poetry. Classified and partially annotated.

2017. Newberry Library. Dictionary Catalog of the Ed. E. Ayer Collection of Americana & American Indians in the Newberry Library. Hall, 1961. 16v.

Arranged by subject. Imprints as late as 1951 under subject, Indians of North America--Poetry.

2018. O'Brien, Lynne Woods. Plains Indian Autobiographies. Boise State College, 1973.

A bibliographical essay which is a good starting point for one interested in the subject. Momaday is the only contemporary included.

2019. Perkins, David & Norman Tanis, comps. Native Americans of North America; Based on Collections in the Libraries of California State University, Northridge. 1975. Reprinted, Metuchen, N.J.: Scarecrow Pr.

Compiled for the students at the University. The areas which have some usefulness for my bibliography are Literature, Music, Dance and Religion. However, few recent titles are included. There are no annotations. Materials are arranged first by subject, then by tribe. There is also an author and title index.

2020. Stensland, Anna Lee. Literature by and about the American Indian; an Annotated Bibliography for Junior and Senior High School Students. National Council of Teachers of English, 1973.

Extremely useful, not only for the Junior and Senior High School levels but for the general reader interested in the subject. Pages 167-77 contain brief biographies of American Indian authors, which are sometimes difficult to locate.

2021. Tacoma Public Library and Tacoma Community College Library. A Selected Sample of Books by and about American Indians, with Special Emphasis on the Pacific Northwest. 1970.

Arranged especially for clients of the Tacoma libraries. Tribal affiliation of Indian authors is not given. Classified, but not annotated.

2022. Townley, Charles. American Indians; a Selective Guide to the Resources of the USCB Library. University of California, Santa Barbara, 1971.

Considers reference sources, general and specific, as possible resources for aspects of information on the American Indian. Of special interest: Music, Folklore.

2023. Trimble, Martha Scott. N. Scott Momaday. Boise, Idaho: Boise State College, 1973.

Lists Momaday's writings, including periodical sources.

2024. Ullom, Judith C., comp. Folklore of the North American Indians; An Annotated Bibliography. Washington, D.C.: Children's Book Section,

Gen'l Ref. & Biblio. Div., Library of Congress, 1969.

Attractively illustrated and printed text. More than a bibliography of folklore appropriate for children. It is a study of the folktale from its primitive origins among North American Indians. Arranged by cultural area, and subdivided into Sources and Children's Editions. Lengthy annotations.

Part 10

PERIODICALS ANALYZED

One of the problems and challenges of searching out Native American writers, especially in periodical literature, is that not until about 1960 were they given much, if any, recognition by the world of publishers. Perhaps they had not made attempts to seek recognition. A self-consciousness and shyness was a normal reaction to the treatment historically given them.

The climate of awareness and self-expression ushered in during the 1960's provided a time ripe to voice the suppressed hopes and genius of a people possessed of deep religious feelings and a profoundly democratic philosophy of life.

Innumerable newspaper-periodical-type of publications were launched by tribal organizations and communities and native schools in North America: the United States, including Alaska, Canada and even Mexico. According to _Ulrich's Periodicals Directory, 1975-76_ (Bowker, 1976), about ten titles indicate publication dates before 1960. Approximately sixty others are also listed, some without original publication dates. Nearly 75 additional titles have come to my attention via other sources. Those which were described as including poetry formed the nucleus from which selections were made. Unfortunately most of these newspaper-periodicals were not indexed.

It is gratifying to note from the following list that a number of current general periodicals are printing the prose and poetry of Native Americans. This particular group of titles emerged from bibliographies, indexes and university library card catalogs in addition to the above mentioned sources; plus the following standard indexes: _Index to Little Magazines_, _Readers' Guide to Periodical Literature_, and _Social Science and Humanities Index_. Only the better known poets, e.g., Ted Berrigan, N. Scott Momaday and James Welch, were searched in the two last-named indexes. There is no doubt but that there are other authors whose poetry has been included. Identifying names of Native Americans is one of the problems of the bibliographer in this area of study.

This selection of periodical titles is considered a suggested list of possible sources. Akwesasne Notes and The Indian Historian are the only two titles which have been indexed from volume one up to mid-1976. To index others listed from first publication date would involve finding locations where they have been preserved. Hopefully, in the future efforts will be made to do this.

In addition to title of each periodical, the date from which each was indexed is given; also address and frequency of publication. Distinctive information is added when deemed significant.

Akwesasne Notes. 1969-
Mohawk Nation
via Rooseveltown, N.Y. 13683
Published seven times a year.
Includes articles and news items on the contemporary Native American and his problems, book reviews and at least one page of poetry by today's young Native Americans.

Alcheringa. 1971-
Jerome Rothenberg and Dennis Tedlock
600 W. 163rd St., New York, N.Y. 10032
Published twice a year.
Proposes to translate and make available portions of the traditional literature of the world's primitive people. Includes poetry of contemporary Native Americans.

American Anthropologist. 1964-
American Anthropological Association
1703 New Hampshire Ave., N.W.
Washington, D.C. 20009
Quarterly.
Includes articles by and about Native Americans. Of special interest are contributions in the area of mythology and religion.

American Indian Crafts and Culture. 1971-
1518 S. Owasso St.
Tulsa, Okla. 74120
Monthly, except July and August.

American Indian Culture Center. Journal. 1971-
3221 Campbell Hall
University of California at Los Angeles.
Los Angeles, CA 90024
Quarterly.
Includes poetry and short stories by Native Americans.

Arizona Highways. 1958-
2039 W. Lewis Ave.
Phoenix, Ariz. 85009
Monthly.

Arkansas Historical Quarterly. 1967-
Arkansas Historical Association
University of Arkansas
Fayetteville, AR 72701

The Blue Cloud Quarterly. XIV-
Blue Cloud Abbey
Marvin, South Dakota 57251
A publication of the Benedictine Missionaries. [1954]-
Published four times a year.
Publishes literature by and about Native Americans.

Chronicles of Oklahoma. 1964-
Oklahoma Historical Society
Historical Bldg.
Oklahoma City, Okla. 73105
Quarterly.

Common Ground. 1948-
Common Council for American Unity
New York
Quarterly.

Expedition. 1970-
University of Pennsylvania
University Museum
33rd & Spruce Sts.
Philadelphia, Pa. 19174
Quarterly.

Great Plains Journal. 1965-
Institute of the Great Plains
Box 1122
Lawton, Okla. 73501
Published twice annually.

Harper's Bazaar. 1970-
Hearst Corp.
717 Fifth Ave.
New York, N.Y. 10022
Monthly.

The Indian Historian. 1968-
1451 Masonic Ave.
San Francisco, Calif. 94117
Voice of the American Indian Historical Society. 1968-
Quarterly.

Publication features articles of historical and current interest, stories, poetry and translations of traditional literature.

Indian Voice; America's Only Indian Magazine. 1971-
Native American Publishing Co.
Box 2033
Santa Clara, CA 95051
Monthly.

Life. 1971-
Time, Inc.
New York, N.Y. 10020
Weekly.

The Little Square Review. 1968-
770 Ladera Lane
Santa Barbara, California

"Devoted to authors not in the editor's opinion granted sufficient recognition by the larger magazines."

Nos. 5 and 6 Spring-Summer 1968. American Indian Issue.

Many Smokes. 1972-
P.O. Box 5895
Reno, Nevada
Quarterly.

Masterkey; for Indian Lore and History. 1970-
Southwest Museum

Highland Park
Los Angeles, CA 90042
Quarterly.

Native Nevadan. 1973-
The Native Nevadan
98 Colony Road
Reno, Nv. 89502
Organ of the Inter-Tribal Council of Nevada, Inc. 1966-
Monthly publication which informs Native Americans of Nevada concerning contemporary events. Occasionally includes poetry.

New Mexico. 1973-
New Mexico Department of Development.
113 Washington Ave.
Santa Fe, N. M. 87501
Published six times a year.

New Mexico Quarterly. 1959-
University of New Mexico
Albuquerque, N. M.

New Yorker. 1970-
New Yorker Magazine, Inc.
25 W. 43rd St.
New York, N. Y. 10036
Weekly.

North American Review. 1968-
University of Northern Iowa
Cedar Falls, Iowa 50613
Quarterly.

North Dakota History: Journal of the Northern Plains. 1971-
State Historical Society of North Dakota
Liberty Memorial Building
Bismarck, N. D. 58501
Quarterly.

Paris Review. 1965-
4539 171 Place
Flushing, N. Y. 11358
Quarterly.

Pembroke Magazine. 1969-
Pembroke University

Pembroke, N.C. 28372
Annual publication.
Publishes for the most part poetry of contemporary writers: Native Americans and those who are involved in the Creative Writing Programs.

Poetry. 1968-
1228 N. Dearborn Pkwy.
Chicago, Ill. 60610
Monthly.

Poetry Northwest. 1967-
University of Washington
Parrington Hall
Seattle, WN 98195
Quarterly.

Prairie Schooner. 1961-
University of Nebraska
Nebraska Hall 318
Lincoln, NB 68508
Quarterly.

Quetzal. 1971-
7845 Lilac Way
El Paso, TX 79915
Three times per year.

Ramparts. 1963-
Noah's Ark Inc.
2054 University Ave.
Berkeley, CA 94704
Monthly.

South Dakota Review. 1968-
Box 111, University Exchange
Vermillion, South Dakota 57069
Quarterly.

Southern Folklore Quarterly. 1965-
University of Florida
Gainesville, Fla. 32601
Quarterly.

Southern Indian Studies. 1964-
Archaeological Society of North Carolina
University Laboratory of Anthropology and Archaeology
Chapel Hill, N.C.

Southern Review; a Literary and Critical Quarterly Magazine. 1965-
Louisiana State University
Drawer D, University Station
Baton Rouge, La. 70803

Sun Tracks. 1965-
University of Arizona
Tucson, Arizona
Quarterly.
Literary voice of Native American students at the University.

Tlalocan. 1970-
Mexico 4, D.F. Mexico
Irregularly published.

United Scholarship Service News. v. 1, no. 5
Bx 18285 Capitol Hill Station
Denver, Colo. 80218
A private agency for purpose of counseling, securing scholarship and placement service for Native American High School, undergraduate and graduate students. Occasionally includes poems of Native Americans.

Warpath. v. 4- 1969-
United Native Americans Inc.
P.O. Box 26140
San Francisco, Ca. 94126
A non-profit and non-partisan Indian organization.
Monthly.
Occasionally includes poetry.

Wassaja. v. 1- 1973-
The American Indian Historical Society
1451 Masonic Avenue
San Francisco, Ca. 94117
Monthly.
"A National Newspaper of Indian America." Excellent, detailed coverage on all aspects of Native American life and problems (Canadian, Mexican, South American and of the United States). Includes book reviews and poetry.

Part 11

TITLE AND FIRST LINE INDEX TO SINGLE POEMS

Part 12

AUTHOR INDEX

*Asterisks indicate non-Indians.